Theology Is for
Proclamation

Theology Is for Proclamation

Gerhard O. Forde

Fortress Press

Minneapolis

THEOLOGY IS FOR PROCLAMATION

Cover design: Mark Stratman

Library of Congress Cataloging-in-Publication Data

Forde, Gerhard O.
    Theology is for proclamation / Gerhard O. Forde.
      p. cm.
    Includes bibliographical references.
    ISBN 0-8006-2425-4 (alk. paper)
    1. Preaching.   2. Theology, Doctrinal.   I. Title.
  BV4211.2.F68   1990
  251—dc20   90-33374
                                            CIP

Manufactured in the U.S.A.   AF 1-2425

94   93   92   91   90   1   2   3   4   5   6   7   8   9   10

Contents

Preface

*T*he thesis of this book is straightforward. Systematic theology, whatever else it might be for, has to be for proclamation. Not, heaven forbid, that systematic theology is what is to be proclaimed! That, I contend, is precisely one of the more persistent misadventures. Systematic theology, whether good or bad, gets substituted for and displaces proclamation. I contend here that systematic theology, while not itself to be confused with proclamation, should be the kind of thinking that advocates, fosters, and drives to proper proclamation of the gospel of Jesus Christ; it should be a systematic reflection that promotes the speaking of the promise. Such a systematic theology should be for proclamation in a double sense: it insists on proclamation; and it recognizes such insistence to be its ultimate purpose. That is, if systematic theology is done properly it will leave its practitioners in a position where they can, in order to complete their own task, do no other than proclaim.

My interest in such thought arises from some twenty-five years of teaching in theological institutions. Viewing the outcome of such splendid and strenuous effort one sometimes wonders why the results are so meager. There are always those, of course, who begin to see.

They are the singular joy of the profession. But less than entirely happy results lead one to ask not only about one's ability as a teacher but also about what good one's particular discipline is doing. More seriously, the question is not only whether the discipline is doing good but whether it might actually be doing some harm. Could it be that systematic theology as usually practiced actually frustrates the proclamation of the gospel? Such questioning may lend solace to those who have always thought evil in their hearts of the discipline, but the intent here is quite the contrary. As the stock rejoinder has it: Every Christian who thinks at all about the faith or about what he or she is going to say or do, does systematic theology. It is done either well or ill, but done nevertheless. So the question raised here is directed to anyone who thinks at all about the faith and contemplates saying or doing something about it. Anyone who does such thinking and contemplation has to do some sort of systematic theology and should be concerned about doing it properly. That is the concern of this book.

Gratitude is due many people and institutions who helped to make this book possible. First, to my wife, Marianna, for her help and encouragement in the project and especially for her long-suffering in keeping house and home together while I was absent, in addition to her own teaching duties. Second, to my students through the years whose questions, stimulation, and encouragement have contributed more than they know to this book. Third, to Luther Northwestern Theological Seminary for its generous sabbatical program, which gave me the time to write. Fourth, to the Aid Association for Lutherans for honoring me with its Fredrik A. Schiotz Award and its stipend which enabled and supported the writing. Fifth, to the Institute for Ecumenical and Cultural Research at Collegeville, Minnesota, for accepting me as one of its fellows and providing a most pleasant place and stimulating atmosphere in which to do research and writing, as well as the support of its director, Patrick Henry, its fellows and staff. Sixth, to my good and kind colleagues, Donald Juel, James Nestingen, Sheldon Tostengard, Patrick Keifert, and Todd Nichol, for reading the manuscript and making helpful suggestions. Finally, to the editors at Fortress Press, especially to John Hollar, now deceased, and to Timothy Staveteig for their encouragement, care, and painstaking effort in bringing the work to the light of published day.

Introduction

S ystematic theology is for proclamation. When properly done, it fosters, advocates, and drives to proclamation. This presupposes at the outset a basic distinction between systematic theology and proclamation. Indeed, a major difficulty in usual discussions of the matter is that systematic theology and proclamation tend so easily to be confused. When that happens it is invariably proclamation that is obscured. Proclamation gets displaced by explanation, teaching, lecturing, persuasion, ethical exhortation, or public display of emotion about Jesus. So at the outset we need to distinguish between systematic theology and proclamation and to relate them in at least a preliminary fashion.

Proclamation, as we shall use the term in this study, is explicit declaration of the good news, the gospel, the kerygma. It is at once more specific and more comprehensive than preaching, even though, as will also be the case here, we often use the two terms interchangeably. Proclamation is more specific than preaching because not all that we ordinarily call preaching—teaching, edifying, ethical exhortation, persuasion, apologies for Christian living—is necessarily proclamation. At the same time, proclamation is more comprehensive because it occurs apart from formal preaching, most notably in the sacraments and the liturgy, but also in the everyday mutual conversation of Christians.

How is such proclamation to be distinguished from systematic theology? It is helpful at the outset to make a distinction between primary and secondary discourse. Proclamation belongs to the primary discourse of the church. Systematic theology belongs to its secondary discourse. Primary discourse is the direct declaration of the Word of God, that is, the Word *from* God, and the believing response in confession, prayer, and praise. Secondary discourse, words *about* God, is reflection on the primary discourse. As primary discourse, proclamation ideally is present-tense, first-to-second person unconditional promise authorized by what occurs in Jesus Christ according to the scriptures. The most apt paradigm for such speaking is the absolution: "I declare unto you the gracious forgiveness of all your sins in the name of the Father, the Son, and the Holy Spirit." Proclamation is not "about" something other than itself. It does not point away from itself. It does not signify some other thing. It is the saying and doing of the deed itself, for example, "*I* baptize *you* . . ." The deed is done, unconditionally. It is not an account of what happened in the past, such as, "God so loved the world that he gave his only begotten Son," true as that is and, indeed, as much as it authorizes the primary discourse. Such accounts are past tense. Proclamation is present tense: I here and now give the gift to you, Christ himself, the body and blood of the Savior. I do it in both Word and sacrament. This is God's present move, the current "mighty act" of the living God.

The only appropriate response to such primary discourse is likewise primary: confession, praise, prayer, and worship. Proclamation as primary discourse demands an answer in like discourse be it positive or negative: "I repent, I believe" or "I don't, I won't, I can't." In other words, when the proclamation announces, "I declare unto you the forgiveness of all your sins," the appropriate response is not, "Well, that's your opinion!" Perhaps the only thing the absolver could say to such irrelevancy would be, "No, that's not my opinion. If I were to give my opinion about you it would likely be something else! We are not dealing with human opinion here, but with the Word of God!" The only appropriate response has to be primary: "I believe" or "I don't believe it." The primary language of proclamation evokes and expects the primary response of confession and worship or its refusal.

Systematic theology, however, belongs to the sphere of secondary discourse. It is not the Word of God, it is words about God, reflection on what has been heard. Above all we must be clear that systematic theology is not what is to be proclaimed. To use an analogy, proclamation is like saying, "I love you." Systematic theology is like a book on the nature of love or the art of loving. It is secondary discourse. It attempts to put things in order, to focus, to lend coherence, and to measure the church's discourse on the basis of its established norms, scripture, the creeds, and confessional documents.

It is essential that these two kinds of discourse not be confused or that one gets substituted for the other. Perhaps this can be clarified by pressing the love analogy further. Imagine the lover and the beloved at a critical moment in which the primary language is to be spoken. "Do you love me?" asks the lover. And the beloved answers, "Well, that is an interesting question. What is love after all?" And so launches into a discussion about the essence of love. After patient waiting, the lover finally gets another chance. "Yes, that's all interesting, but do you love me?" Then the beloved takes another diversionary tack and says, "Well, yes, of course. You see, I love everybody!" (A universalist!) The lover protests, "That's not what I mean! You haven't answered the question! Do *you* love *me*?" So it goes. In spite of all the helpful things it does, secondary discourse makes the would-be lover look ridiculous when substituted for primary discourse.

There is only one type of discourse that will do the job in the case of the lovers: primary discourse, the proclamation, the self-disclosure in present tense, first-to-second-person address, the "I love you," and the subsequent confession, "I love you too!" What happens in the church's proclamation is often similar: secondary discourse gets substituted for primary and so proclamation never occurs. Proclamation as primary discourse must be carefully distinguished from and not confused with systematic theology as secondary discourse. In spite of much apparent antipathy to systematic theology today, that is what is heard mostly from our pulpits—albeit systematics of a second-rate or rather unsystematic sort!

If proclamation and systematic theology are to be distinguished, then how are they to be related? They are necessarily correlated: one is impossible without the other. Without systematic reflection there will be no conscious proclamation. Proclamation may perhaps happen instinctively. But this is more accidental than purposed. Systematic reflection is necessary to make the move to proclamation conscious and explicit. This is entailed in the contention that systematic theology is for proclamation. It ought to be the kind of reflection that fosters and drives back to the proclamation. Indeed, to make distinctions as I have done here is to begin such systematic reflection. Without such reflection one would probably not come to a clear understanding of what proclamation is and so would not do it. One might do a lot of things—exegete, lecture, explain, persuade, teach, orate effectively or poorly, edify—all of which may be fine in their place, but one will not proclaim.

I take systematic theology, therefore, to be the kind of reflection that takes place between yesterday's and today's proclamation. One who hears the proclamation reflects on it so as to say it again in a different time and context. It is a reflection that takes place between the ear and the mouth. If nothing happens there, one is not needed and would best just get out of the way. The hearers would be better advised to read the Bible or yesterday's sermons. But then there will likely be no proclamation for today. Systematic theology is indispensable for such proclamation.

But with such assertions, the correlation is not yet complete. For without the proclamation and an understanding of its place, systematic theology will either not be done at all or is likely to go wrong. Everyone knows and generally agrees that systematic theology exercises a critical function over against the proclamation of the church. But if there is a genuine correlation the proclamation needs to reflect back on and raise critical questions about systematic theology. If today's proclamation does not turn out right, or is not really done at all, something went wrong with the reflection. All too often what happens is that the systematic theology short-circuits the process and usurps the place of the proclamation. The secondary discourse about love displaces the "I love you." One ends then by delivering some species of lecture about God and things rather than speaking the Word from God. When this occurs it matters little whether the lecture in question is conservative, liberal, evangelical, or fundamentalist. That only means the lecture is to one degree or another theologically correct. But that is of no great moment if it does not issue in proclamation.

The secondary discourse is relatively pointless if it does not drive to proclamation, to actual primary discourse. A central concern of this study is to show that proclamation is not just practical or pastoral application of arguments already completed and wrapped in neat packages in the systematic, but that *the move to proclamation is itself the necessary and indispensable final move in the argument.* If and when systematic theology looks on itself as the conclusion of the argument— the means by which ultimate persuasion is to take place so that there is no room or place for proclamation—it has overstepped its bounds and falsified itself. That is, the systematic reflection should not only leave room for the proclamation but must make the move inescapable. The argument must leave one in a position where proclamation is the only move left. If systematic theology does not leave such room and make such a move inescapable, it falsifies itself by denying its purpose. It then usurps the place of proclamation and retreats behind the ivied walls of academia, never to be heard from again except, perhaps, at professional societies where one has long since forgotten its purpose.

Thus proclamation and systematic theology must be intimately correlated: Without systematic theology there will be no proclamation; but without proper understanding of proclamation, systematic theology will overstep its bounds and falsify itself. I intend to show that both proclamation and systematic theology will be understood and done differently where such correlation is observed and maintained. Proclamation is neither second-rate or popularized systematic nor the practical application of systematic arguments. Systematic theology, likewise, will operate under certain critical limits. It will insist on and leave room for the proclamation. In following out its reflective task it will make certain characteristic moves and refuse to make others, realizing that it cannot usurp the place of the proclamation. Proclamation has to be the final step and thus set a critical limit to the systematic. The purpose of this study in this regard is to point out how this happens and thus to establish the critical function of proclamation vis-à-vis systematic theology.

When one looks at the history of the church from the perspective of the relation between proclamation and systematic theology, it becomes apparent that a perpetual problem has been the eclipse of primary discourse, especially in the form of proclamation, so that it tends to get truncated or to survive only marginally. Almost from the start the gospel proclamation tended to lose its present tense. It was thought that the eternal Logos made a one-time appearance, came down, acquired a body, was crucified and raised, and then absconded with his body, never to be heard from again. The heavens were silent, the great acts of God were over and done with, and there were no more prophets. Jesus became, in today's parlance, "history," past tense. The good news became old news. The only place where the present tense survived in some fashion was in the sacraments. That is why they became so important. But even in sacraments specially authorized successors of the dead-and-gone Jesus were necessary to perform the miracle of making him present tense again. Meanwhile, the discourse of the church, its proclamation, became more and more just secondary, past tense discourse about God and his Christ. However, as long as such secondary discourse was an ecclesiastical affair, done by the bishops and catechists and doctors of the church, and ancillary to the church's liturgy, it did stay tied to the church's mission. When it later became oriented mainly to the schools the relation began more and more to unravel. The direct proclamation survived at best only as a part of the Sacrament of Penance where it was carefully hedged by conditions and kept in the closet of the confessional.

The Reformation was at best a temporary interruption in this tendency to concentrate on the secondary discourse of the church. It was an attempt to get the primary discourse out of the closet of the confessional into the common discourse of Christians and into the public pulpit. It survived by fits and starts in the churches, but increasing separation between university and church could only mean that theology would become more and more an academic rather than an ecclesiastical discipline. Secondary discourse again crowded out primary discourse.

Through it all, in varying degrees in both Protestantism and Roman Catholic camps, the secondary discourse—the words about God, the history, the infallible facts of the Bible, the old news—properly attested ecclesiastically tends willy-nilly to become the object of faith in place of the promise, the proclamation. The great crisis for the church is that the modern world since the Enlightenment sets serious question marks over this past-tense, secondary discourse. Not only does its historical veracity come under critical scrutiny, but even more seriously, its heteronomous character becomes odious. In other words, as a teaching about a past event it partakes of the uncertainty of all such past events. But even if true, it appears heteronomous (that is, an arbitrary or alien law imposed from without).

The Enlightenment sought to liberate the world from such heteronomy. It saw clearly that old news was bad news. Those who think that an inerrant or infallible historical record solves the problem mistake the gravity of the crisis. An inerrant record only makes matters worse. Old news remains bad news even if it is inerrant. Gotthold Lessing put the question that hangs over the modern era like a marsh gas: How can accidental truths of history be proofs of eternal truths of reason?[1] The Enlightenment rejected such heteronomous "positive" historical religion for "natural" religion, a religion fitted to the autonomy of enlightened and rational beings—as Immanuel Kant was to put it, a "Religion Within the Limits of Reason Alone."[2]

For theology that was a fateful moment. It put an end to ecclesiastical hegemony and demoted theology to one among many academic disciplines. It signified in turn a hermeneutical divide: from that moment on, Scripture would have to be interpreted according to the canons of practical reason. As a result, academic theology tries to manufacture a gospel by turning accidental truths of history into eternal truths of reason, even if only "practical reason." This is the triumph of secondary discourse. Whatever has to do with proclamation is banished to the realm of "practical theology."

Ever since, the church has been on the defensive. On the "left," the strategy of theology has been that of accommodation, apologetics, and theological cosmetics. It has been engaged in a valiant effort to rescue the secondary discourse itself from complete demise by attempting to make it acceptable, credible, palatable, and amenable to human autonomy, to hone down and blunt the sharp edges of the message. The nagging question of what this accomplishes still remains. Does the defensive strategy actually defend anything? Or does it gradually erode the faith?

But how is the problem to be met? On the "right," conservatives and reactionaries insist that we are safe only if everything is, so to speak, set in stone. We are protected from the erosions of time only by an inerrant scripture, infallible secondary discourse. But this is likewise an undermining of the present-tense proclamation. Old news remains bad news even if it is supposedly inerrant or infallible.

The ecumenical question in many ways only highlights and aggravates the problems. As long as one operates on the assumption that the secondary discourse is the object of faith and hence a species of "absolute truth," one can only choose up sides and compare such secondary discourse and hope to reach some "convergence." Failing that, one can only surrender to pluralism—all too often just a plea for the right to hold a private opinion without subjecting it to rigorous public scrutiny. Theology then becomes a matter of taste. There can, of course, be no argument about taste! *De gustibus non disputandum est* (taste cannot be disputed) becomes the final authoritative utterance in theology.

Recapturing the distinction and proper correlation between primary and secondary discourse and, with it, the idea of a systematic theology that is for proclamation promises help not only in ecumenical conversation but also in the church's conversation with the contemporary world. The defensive strategy of theology in the modern world has resulted not in saving but rather in eroding the faith. The conservative and reactionary right has correctly seen that. But its attempt to avert erosion by insistence on setting the secondary discourse in stone is only postponement of eventual disaster. It is time to take a different tack. What the church has to offer the modern world is not ancient history but the present-tense unconditional proclamation. The strategy of accommodation and defense has resulted in the sentimentalization and bowdlerization of almost everything. It is time to risk going over to the offense, to recapture the present tense of the gospel, to speak the unconditional promise and see what happens. To do that it will be necessary to construct a theology that is for proclamation, for going over to the offense, not for defense.

This book, an attempt in that direction, is something between an essay and what used to be called an outline of systematic theology. It is like an essay because it represents an initial testing of a thesis. I have not attempted to argue the case by meticulous comparison with other systematic works since that would disproportionately increase the length of the work. At the same time it is something of an outline (what German systematicians call a *Grundriss*) because it traverses traditional dogmatic topics and tries to show how a systematic theology that is for proclamation might look. It does not pretend to be rigorously systematic in the sense often employed among academics, but a serious systematic proposal is being made. The term systematic theology is used more to indicate the arena and type of reflection required than to claim that a seamless web is being woven. Nor does the work by any means claim to be a complete systematic theology. Since it concentrates on proclamation and the related problematic, it has a somewhat limited scope.

This book is, furthermore, a preliminary sketch. This is not to imply that some dogmas or doctrines are of more importance for proclamation than others. It is simply that the matter must be presented within certain limits of time and space. There is, for instance, no complete or explicit discussion of the doctrine of the Trinity, but the substance is radically trinitarian throughout. The very understanding of proclamation it proposes is radically trinitarian: that God speaks to me in the address of a fellow human today is possible only if God is triune, only if that person can speak to me in the Spirit the Word of the God who does himself to us in Jesus. The logic of the argument would not, I suspect, allow for the easy collapse of the immanent into the economic trinity inspired by Karl Barth and Karl Rahner and prevalent in much current systematic reflection. But this awaits further work. In some instances where a more complete investigation of my own views is possible the reader is directed to other writings and articles. Such expositions do not yet exist, however, in every case. Omissions will have to await a more complete treatment in subsequent work.

Prolegomenon

For since, in the wisdom of God, the world did not know God through wisdom, it pleased God through the folly of what we preach to save those who believe.

(1 Cor. 1:21)

1

The Preached God

And how are they to believe in him of whom they have never heard? And how are they to hear without a preacher?

(Rom. 10:14)

Systematic theology is reflection between yesterday's and to-day's proclamation. Having heard and been claimed by the Word of God, we reflect on how to say it again. We begin such reflection with the God we have heard. That is proper since "God" is the word we use for the beginning, as well as the ending, of all things. "In the beginning, God . . ." (Genesis 1), and in the end God shall be all in all (1 Cor. 15:28). Having heard the word of God we are, in turn, impelled to speak it, to proclaim it. But how shall we reflect on God so as to foster proclamation? That is the fundamental question for systematic theology.

God Not Preached

It is customary in systematic theology to begin with a discussion about how we can know and speak of God. We investigate possible sources for the knowledge of God: nature, experience, reason, and finally special revelation in the scriptures of the church and its traditions. We review the norms for our speaking of God: the canons of the church, its scriptures, its creeds, and its liturgies. Such surveying and reviewing have their rightful place in the theological enterprise. When systematic theology is understood as the kind of thinking that takes place between yesterday's and today's proclamation, however, reflection about God takes a shape different from the usual. Being captivated by the proclamation, our thinking about God is radically altered. We encounter not just talk about God, but God speaking to us.

Getting God Off Our Backs

The hearing of the proclamation makes us aware of a fundamental distinction, as Luther once put it, between God preached and God not preached. In the proclamation we hear something we have not heard before and cannot hear elsewhere: "What no eye has seen, nor ear heard, nor the heart of man conceived, . . . God has prepared for those who love him" (1 Cor. 2:9). The distinction between God not preached and God preached helps us to reflect and speak honestly about God.

To begin with, assuming we have heard God in the proclamation, we can be honest about the fact that outside the proclamation God is something of an onerous burden. We see that apart from God preached, we are estranged from God. Rather than being the one we are allegedly always seeking, God not preached appears more as the one we can never quite get off our backs. As such, "God" is the name for whomever or whatever is "out there," "up there," "in the depths," "transcendent to us," and messing with us. "God" is the place where the buck stops. "God" is responsible for it all. God is an enigma for us. Is there anyone, anything, "out there," "up there"? We are not quite sure, and our attempts to either prove it or to disprove it fall short. Outside the proclamation both theistic and atheistic theologians are strangely one. Both are trying to get God off our backs. The theist most often does it by trying to make God "nice," to bring God "to heel," so to speak, and the atheist does it by trying to make God disappear. Both attempts have a similar outcome from the point of view of the proclamation: they only subvert it.

Nevertheless, for better or for worse, neither theistic nor atheistic appeals seem to work for long. We may find an argument temporarily convincing, but then something else overtakes us—some tragedy, some joy, some fortune or misfortune, some deed or happening that inflates or deflates our ego—and we are back where we started. No matter how persuasive the argument, the next generation, even the next thinker, acts as though it had never been made, or it could not be done, or it did not really work because there were some "holes" in it. The arguments are done, redone, and redone again. We never seem to get God off our backs. God just persists. And that is our problem. That is, in part, what it means to say that we live under the wrath of God and cannot escape.

Thus God apart from proclamation is a rather intractable problem for us. We neither get along very well with God, nor without God. We are at best ambivalent about God. On the one hand, we like the idea of an eternal "anchor" to things, or an eternal goal that is also the source and guarantor of all the things we seek: eternal truth, goodness, beauty, and so on. On the other hand, God is a threat to us: the ruler, the judge, the almighty One who has the final say. We are caught between seeking and fleeing God's presence. The psalmist sings, "As a hart longs for flowing streams, so longs my soul for thee, O God" (Ps. 42:1). But then, "Whither shall I go from thy Spirit? Or whither shall I flee from thy presence?" (Ps. 139:7). Our thinking does not exactly help us, at least not in a direct positive sense. The problem is that when we think "God" we come up against an awesome string of sheer abstractions, what Luther meant, perhaps, by the "naked God in his majesty" (*deus nudus in sua maiestate*), the "bare idea" of God. God is absolute, immortal, immutable, infinite, timeless, passionless (*apathos*), omnipotent, omnipresent, and omniscient; God is the eternal ruler, judge, and disposer of all things, by whose power and will all things come to be and not to be. God is, by definition, God.

It is the very godness of God that causes all the difficulty in our thinking. For if those fearsome abstractions convey truth, "God" is the end of us. That is, should God be all those things, we are left with nothing—no significance, no freedom, no place to stand. God as sheer abstraction, as "the naked God," is an inescapable terror for us. God "not preached" is a God of wrath. This concept may be unpopular but it is true. Otherwise, people would not feel the need nervously and desperately to hide it, to cover up or paper over the naked God with pages torn from theology texts. Outside the proclamation God is unavoidably wrathful.

God the Absconder

God not preached is therefore a confusing, nefarious brew of presence and absence, of sheer timeless abstractions. Yet the abstractions do not reveal so much as hide God from us. They tell us more about what God is not than what God is. God is infinite (that is, not finite), immutable (that is, not changeable), not mortal, not suffering, not limited by time or space, not relative to anything. As such, God amounts to a deified minus sign.

So even though inescapably present, God is terrifyingly absent in this presence. God is, as the tradition (especially Martin Luther) put it, "hidden" (*absconditus*). The Latin has a more active flavor to it than the English, as when someone absconds with the "goods" and leaves behind only an absence, an emptiness, a nothingness. Moses experienced this active absence when he asked to see the divine glory: And the Lord said, "Behold, there is a place by me where you shall stand upon the rock; and while my glory passes by I will put you in a cleft of the rock, and I will cover you with my hand until I have passed by; then I will take away my hand, and you shall see my back; but my face shall not be seen" (Exod. 33:21-23). Not preached, God is the absconder, the one who will not be seen and leaves behind only an emptiness, a blank space. In that sense, God is not merely "hidden" (that is, more or less passively unseeable or unknowable), but the one who actively hides from us, always "gives us the slip."

There is, of course, both a positive and negative aspect to this absconding. On the one hand, that the naked God hides from us and saves us from destruction: "No one can see God and live." The constant temptation of the theologian of glory in us is to try to penetrate the "hidden majesty" of God. Were we able to do that this side of the Parousia, nothing but destruction would result. Enough mischief is accomplished by our unsuccessful attempts to do so. There is a "hidden grace" in the hiddenness of God. On the other hand, the negative aspect is that apart from the proclamation we live under the wrath of the divine hiddenness—the terror of the naked abstractions, the divine absence, the nothingness. As the ever-present absent One of the terrifying abstractions, the One who is the end of us, God not preached merges into and becomes confused with Satan, the accuser and destroyer. This is suggested in the idea of the "masks" (Latin, *larva*) of God. The Latin word also means "ghost" or "demon." The masked God—the God not preached—is hardly distinguishable from Satan.

We can, of course; become fascinated with the emptiness, the nothingness, thinking perhaps that it in itself provides some avenue of escape from the burden of God. Those so fascinated can become enticed by a living negation, a mystical way of self-denial by which one becomes something of an abstraction oneself. Piety becomes almost a holy suicide. Thus even in this there is no escape from the wrath of God. God not preached remains an intractable problem for us.

Shuffling the Masks

God not preached is the absconder, one who hides behind the naked abstractions, and there is nothing theology as such can do about that because theology is a collection of abstractions. It is only in the concrete proclamation, the present-tense Word from God, spoken "to you" the listener, that the abstraction is broken through for the moment and God no longer absconds but is revealed. This is what theologians with too few exceptions through the ages have either failed or refused to see. When the distinctive correlation between systematic theology and proclamation is overlooked, the theological impulse will of necessity be to attempt the impossible: to go to work on the abstractions, to attempt to remove or see through them, to tear the mask from the face of the "hiding" God. When the proclamation is not heard, there is no other recourse. One attempts, against Luther's frequent caveat, to "peer into the hidden majesty of God."

Systematic theology has lately subjected itself to futility because of its preoccupation with such attempts. The attempt is futile because it only shuffles masks. Just when one thinks that he or she has removed one terrifying mask, another mask emerges and turns out to be even more threatening, though the perfidy may not be immediately apparent. Such theologizing only substitutes another seductive abstraction for the proclamation. For example, nineteenth-century liberalism proposed Jesus' proclamation of "the Fatherhood of God" as a surrogate for the gospel. Yet "Fatherhood," severed from its trinitarian moorings, has turned out to be just another frightening mask to many in our day. We should learn from this that similar masks such as "the Motherhood of God" will turn on us as well. They turn on us because the abstraction replaces the proclamation. Instead of the "I love you," of the almighty one, we hear a lecture on a God who is in general "love." The "solution" only creates an even greater problem. Instead of a word from God we hear theological opinions about God. We go out of the frying pan and into the fire! Recall our lover who at the crucial moment claims, "Of course, I love everybody!" or even perhaps "I am love," instead of saying, "I love you!" What is the beloved to say or do about that? If the message is merely that God is love in general, then everything is turned back on us. "If God is love, what is the matter with me? Why am I such an unloving clod?" The generality, the abstraction, whatever its place, only turns on us because it can never do the job of the concrete, self-revealing proclamation. Theology simply cannot unmask God.

This move to tear away the masks, to penetrate, modify, or erase the abstractions, has reached epidemic proportions in the last century. This is no doubt a consequence of the demise of proclamation among us. We seem to have become very sensitive about a timeless, immutable, impassible, and omnipotent God, and have attempted to replace these "masks" with those of suffering and self-limitation. Ronald Goetz sets the issue clearly:

> The age-old dogma that God is impassible and immutable, incapable of suffering, is for many no longer tenable. The ancient theopascite heresy that God suffers has, in fact, become the new orthodoxy.[1]

Goetz's list of theologians attacking the impassibility and immutability reads virtually like a "who's who" of contemporary systematic theology: Karl Barth, Nicolas Berdyaev, Dietrich Bonhoeffer, Emil Brunner, John Cobb, James Cone and liberation theologians generally, Hans Kung, Jurgen Moltmann, Reinhold Niebuhr, Wolfhart Pannenberg, Rosemary Ruether and feminist theologians generally, William Temple, Pierre Teilhard de Chardin, and Miguel de Unamuno.[2] Others could be added.

Indeed, Goetz finds this move to a suffering God to be the one point of consensus today in an otherwise discordant and chaotic pluralism. It is, he avers, a "doctrinal revolution" the implications of which are "enormous," affecting every classical Christian doctrine.[3] Particularly remarkable, Goetz finds, is that this "theopascite mind-set" has developed as a kind of "open secret."

> The doctrine of the suffering God is so fundamental to the very soul of modern Christianity that it has emerged with very few theological shots ever needing to be fired. Indeed, this doctrinal revolution occurred without a widespread awareness that it was happening.[4]

Goetz lists a number of factors which he thinks have contributed to the rise of contemporary theopascitism: the decline of Christendom; the rise of democratic aspirations; the problem of suffering and evil; and scholarly critical work on the Bible in the light of the foregoing.[5] While Goetz does not claim his list to be exhaustive, it seems apparent from the point of view of this study that something more internal to theology itself is a major cause: the failure to see that proclamation is the only vehicle for reconciliation with God. Systematic theology, consequently, has thought itself obliged to repair God's damaged reputation.

The problem is at least twofold. On the one hand, a God stripped of the masks and abstractions is no longer worthy of the name. On the other, such a God ultimately turns out to be more reprehensible and frightful than before. The logic of the masks plays itself out. In Goetz's words:

> The doctrine that God is limited in power solves the problem [of evil] by sacrificing God's omnipotence. However, to my mind, any concept of a limited deity finally entails a denial of the capacity of God to redeem the world and thus, ironically, raises the question of whether God is in the last analysis love, at least love in the Christian sense of the term.[6]

There is no doubt a sense in which theology will want to speak of God's suffering. This needs to be done more carefully, however, in terms of the trinitarian relations and the difference between God not preached and God preached. Why, for instance, do the systematic attempts to displace the impassible God always fail? Why do they have to be done and redone and redone again? What impels us forever to keep trying unless it is that, no matter what, the impassible God "sticks in our craw"? Do we sense that the mask remains in spite of all our efforts? Has systematic theology not demonstrated its futility in the matter? The point is that frontal attacks on the naked abstractions do no good. The assertion that God suffers accomplishes nothing apart from a systematic theology that fosters a reconciling proclamation. The assertion that God suffers tends to degenerate into sentimental drivel about how God somehow identifies with us in and is supposedly enriched by our suffering. The result is little more than a kind of "misery loves company" theology that is much worse than belief in an impassible God. Again in Goetz's words, "God the fellow sufferer is inexcusable if all that he can do is suffer."[7] The frightful logic of the

masks works itself out. God the sufferer is in the end more offensive
than the impassible God.

> The fact that God, though sympathetic with the suffering of humanity,
> is nonetheless enriched by it, would seem little more impassive than
> the bathos of the sentimental butcher who weeps after every slaughter.
> If the purpose of our life and death is finally that we contribute to "the
> self-creation of God," how, an outraged critic of God might demand,
> does God's love differ from the love of a famished diner for his meat
> course?[28]

The impassible God is indeed frightening enough, but at least
that God did not eat us for lunch! Theology—biblical, systematic, or
otherwise—cannot tear the masks from the face of the absconding
God. If it does not see itself as driving to proclamation it succeeds
only in shuffling masks and making matters worse.

The problem here is deeper than the reasons suggested by Goetz.
It is not just that certain peculiarly modern misfortunes have happened
to theology more or less from without, but that there has been a
fundamental miscalculation about the very purpose and limitations of
the systematic enterprise itself. Theology undertakes to reconcile us
to God by seeking to penetrate the masks, to get behind the abstractions. The result, however, is only to disenfranchise God and water
God down. But God is not mocked. We do not by such artifice escape
the divine wrath. We are delivered willy-nilly into the hands of "the
judge" or perhaps of Satan, the accuser, the "attorney for the prose-
cution." For apart from the proclamation God and Satan are virtually
indistinguishable.

Who Killed Cock Robin?

Who is responsible for the demise of God in the modern era? The
intellectual historian James Turner tracks down the culprits for the
modern American scene in *Without God, Without Creed.*[9] Traversing
American intellectual history and particularly the work of nineteenth-
century theologians and preachers, Turner concludes that the theologians and preachers themselves were the real cause of unbelief.
Adapting belief to modernity, they succeeded only in reducing God
to human dimensions, and in doing so,

> [they] made unbelief a more attractive possibility. Put briefly, unbelief
> was not something that "happened *to*" religion. . . . On the contrary,

religion caused unbelief. In trying to adapt their religious beliefs to socioeconomic change, to new moral challenges, to novel problems of knowledge, to the tightening standards of science, the defenders of God slowly strangled Him. If anyone is to be arraigned for deicide, it is not Charles Darwin but his adversary Bishop Samuel Wilberforce, not the godless Robert Ingersoll but the godly Beecher family.[10]

What the theologians and preachers muted or jettisoned altogether tended to be those aspects most closely associated with the terrifying masks and naked abstractions—the transcendence, incomprehensibility, and hiddenness of God. This occurred in three dimensions. First, God the Ruler of nature was abstracted into naturalistic scientific explanations. Second, God the moral Governor was identified with purely human activities and aspirations. Third,

> and most importantly for our purposes here, God—the mysterious Lord of Heaven Who struck human beings with awe and humility—was much diminished, as believers shifted the main focus of their concern from God's transcendence of earthly things to His compatibility with humanity, its wants, its aspirations, its ways of understanding. What remained of awe before divine mystery was transformed into reverence for such surrogates as nature, art, and humanity itself.[11]

The "fatal slip" of many religious leaders, in Turner's view, was that they forgot "that their God was—as any God had to be to command belief over the long term—radically other than man."[12] It is to be expected that Turner's analysis would fit in cultures other than the United States'. It is, after all, a very old game. As St. Augustine remarked long ago of Cicero's attempt to enhance human freedom by rejecting divine providence, "Seeking to make men free he succeeded only in making them sacrilegious."[13] Or as Luther put it when Erasmus attempted the same thing, "The gouty foot laughs at your doctoring!"[14] The "God-pain" is like the gout. The more theological doctoring is attempted, the worse it gets.

The Classic Distinction

The only solution to the problem of the abstract, naked, absconding God is the proclamation: God preached. The failure in systematic theology to attend to the fundamental distinction between God not preached and God preached has been disastrous. This distinction comes from Luther, though perhaps not even he exploited its full

significance. Luther's distinctions in the doctrine of God are well
known. God clothed in the flesh is set against the naked God (*deus
indutus* versus *deus nudus*) and the revealed God against the hidden
God (*deus revelatus* versus *deus absconditus*). The distinctions were
made with such gusto and confidence because he knew that no one—
no earthly theologian certainly—was going to dislodge, spy out, or
unmask the naked, hidden God. The naked, hidden God needs no
theological proof, apology, or defense. The problem, Luther saw clearly,
was neither how to find God nor even to prove God's existence, but
how to get God off our backs. Yet only God could do that. The distinctions are not theoretical but descriptive. They are accurate descriptions of the way things are. Only God can deal with God.

Thus there is a battle. It is God against God. The abstract God
cannot be removed but must be dethroned, overcome, "for you" in
concrete actuality. The clothed God must conquer the naked God for
us. We can never escape on our own. The revealed God must conquer
the hidden God *for you* in the living present. Faith is precisely the
ever-renewed flight from God to God: from God naked and hidden to
God clothed and revealed. Thus Luther insisted that we must cling to
the God at his mother's breasts, the God who hung on the cross and
was raised from the tomb in the face of the desperate attack launched
from the side of the hidden God/Satan. There just is no other way. The
question at stake is whether one will believe God in face of God.[15]

All of that is common knowledge. Less well known, however, is
that there was a third pair of concepts in Luther's "dialectic of God"
which set the preached God over against God not preached. This third
pair is at once the most neglected by systematic theology and the most
critical, for it determines the way one does theology. Systematic theology can cope with distinctions between the naked and clothed God
or between God hidden and revealed. These distinctions can be reduced, supposedly, to reasonably approximate "abstractions," permit-
ting systematics to straddle the dialectic in some fashion, even though
it complains a bit and puzzles about what is hidden and what is revealed
in our "knowledge" of God. Indeed, howls of dismay are often heard
when a theology is questioned for removing the "masks" that are its
particular targets. So the protest often runs, "How can Luther know
so much about the hidden God?" The question betrays a common
theological myopia resulting from failure to see that the naked God,

the hidden God, can and is to be left alone only when one has heard and knows the place of the proclamation. From the point of view of the proclamation alone one can "let God be God." Not only is it impossible to dislodge this God, but also, the proclamation itself gains warrant and authority only if we let God be God.

But if the hidden/revealed dialectic is puzzling, what is systematic theology to make of God not preached versus God preached? Where does systematic theology place itself? It would be unseemly for it to place itself on the side of God not preached, for then it would open itself to the suspicion of being an abstraction with little to say. Yet if it were to place itself on the side of God preached it would seem to reduce itself to homiletics. The distinction is difficult for systematics because it calls for a different understanding of the function of theological discourse. Indeed, it calls for two different types of discourse—that which preaches God versus that which does not and neither pretends nor aspires to do so but sees its purpose as serving and fostering the preaching. Systematic theology does not seem to like such distinctions—perhaps because it is unwittingly accustomed to putting itself in the place of preaching.

The Source of the Offense

A principal reason why the distinction has been ignored and neglected, however, is the perplexing and even offensive context in which it finds its classic statement: Luther's disagreement with Erasmus over the bondage of the will. The discussion in which it appears turns on some biblical passages that Erasmus believed allowed him to infer freedom of choice. The specific passage in question is Ezek. 18:23: "I desire not the death of the sinner, but rather that he should be converted and live."[16] Erasmus argued that if God does not desire the death of the sinner, such death can only be due to the wrong exercise of free will. In other words, since God does not desire it, human free will must be the reason for it. If, Luther was right in saying that all things happen by divine necessity, Erasmus reasoned, then God would be the ultimate cause of the sinner's death, and the claim of the passage that God "desired not the death of the sinner" would be absurd.

Luther, however, claimed that Erasmus's inference of free choice made a horrible confusion of law and gospel.[17] It turns a sweet proclamation of the gospel promise into a terrible statement of law: "If you want to escape death, you had better exercise your free will, stop sinning, and convert!" One may as well exhort the alleged free will to stop our dying! The inference of free choice always has the effect of turning gospel into law, turning the proclamation into a project to be accomplished rather than a promise freely given. Moreover, if the inference is true at all, it proves too much even for Erasmus. It proves only that Pelagius was right: the will is free enough even to avoid sin and death and thus to dispense with the Spirit and grace altogether.

As one would suspect, the consequences of such a move for systematic theology are serious as well. If the Word "I desire not the death of the sinner . . ." is taken as a statement about God in the abstract, a general or universal truth about God not preached, both the need for proclamation and the very godness of God are undercut. If it is generally and universally true that God does not desire the death of sinners, then proclamation is not needed, for surely the desire of God will be realized. The difficulty, however, is that reality undercuts confidence in such generalities, for in fact, sinners are dying like flies! Either they are dying without God's knowledge, or God is unable to do anything about it. In either case, the very godness of God is sacrificed. We are left with a God who "desires not the death of the sinner" but either is ignorant of or cannot—or will not—do anything about it.

The point of Luther's argument is that proclamation cannot be confused with or turned into abstract, general statements about God. Luther insists that the "I desire not the death of the sinner . . ." is the sweet voice of the gospel, that it is true of the preached God, but is not to be construed as a general truth any more than, for instance, "I forgive you all your sins." Luther saw that the Ezekiel passage was in fact not a general statement about God in the abstract but part of God's instruction to the prophet on what he should preach to the house of Israel. One should no more make a general statement out of that than out of a prophecy of doom and destruction. Theology needs to recognize the difference between God not preached and God preached, between our general, abstract statements about God and the proclaimed Word of God to us. Theology that attempts to make God "nice" ends only with a polite, societal deity whose "goodness" is at once ineffectual, patronizing, oppressive, and ultimately terrifying.

A viable doctrine of God requires the distinction between God not preached and God preached. The classic statement of the position comes at that point in the argument between Erasmus and Luther where the question arises as to why, if there is no freedom of choice, some believe and others do not. The proclamation of the gospel comes effectively to those who have been brought to despair over sin through the law. Why then are some touched by the law and others not? Here, Luther insists, our theologizing has reached its limit. The ultimate answer to the "why" lies in

> that hidden and awful will of God whereby he ordains by his own counsel which and what sort of persons he wills to be recipients and partakers of his preached and offered mercy. This will is not to be inquired into but reverently adored, as by far the most awe-inspiring secret of the Divine Majesty, reserved for himself and alone and forbidden to us.[18]

This is a crucial moment for systematic theology because a limit has been reached. Theologies can be characterized by whether they observe this limit or not. The limit means that discourse about God breaks into two different sorts. The distinction between God preached and not preached is added to the dialectic of God and explicitly heads the list.

> We have to argue in one way about God or the will of God as preached, revealed, offered, and worshiped, and in another way about God as he is not preached, not revealed, not offered, not worshiped. To the extent, therefore, that God hides himself and wills to be unknown to us, it is no business of ours. For here the saying truly applies, "Things above us are no business of ours."[19]

We can, indeed we must, talk about God in two different ways. In the one we have to do with God preached, revealed, offered to us, and worshiped by us, while in the other we have to do with God not preached, not revealed, not offered, not worshiped. Care must be taken that we speak properly in these two different ways.

But just here we come to the critical point. For it is precisely Luther's talk about the preached and not preached God and especially the way the two kinds of talk are related that have provoked vehement protest. Here just about everybody, including most Lutherans,[20] abandon ship. Let us look carefully at the source of the offense in the passages immediately following the quote above.

And lest anyone should think this a distinction of my own, I am following Paul, who writes to the Thessalonians concerning Antichrist that he will exalt himself above every God that is preached and worshiped [2 Thess. 2:4]. This plainly shows that someone can be exalted above God as he is preached and worshiped, that is, above the word and rite through which "God is known to us and has dealings with us; but above God as he is not worshiped and not preached, but as he is in his own nature and majesty, nothing can be exalted, but all things are under his mighty hand.

The God who is to be preached is the God who comes in lowliness and humility. It is possible for human and satanic perfidy to vaunt itself above the preached God, as exemplified by the antichrist. God not preached, revealed, offered, or worshiped, however—"God as He is in His own nature and majesty"—poses a particular kind of limit for us and consequently for proper theological discourse. If one is to speak properly about this not-preached God, one must recognize that such a God simply is the limit. In other words, we do not have to do with a limit that theology may or may not choose to impose on itself, but one about which it can, finally, do nothing. "Above God as he is not worshiped and not preached . . . nothing can be exalted." Luther means that we simply can do nothing about the not-preached God. Such a God just remains God "in his own nature and majesty." God not preached is the God we can never get off our backs, the God who always comes back to haunt us when we think we have at last managed to escape by theological artifice, the God we invoke in curses even when we do not believe, the God about whose existence or nonexistence we argue in vain, the God whom we absolve from evil in our theodices but in whose face we must shake our fist anyway, even the God to whom Jesus cried, "Why have you forsaken me?" and received no answer.

But how then are we to regard the not-preached God? How then is God not preached to be related to God preached? This is the most critical point in the discussion.

> God must therefore be left to himself in his own majesty, for in this regard we have nothing to do with him, nor has he willed that we should have anything to do with him. But we have something to do with him insofar as he is clothed and set forth in his Word, through which he offers himself to us and which is the beauty and glory with which the psalmist celebrates him as being clothed. In this regard we say, the good

God does not deplore the death of his people which he works in them, but he deplores the death which he finds in his people and desires to remove from them. For it is this that God as he is preached is concerned with, namely that sin and death should be taken away and we should be saved. For "he sent his word and healed them" [Ps. 107:20]. But God hidden in his majesty neither deplores nor takes away death, but works life, death and all in all. For there he has not bound himself by his word, but has kept himself free over all things.[21]

What are we to do about God not preached? Nothing. We are to leave the not-preached God alone and pay attention to the God clothed and displayed in the Word. But how can we do that? Only, of course, to the degree that we are grasped by the preached God. In Luther's terms we cannot—will not—do it by ourselves, not apart from the proclamation. To put it bluntly, everyone theologizes here as they must. A veritable battle is being fought over us between God not preached and God preached. God not preached devours sinners without regret, but the preached God battles to snatch us away from sin and death.

All that, though difficult to swallow theologically, is understandable and perhaps acceptable. What puts everyone off, however, is the last sentence: the assertion that God hidden in majesty "has not bound himself by his word, but kept himself free over all things." The usual objection is this: if God not preached (God hidden in majesty) is not bound by God preached (by the Word of promise) but is free over all things, then there is no basis for certainty or confidence that the promise of the preached God will stand. The fearsome specter of a God hidden in majesty who can arbitrarily wipe out the promise has haunted theology ever since.

The driving impulse of this haunted theology has been the persistent attempt to banish the specter of this terrifying absolute God (*deus ipse*) from sight, to try to bind this God not preached to theology's understanding of the revealed Word. But the only result of this attempt has been to forsake proclamation for an explanation. Ironically, such theology abandons the real weapon it has against the unpreached God. For the point is that not theology, but God preached is the only defense against God not preached.

What prompted Luther to leave the specter of a God who has not "bound himself by his word, but has kept himself free over all things" to haunt us? There are at least three major reasons that should now be obvious. First and foremost, Luther recognized the primacy of the oral, spoken word, that particular type of discourse called proclamation, the living voice of the gospel. The burden of the passage quoted above is his insistence that we must take explicit theological note of this primacy and observe careful distinctions in our speaking between God not preached and God preached. Luther let the absolute God be, precisely to make room for the proclamation. So we have the remarkable circumstance that the argument Luther used to save the proclamation is the very one most systematic theologians since have thought would endanger it. The antithesis could hardly be more clear.

This is the classic illustration of how a theology that understands the place of proclamation will make certain moves and refuse to make others. Luther knew that only the proclamation—only the preached God, the living Word here and now—could save us from the God not preached, the absolute God. A theology that intends to save us by attempting to remove or render the God not preached harmless in the system makes just the wrong move. It fails to recognize the nature of the battle for the human soul. It maintains that it can bind God not preached to the Word and so "save" us. It makes the fatal assumption that it can accomplish more that the living Word. Theology must recognize its limits. It must understand that only the concrete address, the "I absolve you," the "I baptize you," will save us from the threat of the absolute God. Absolution is the only solution to the problem of the absolute!

The second major reason why Luther did not banish the absolute God from his theology is already implied in the first. Such banishment cannot be accomplished by any kind of theological artifice. Luther left the absolute God there in his theology because he knew he could do nothing about it. Nothing can be exalted above the absolute God. It simply is not true that God in general is bound even to an abstraction called the revealed Word. As Luther put it, "God does many things that he does not disclose to us in his word; he also wills many things which he does not disclose himself as willing in his word."[22] What would happen if we were to claim that the absolute God is bound and limited by the Word? We would revert to the situation in which the preached Word—"I desire not the death of the sinner"—becomes a general statement by which God is bound and limited. But that is not true, nor does it accord God any particular honor. For sin and death continue, and nothing—certainly not theology—alters the reign of the absolute God except ("when and where it pleases God!") when the concrete proclamation interrupts and creates faith. Not even God can do anything about wrath in the abstract. Not even God can somehow unmask God in the abstract. The proclamation of the concrete, incarnate word set against the absolute God so as to create faith is the only way out. Faith means precisely to be grasped by the proclamation in the face of the terror of the absolute God, in the face of tribulation (*Anfechtung*), as Luther put it. Theology, no matter how sweetly done, does not cure tribulation. Theological opinion may provide momentary relief, but rarely does it survive the heat and evil of the day.

The third reason that prompted Luther to leave the specter of the absolute God alone is his knowledge that we as sinners live under the wrath of God. Our efforts—even the best of them—afford no escape. Theology, no matter how cleverly devised, cannot deliver us from the wrath of God. It may twist and turn to remodel God, try by every artifice to fashion less frightening masks, but in the end such masks only turn on us. We are sinners confronted by masks we cannot see through. We cannot see God. Luther was not merely stating opinions at this point. He was describing as honestly as possible the actual state of things. No doubt only faith can risk such honesty.

Faith itself is endangered when the attempt is made theologically to bind the hidden God to the Word as abstraction. The nature of faith is transformed. Faith strives to become sight, to render the hidden God visible. Faith's object is not the proclaimed God, not the sacramental deed of God "for you" in the living present, but certain alleged truths about God in the past tense. Indeed, the very freedom of faith is consequently lost. Theology becomes a tour de force, an attempt to induce or perhaps even subtly force belief in the God one has conjured up. But faith is a matter of being set free from the God of the past tense. It is not a matter of deferring to the authority of this or that theologian, but a matter of being set free by the proclamation itself, by an actual word from God. Faith comes by hearing and being grasped by the proclamation. God speaks to you. Faith is the Spirit-fired free flight from the hidden to the revealed God.

The fact is that the terror of the absolute God reigns until the proclamation that creates faith announces its end and liberates the believer from it. Theology must learn to speak the truth about this. Theology must know its own limitations and speak honestly about the way things are. It must not tell sweet lies about God. It must assess the true nature of the battle so that it can be joined in proper fashion. Ironically, a theology that sets out to protect the proclamation by tying the absolute God to the revelation only undercuts the proclamation itself and bowdlerizes God. Small wonder that we find ourselves today with only tenuous belief in a platitudinous God and little consciousness of what God wills to say to us. So we talk mostly about ourselves. Where the distinction between God not preached and God preached is not observed, we are gradually reduced to complete silence.

Where systematic theology is informed by the distinction between God not preached and God preached, however, the way is open for a profound and exciting view of the nature and place of the act of proclamation. The deed of proclamation in the living present is the deed of the living God! It is what God has in mind for us. The mighty acts of God are not over, not relegated to the past or to some philosophy or theology of history. The proclamation itself is the mighty act of God in the living present. Everything that God has done in Jesus Christ has been poured into this moment. The incarnation, death, and resurrection of the Son of God in Jesus is the authorization for the proclamation of the will of God in the living present. The preacher needs the "nerve"—the Spirit—to act on that. Systematic theology needs to understand itself so as to drive the preacher to that point. It must be constructed so as to leave its practitioners at a point where they can do no other than proclaim. Where systematic theology overlooks or blurs the distinction between God not preached and God preached, thereby usurping the place of proclamation itself and leaving us with a lecture instead of the promise, all will be lost.

The Electing God

If we are to proclaim and not merely explain God, what are we to say? In speaking of God it is important to start with the very first principle: What is to be proclaimed is what God has decided, in fact, to do. The word for what God has decided to do is election. The God of the Scriptures is an electing God. The God of the Scriptures is "the God of Abraham, Isaac, and Jacob," the God who chooses Israel and disposes over its entire history, the God who comes in Jesus to break down the wall of separation between Jew and Gentile so that the election shall know no bounds, the God who sends apostles so that this "mystery hidden for ages in God" may now be revealed to all, even the "principalities and powers in the heavenly places," through the ministry of the church and its proclamation (Eph. 3:7ff). The God of the Scriptures is an electing God and, therefore, a God who speaks and enjoins those who hear, believe, and follow to speak the Word of God, to go and do the electing.

This sending forth of preachers to do the electing is the aim of the God of the Scriptures (the proclaimed God) as distinguished from all the gods of idealisms (the explained God). The explained God is the God not preached who does everything in general, and so in the end does nothing in particular, no matter how much one may talk about the "mighty acts of God in history." These "mighty acts" are all turned into the past tense, and thus treated as mere occasions for further explanation. The history finally becomes material from which one distills one more explanation, as the philosophers of old did from the myths. Whether the material comes from biblical history or from the myths makes little difference if all that comes of it is one more explanation. That is why arguments between revelation in history and in nature soon become sterile. The explained God always turns out to be one of the gods of idealism, the alleged goal and rewarder of the idealist project, as Regin Prenter points out.[23] The explained God is not the God who seeks the lost, but the God whom the lost (even if with the aid of grace) must seek and attempt to appease, the just rewarder of pious effort, the God of law who always turns against us.

Predestination, a Test Case

The electing God of the Scriptures is the God of predestination. Such an assertion, however, puts systematic theology once again at a crossroad, facing the question of the next move. Election or predestination is a crucial test case because it is such a persistent, intractable, and offensive problem for us. The usual move is predictable: attempt to remove the threat or domesticate the offense by systematic adjustment, to pretty up the mask, so to speak, with theological cosmetics. The most direct and honest move is to obscure predestination altogether. The scriptural evidence is ignored, explained away, or treated perhaps as a species of ancient mythology to be demythologized in some fashion. The most subtle move is to fabricate some kind of synthesis between divine election and the idealist project. God obligingly elects those who in one way or another fulfill the necessary conditions. One then only needs to negotiate minimal or maximal conditions.

Such moves are, of course, quite natural. Election—predestination—as a general or abstract idea is threatening to us. Even if it is a "revealed" truth, it remains an idea and as such carries no comfort. Once again we encounter at the outset one more frightening mask of God. We know the "that" of it but we do not know the "why" or the "who." Added to the list of magnificent abstractions, it becomes the last straw. The idea that the almighty, timeless, immutable, impassible, infinite, immortal, omni-everything God also elects can only be taken to mean that such a God has decided things in eternity once and for all, and there is absolutely nothing further to be said or done about it.

Such a God is the end of us, the absolute end of all our idealistic hopes and aspirations. Kant, the father of modern idealism, saw the matter with chilling clarity in his attempt to construct a *Religion Within The Limits of Reason Alone.* Speaking of the possibility of faith in a God who is no longer within the limits of reason alone, but who actually invades time and history to create faith, Kant says,

> Yet were this faith to be portrayed as having so peculiar a power and so mystical (or magical) an influence that although merely historical, so far as we can see, it is yet competent to better the whole man from the ground up (to make a new man of him) if he yields himself to it and to the feelings bound up with it, such a faith would have to be regarded as imparted and inspired directly by heaven (together with, and in, the historical faith), and everything connected even with the moral constitution of man would resolve itself into an unconditional decree of God: "He hath mercy on whom he will, and whom he will be hardeneth," . . . which, taken according to the letter, is the *salto mortale* [death leap] of human reason.[24]

Kant saw with utmost clarity that the actual intrusion of God into time to create faith meant election and that to admit to it is the "death leap" of human reason, the end of the "old being." Kant, of course, resolutely turned his back on the prospect. In so doing he made the only move humanly possible. For there is nothing we can do but deny, disown, or dismantle such a God. It is a matter of self-defense. This fact describes what is called the bondage or servitude of the will. It is the essence of sin: We are unreconciled to and will not trust such a God. As such it is the presupposition disclosing the need for proclamation. Were there no such bondage there would be no need for proclamation. An explanation would do.

A systematic theology that understands the place of proclamation will make a quite different move. It will understand that there is no "abstract" theological cure for the problem of the electing God. It will realize that attempts to remove the electing God are futile. It knows that no amount of persuasion can prevent the idea from returning to haunt us—"What if . . . ?" It knows that anyone who reads the Bible with faithful discernment will soon lose confidence in theological cosmetics.

What is to be done about an electing God? Our only recourse is to make the move to proclamation. We are not, of course, to proclaim that God is an electing God; everybody knows that already and is scared to death by it. Rather, we must do the electing ourselves. One must have the nerve—or better, the Spirit—to do the unheard-of thing and say to those listening "You are the elect!" or "You are the one." "Just as surely as I am here and you are there, this is the moment the almighty, eternal, electing God has planned on, the 'mystery hidden for ages' and now revealed 'through the church,' the actual revelation of the will of the hidden God!" We have to do with that shepherd (Matt. 18:12-14; Luke 15:3-7) who left the ninety-nine and went after the one that was lost! The point is that since God is an electing God, the only real solution to the problem of being unreconciled to the God not preached is to do the deed of the preached God: "Once you were lost but now you are found."

Two False Solutions

The two most prevalent attempts of idealism to reach a solution must be rejected. The first is universalism: the idea that we can defuse the dynamite of election and predestination by saying that God "elects" everyone. Quite apart from the fact that the Scriptures give us no particular warrant for asserting this, the idea does no real good at all. It substitutes an abstract idea about God for a concrete self-disclosure of the divine will, leaving the hearers under wrath. The error is not in the hope it expresses. It is certainly more legitimate and gracious than a so-called evangelical theology that insists hell must be populated to complete the divine plan. The error of universalism is that it simply cuts off the move to proclamation. As a result, the God who supposedly loves and elects everyone never gets around to saying it to anyone. The opinion of the "universalist" is no better than that of the double predestinationist who likewise subverts the proclamation by the abstract notion that the election of some to heaven and others to hell has been determined before all time. Ideas of universalism do not save anyone. Even the slightest hint in the Scriptures of the possibility of a different outcome is enough to shatter one's confidence in such ideas.

> The argument about universalism is usually wrongly stated and takes different shape when one thinks in terms of proclamation. The scriptures do indeed contain statements which appear universalist. But like the "I desire not the death of the sinner" discussed above they are misused if taken as abstract general statements or ideas about God. If one interprets scripture in that fashion, one will then have to find some way to cope with other statements as well that seem to indicate different ideas about God—the possibility, for instance, of being cast into the "outer darkness" where there is "weeping and gnashing of teeth." The point is that ideas afford no real comfort when one's ultimate destiny is at stake. Searching for a "general consensus" in scripture or counting passages for or against an idea is no protection for the "conscience." One is not saved by a scriptural consensus. The smallest hint or just one passage is enough to shatter confidence and to raise the specter of being lost.[25]

Once again, the move must be made to the proclamation. The element of truth in the universalist position is that the gospel demands to be proclaimed universally, that it knows no bounds, imposes no conditions. The preached God comes to do battle against sin and death precisely through such limitless proclamation. The preacher is authorized to say it—to do the election—to everyone within earshot.

The second attempt to defuse the dynamite is to fall back on some version of human responsibility or "free will" as an explanation for the gospel's success or lack thereof among us. Election is discounted since we are the ones who make the ultimate decisions. The reason why some are "saved" and others not rests in our hands. At first this seems to remove the threatening mask from the face of God, but in the end it only makes matters worse. "See to it yourselves then!" would be the divine message to us. The result, once again, is the loss of the proclamation. Instead of the Word that does the deed here and now, the hearer gets explanations about how "nice" this God is who does not elect anyone. A "systematic theology" that thinks itself able to persuade supposedly free beings gets substituted for the proclamation. Exhortations abound—all prettied up in high-sounding phrases like having Jesus as "your personal Savior," or "letting Jesus into your heart"—to choose this abstraction.

A systematic theology that understands the nature and place of proclamation consequently will not waste its time trying to avoid or explain the election away. Instead it will endeavor to get preachers to go and do it. It will recognize precisely that systematic theology has to make room for the proclamation, foster it, drive to it, leave its practitioners with no other recourse but to do it.

The Place of the Preacher

A systematic theology so constructed will understand that to be of any use the proclamation must be able authoritatively to answer the crucial question about what God has decided to do here and now, that is, about election or predestination. The crucial question is not the whether or why of it, but the who. The preacher must claim the audacious and unheard-of authority to say who is intended, to actually speak for God. The answer, to anticipate, is always you: "You, now that you are here within earshot." This is the place of the preacher. There is only one question about predestination we can answer with any authority, and it is the only one that matters: Who?

The preacher acts on the presupposition that only the present-tense, here-and-now deed of God, the proclamation itself, can be the solution to the problem of God. The proclamation is the end result, the culmination, of the great acts of God in history. The preacher ought to have the consciousness of standing in that place knowing that the Word and sacrament are themselves the end (*telos*), the purpose of it all. The concrete moment of the proclamation is the doing of the mighty act of God in the living present. It is not a recital of past acts, but the doing of the act itself now. Only when there is an authoritative Word from God in the present tense do we escape the threat of the hidden God. Only then can a faith be created to stand in the face of that threat. As Paul wrote, "Faith comes from what is heard, and what is heard comes by the preaching of Christ" (Rom. 10:17), "for ... it pleased God through the folly of what we preach to save those who believe" (1 Cor. 1:21).

Let God Be God

Now we can see what is to be gained by leaving the absolute God alone, by not attempting systematically to tear the mask from the face of the hidden God. Precisely because one allows God to be God, by whose will and appointment all things happen, one is able to declare that the concrete moment of the proclamation (the absolution, the sermon, the baptism, the supper; all given *for you*) is the divine act of God in the living present. Of course that "for you" cannot be spoken except in the proclamation. We are left in the position where we can only move to the proclamation because it is a matter of the present tense, here and now. The moment of proclamation is the revealed will of God "for you." When you are there, when you are within earshot, you are the target. The almighty, immutable, God breaks through the hiddenness to speak the concrete word of election to you.

Faith comes by hearing! One must be still and listen (cf. Ps 46:10). Faith alone hears and trusts that the unchangeable God of election stands behind the proclamation. That is the mystery hidden in God, now revealed in the church. Where the electing God, the hidden God, the absolute God has already been dismantled, we are not dealing with the Word "of" God, but only our words and opinions "about" God. There everything collapses into uncertainty. Perhaps it was just by social custom or parental whim that we were hauled before the congregation and doused with water, or only an accident that we happened to hear the gospel word. We cannot be certain we were intended to hear it. Where one allows God to be God—whatever that may cost or entail in subsequent theological consequences—the moment of proclamation is the doing of what God has in mind for us. God makes no mistakes. Were this not the case, all would be lost in the arbitrariness of opinion and the black hole of the self.

A systematic theology operating under such auspices will take a different shape from what usually trades under that name, though it needs to cover much the same ground. Since the question is not whether but who God elects, a different set of questions becomes central. Who has the authority to say so? Where does such authority come from and how is it granted? Who are the hearers of the proclamation? How can one announce with such confidence, "You are the elect"? What does one presuppose about such hearers and what shape must the proclamation consequently take? What is the expected and hoped-for outcome of the proclamation? Such questions abound. Systematic theology has to deal more intentionally with questions about the presuppositions for and the authority of the present-tense proclamation.

2

The Hard of Hearing

Do you not yet perceive or understand? Are your hearts hardened? Having eyes do you not see, and having ears do you not hear?

(Mark 8:17-18)

*E*xamination of the way in which systematic theology is correlated with proclamation affects the way one views the predicament and prospect of the hearer. This necessitates sketching a theological anthropology. Such an anthropology must first unfold presuppositions for the proclamation.

It may be a bit misleading to speak about strict *pre*suppositions here, since there is a hermeneutical circle. The systematic undertaken comes from the already heard proclamation that has shaped the presuppositions. That is, proclamation heard and believed shapes a confession upon which one reflects in order to return to proclamation again. Our concern is for the hearer in the light of this "circle." What do we who have heard the proclamation presuppose about the hearer whom we will in turn address?

Given the distinctions between God not preached and God preached, what is the actual predicament of those who are to hear the proclamation? Why can they not hear without a preacher (Rom. 10:14)? Would not a teacher or a purveyor of wisdom do as well? When the question of the human predicament is put in this fashion it will not only lead us to a more accurate assessment of who we are and where we stand over against the electing, preached God, but it will also play a significant role in shaping the proclamation itself.

The Grand Scheme

What does theology have to say about the human predicament? It is customary in both dogmatic and systematic theology to introduce at this point an interpretation of the great scheme of creation, fall, and redemption. Some assessment of the degree of fallenness from created innocence or perfection is usually offered and a corresponding redemption proffered. The neatness, order, and utility of such schemes is not to be denied. But it is too early for us to move directly to that scheme. A systematic that seeks to promote a vital proclamation has some very basic questions to answer about presuppositions before it can paint a broader picture.

Actually, most interpretations of the creation, fall, redemption scheme already rest on presuppositions detrimental to the proclamation. It was proposed way back in the days of the early church as a defense against gnostic teaching—ideas that the soul, due to some cosmic bungle, had become fatally trapped in a material world not created or ruled by the God made known in Jesus. Gnostic views tended toward metaphysical dualism (a world split between spirit and matter and ruled by opposing powers) and fatalism (the human spirit or soul was involuntarily trapped in a hostile world). The creation, fall, and redemption scheme countered such views. Seeking quite rightly to avoid gnostic dualism and fatalism, the church fathers insisted on the goodness of creation and tended to interpret the fall as a free act entailing a partial—though serious—loss of such freedom. Redemption could then be interpreted as a restitution of original integrity accomplished by the corresponding degree of cooperation of the will with divine grace. While this scheme refuted gnostic heresy, it unfortunately tended at the same time to undercut the newness of the eschatological proclamation and to overestimate the place of human free will with respect to salvation. The metaphysical dualism of gnosticism was controverted, but the eschatological "dualism" of the New Testament became a casualty. The proclamation tended to lose its character as the radical word that brings the end of the old age and the beginning of the new, and was instead replaced by venerable and ancient orthodox teaching that was to be accepted by "free choice." In other words, the distinction between God not preached and God preached was overlooked and lost. Ironically, orthodox Christianity became suspicious of the new. The result was that proclamation and sacrament lost their cutting edge as bringers of the new eschatological kingdom, and became instead "graces" offered to the "damaged" will so it could cooperate in the restoration of the original creation.

In such a "system," proclamation itself tends to become just more information about what God has done to repair the damage to this grand scheme of things. A Christian "gnosis" appears in opposition to heretical gnosticism. Christianity mirrors its enemy. Christian discourse is taken captive almost entirely by doctrine, right teaching, "orthodoxy."

The move to "right teaching" is not in itself a bad thing, of course. There must always be such, at least on this side of the Parousia. Disaster occurs, however, when awareness of the purpose of such teaching is eroded, when no distinction is made between such teaching and proclamation, between God not preached and God preached. Doctrine and proclamation get run together, most always to the detriment of proclamation because—identified with doctrine—it loses its status as a "means of grace." Doctrine is generally past tense. It is built on and interprets the great acts of God in past history. Proclamation as present-tense declaration wanes and even disappears as a result. The sacraments become the only remaining instances in which the gospel retains its present tense. But even the sacraments are captive to the ancient scheme when viewed as purveyors of the grace that makes it work.

The eschatological finality of the sacraments always causes difficulty for the ordinary time line of our lives. Sacraments break into our lives, bringing an end and new beginning. We do not know how to cope with such finality. So, for instance, there was a tendency in the early church to postpone baptism until one's deathbed. Even when that practice was later discouraged, uncertainty and anxiety remained about what kind of "end" baptism was supposed to effect. What was one to do about sins committed "after" baptism? So the practice of penance developed to fill in the time gap. More recently difficulty with the time question surfaces in debate about whether baptism should be performed before (infant baptism) or after (believer's baptism) one has "come to faith." The question, however, remains: Is baptism itself the bringer of the eschatological end, or is it a symbol of some sort marking the fact that the end has not yet taken place or supposedly taken place in some other way?

Similar problems arise with regard to the last supper. The very title introduces the time problem: how is the time gap to be bridged between that last supper and subsequent repeated suppers? Attempts to fabricate such bridges have been the cause of much theological and liturgical misadventure. (See below, pp. 158–78, where these matters are discussed more fully.)

Here again a systematic theology that seeks to foster proclamation will need to move differently and suggest a somewhat altered scheme in the end.

The Bondage of the Will

The first anthropological presupposition for the proclamation is the bondage of the will. If the human will was not bound there would be no need for proclamation. One could simply explain matters as clearly as possible and appeal to the will for a decision, whatever the will's degree of freedom or unfreedom. The "wisdom" of the theologian or the "gnosis" of the sage would be sufficient. However, a problem arises:

> Where is the wise man? Where is the scribe? Where is the debater of this age? Has not God made foolish the wisdom of the world? For since, in the wisdom of God, the world did not know God through wisdom, it pleased God through the folly of what we preach to save those who believe.
>
> (1 Cor. 1:20-21)

The proclamation is neither an appeal to the wisdom of the age nor grounded in it. Proclamation is folly, an offense. Furthermore, it is the very wisdom of God that has made it impossible for the world to know God through its wisdom. God, we might say, knows that we cannot be saved that way. It pleased God rather through the folly of the proclamation to save those who believe. Proclamation is something other than an appeal to the wisdom and therefore the supposed freedom of this age.

We are dealing with a fundamentally different paradigm here, fundamentally different presuppositions. The presupposition for proclamation is not the free choice of the will, but the bondage of the will. Again we find ourselves in sharp antithesis to the usual manner of thinking. We usually assume that if there is no freedom of will, proclamation is pointless. What is the use of proclamation if there is no free choice? That, however, confuses proclamation with explanation, the wisdom of this age. It confuses God preached with God not preached. Theologically, the situation needs to be reversed. Because there is no freedom, we can do nothing other than proclaim in order that the blind may see, the lame may walk, the deaf may hear, and captives may be set free. Proclamation is the invasion of the house of the "strong man armed" who hopes to keep control of things, not the appeal to a freedom already at hand. Bondage, not freedom, is presupposed, and such a presupposition will not only affect our view of the human predicament but will also deepen the understanding of proclamation itself.

It is important to grasp what is being said here as well as what is not being said. In fact, the bondage of the will is the anthropological counterpart to our discussion of God. In and of ourselves—"in our natural state" or "in our fallen state"—we are "bound to," we "will," or even, we "must," say no to God because we do not know the preached God. Use of the future tense is essential here to avoid some of the abstraction that often accompanies the discussion.[1] "Will" is initially a future-tense action or verb and only subsequently taken as a noun. Strange things happen in language and especially theology when we lose sight of this and take "the will" only as a noun denoting something we "have" at our disposal. The question is really not whether we "have" free wills, but rather what we will do—what we are "bound to" do—when we come up against God. Proclamation presupposes that we cannot, will not, reconcile ourselves to God. But the proclaimer hopes and thus proclaims in the expectation that through the proclamation the "Spirit of the Lord" is at work to set captives free.

A systematic theology correlated with proclamation thus views the questions about the place of natural theology somewhat differently. Systematic theology usually tries either to use natural theology as a presupposition for the subsequent construction of the system or, more recently, as in Barth and his followers, to expel it from the system altogether. Is there such a thing as a natural theology? Does it have a place in "the system"? A systematic theology sensitive to the place of proclamation will take a different road here. On the one hand, it would agree with those who find a natural theology at hand among humans; on the other hand, it would agree with Barth that the aim is to get rid of the natural theology. Against the natural theologians it would argue that the natural theology we have is not the foundation of the system, but rather the source of our trouble. The problem is not so much how to preserve it as how to escape it. Against the Barthian attempt to expel natural theology it would argue that this is an impossible tour de force. Systematic theology cannot get rid of natural theology as such. To presume that it can is only a variation on the old theme: the attempt to get rid of the hidden God by theological artifice. The hidden God only comes back under a different mask. Indeed, just as in the battle with gnosticism, a theology that purports to expel natural theology by a tour de force tends to become too much like one itself. Here also, systematic theology has to realize that only the proclamation and the sacraments are the means of grace through which the captives are set free.

The Nature of Bondage

So we begin by presupposing the bondage of the will. The phrase "bondage of the will" does not mean, first of all, that the will is forced, determined, or frustrated, perhaps by some higher power or fate or god in its attempt to do what it really wants to do. No, the bondage of the will refers to what we will not do, what we are bound not to do in a given instance. The bondage of the will means that we find ourselves in a situation where we simply cannot do what is asked of us, and we cannot do it because we will not. What is being claimed is that there is something we actually cannot do because we do not want to. What is that something?

Second, in the classic argument with Erasmus, Luther made a basic distinction pinpointing just what is at issue here.[2] He said that if we must use the term free will, then we could use it with regard to those things that are below us rather than above us. In this distinction Luther was trying to describe faithfully and accurately just the way things are with us. Obviously there is a large arena in which we do pretty much as we will. Luther calls this arena the things "beneath us (*inferioris*)," that is, those things over which we have dominion because nothing actually stops us. He also speaks of "means and possessions (*facultatibus et possessionibus*)," which one has a right to use or not, things one can do or not do as one pleases. Luther means that we decide what to do with our money and goods, to come and to go, take what jobs we wish, choose our friends, and so on. I expect we could expand the list even to include such things as morality. We can decide or be persuaded whether to act morally or immorally. No doubt we can even decide whether to join or go to a church. Perhaps we could even decide "for Jesus" (whatever that might mean to us) if we happen to find Jesus attractive. In all of that nothing stops us at least from willing what we will. Physical restraint or accident may stop us from doing it now and then, but the will, at least, is not forced. And above all, God does not overtly interfere. God, by definition, does rule all things, of course, but in this sphere apparently does so without direct interference. God, it would seem, is able to rule all things without such overt interference. Luther, in other words, is not interested on this level in the argument about how the divine omnipotence rhymes with the contingency of our acts. What we hold about God makes no direct difference here. One can be a determinist or a libertarian since, either way, one will still do what one chooses. "All you need to know to be free is that nothing is stopping you," states the rather irreverent but in this sphere accurate piece of graffiti on the library wall. The point is to describe what is actually the case.

Third, we are not free in what is above us. That is, there is something we really are not free to do, something we actually cannot, or will not do. It has to do, Luther says, with God and everything that bears on salvation or damnation. Here one is a captive, prisoner, and bondslave, either to the will of God or the will of Satan. In the ordinary course of affairs, when we go about our daily routine, making our choices in those things below, we do not think much about God, and things go as they go. It is when we "stop and think," when we start looking back over our shoulder, so to speak, when we start puzzling about God, that we get into trouble. We start to wonder about what is "above" us. We wonder whether God really determines all things, whether we are perhaps just puppets on a string. When we do that, we enter an entirely different realm, a realm where there is no "free choice," in Luther's words. That may be a shocking concept today because we tend to think that the realm above, the "metaphysical" realm, is more or less a "free space" into which we can project whatever ideas we will. We tend to think that we can make over the gods at will to fit our own fancy (see above, chap. 1). Here, however, the contrary assertion is made: We have no free choice in what is above us.

Why? Because when we enter that realm of "things above," the "die has already been cast." Our minds are made up; the jaw is set. We have no remaining choice, not because we are supposedly forced into something, but because we have already made it. Indeed, the fact that we are there at all means that our choice has already been made. We are there for one reason. We are there to claim our freedom, to declare our independence. We are bound to do so because when we come up against God we come up against those masks, the magnificent abstractions about which we can do nothing. We come up against that which is really and truly above us. The trouble is simply that God is above us. God is simply God and not at our disposal. And we will not have it; we *will not,* cannot, let God be God.

When we come up against the eternal, immutable, impassible God and we hear in addition that this God elects (saves and damns) we simply cannot allow it. We must say to such a God, "God, I don't know what you are up to so I must take my destiny in my own hands. I think it would be safer that way!" This, to be sure, is already blasphemy, but that is the only course open to us. We are bound in this case by the "will of Satan," the adversary of God. We have no choice other than to say no to God.

Fourth, our very claim to "free choice" in what is "above" us is, ironically, the mark of our bondage. In defiance of God we claim to be free. Such "freedom," of course, is only a faith in ourselves over against God, our defense mechanism against God. In effect we say to God, "God, I cannot trust you with my destiny, therefore I must claim at least enough freedom to control it myself." But such a claim to "freedom" only describes our bondage in the things that are "above." To paraphrase St. Augustine's words about Cicero: In thinking ourselves free we only make ourselves sacrilegious.

Creatures, not Gods

So it is that we are not free in those things above us. There is something we actually cannot do. We simply cannot reconcile ourselves to God, nor surrender ourselves to a hidden God. We will not. We must claim the right to control our own eternal destiny over against a hidden

God. But it is important to see that this is a *bondage* of the will, not a forcing of the will. The will cannot be forced, even by God. The will will will what it will! But it is always bound to something or perhaps captivated by something. In some respects, Luther's book against Erasmus might better have been titled *On the Captivation of the Will*. In any case, it is essential to see that the God of the magnificent abstractions is not some transcendent manipulator who secretly pulls strings to make us do something we do not want to do. Our bondage in things above is not of that sort. The trouble is simply that we do just what we want to do, and so find ourselves locked in opposition to God. We will not believe nor trust in God. We cannot reconcile ourselves to the very idea of God.

That is the basic anthropological presupposition for the proclamation. As such it tells us something vital both about the human predicament and about the shape proclamation will have to take. Concerning the human predicament, we become aware that we are not gods, but creatures (see below, chap. 5). The fact of the bondage of the will shows us that we are not gods because we do not have free choice. Our wills over against God are bound, and there is nothing we can do about it. God is free. We are not. So Luther could say that it was not just a logical mistake to attribute free will to us, but finally blasphemy. Only God has free will. Free will is really a divine name.[3] We simply do not have the ability to turn this way or that in what is above us. Perhaps it is, as Philip Watson put it, we simply are not free to choose our own motivation.[4] No matter what we do, we are bondservants to what is above us, either to God or Satan.

Concerning the proclamation, it is only in light of it that we will come to confess the truth. Concomitant with claim to free choice is the idea that we seek to be gods. We will never admit to not having free choice in things above. We cannot bear the idea that only God has free choice; we must claim it, seek it, usurp it for ourselves. So we seek to be gods.[5] We used to be more subtle about disavowing or at least disguising such blasphemy. Of late, however, we seem more bold and open about it.[6] Such audacity may be a more honest expression of our self-esteem, but it is no less reprehensible. And it is no less the target of the proclamation.

The Upward Fall

If our problem is that we aspire to be gods, we must consider the fall and sin differently from the traditional scheme adduced above. The fall is really not what the word implies at all. It is not a downward plunge to some lower level in the great chain of being, some lower rung on the ladder of morality and freedom. Rather, it is an upward rebellion, an invasion of the realm of things "above," the usurping of divine prerogative. To retain traditional language, one would have to resort to an oxymoron and speak of an "upward fall." This, after all, is precisely what the temptation by the serpent in the garden implies: "You will not die . . . you will be like God, knowing good and evil" (Gen. 3:4-5). A line had been drawn over which Adam and Eve were not to step. They were not to eat of the tree of knowledge of good and evil. There was a realm "above" which they were to leave to God; if they did not, their death would result. But the tempter insinuated "Don't believe it for an instant! God is only jealous of the divine preserve! God knows that if you step over the line you will not die but become gods. You have something going for you! You have divine qualities, you have an immortal soul." So the step is taken. It is rebellion, an upward fall.

The Image of God

Some may protest that such talk about an upward fall could be interpreted to suggest that human striving "upward" for cultural and intellectual excellence is associated, perhaps even identified, with the fall. Indeed, a spate of recent theological literature claims that the serpent's temptation was beneficial, the goad impelling humankind out of the naiveté and innocence of nature into the blessings of cultural development. Such views should not be confused with the view of the upward fall suggested here. Apart from or prior to the rebellion, humans are to be fruitful, multiply, take care of the realm of things "below" entrusted to them, and use all their gifts in doing so. The upward fall is not a blessing in disguise. It is not the beginning but the systemic distortion of the human venture. No denigration of human intellectual or cultural endeavor is intended by employing the oxymoron.

Indeed, humans are to "image" God in taking care of creation. In the light of the proclamation the active sense of "imaging God" seems a better way to handle the troublesome question of the image of God. Just as God rules in the realm of things above in perfect peace and harmony, so also humans are to "image" God and take care of things below. Rebellion means refusal, to image God. It is rather the attempt to be God.

The Opposing Image

Does such rebellion mean that the image is lost, either partially or wholly? That question is really not to the point since it comes from the picture of the downward fall. There one treats the image as though it were a faculty or an endowment that could be impaired or lost by falling to a lower place on the scale. Usually the "image" has to do with "reason," on the one hand, and free will, on the other. Humans are "like God" in that they have rational freedom. In the scheme of the downward fall, consequently, one is anxious to protect free will from total corruption or loss. If one cannot, the whole scheme will have to be jettisoned. Those who speak of "total depravity" are thus quite naturally a dire threat and often charged with manicheism and the like.

If one looks at the human predicament as the consequence of an upward fall, however, then much of the difficulty can be avoided. What one "loses" in such a "fall" is faith and trust in God. One becomes, as stated previously, bound against God, indeed, a bondservant of Satan. The image is not lost, but turned to its opposite. One now images not God but the divine adversary. Even though the image is not lost as such, one can see that the predicament is infinitely more serious than the relatively mild impairment or partial loss envisaged by the downward fall. The God-given faculties are not lost, but rather bound to the service of Satan. Succumbing to the temptation, "you shall not die," creatures are driven by their death-denying, self-promoting (*causa sui*) projects. Death reigns in the midst of life.[7] Even so, God does not abandon creation. There is a certain order that continues even when the imaging is turned to its opposite: we have to do well to live. The physician, for instance, still has to perform proper surgery even though he or she may be entirely dedicated to self-aggrandizement. The same is true even of pastors. One cannot stop the imaging even in one's perversity. God will not be mocked.

Original Sin

The theme here, of course, is sin—not "sins," but "sin," what tradition calls original sin. If we have been seduced into the upward fall, if we are bound and cannot, will not, escape, then sin does not comprise discrete acts of will but a predicament, a condition in which we find ourselves. Though a fixture of orthodox Christian theology, the doctrine of original sin has not fared well because it does not work well in the traditional free-will scheme. It undercuts the ability of the system to fix the blame for sin on the supposed free choice of will. If, on the one hand, the will is free, then theoretically, at least, one should be able to avoid sin and exculpate oneself by such avoidance. (So the Pelagians, in fact, held.) Free will, if it is to be maintained, excludes original sin. If, on the other hand (to controvert Pelagianism—semi and otherwise), sin is held to be an unwilled condition, perhaps inherited from our first ancestors, then we could again exculpate ourselves by claiming we never had a chance to exercise free will. We could blame it all on Adam and Eve. Either way, original sin just does not seem to fit the scheme. So the doctrine has remained something of a conundrum. It appears to raise a theoretical issue that never comes to expression in the confession where it belongs.

If, however, we proceed from the premise that the proclamation exposes our upward fall and our bondage at the same time as it delivers from it, then we can perhaps begin to grasp what is intended by the doctrine of original sin. We see that we are trapped in a condition, bound in a predicament we cannot escape. At the same time we see that we cannot escape because we will not. Outside of or prior to the proclamation, this is the way we are. When the proclamation gets through to us, we come to confess our bondage. The confession of original sin is thus more a response to the proclamation than a theoretical deduction from theological or even biblical premises. Only upon release from the bondage do we confess to it. Sin is truly confessed and seen for what it is in the moment of its overcoming.[8] "The highest act of freedom is to recognize our bondage."[9]

The Historicity of the Fall

Whence does such bondage come? Is the upward fall a historical event? The proclamation finds us in the state of bondage, and so we confess it. Is it appropriate or necessary to ask how we got that way? This, of course, has been a persistent problem for any doctrine of the fall, and particularly so since historical and scientific research has led us to question traditional assumptions about the historicity of the ancient story of Adam and Eve and about the possibility of squaring it with contemporary views about human origins in the natural sciences.

If we proceed from the proclamation, however, it is apparent that the confession does not in itself depend on such historical accounts. The confession springs from being set free in Christ. The story of Adam and Eve did not induce Peter to say, "Depart from me, for I am a sinful man, O Lord," nor Isaiah to cry out that he was a man of unclean lips nor Job to repent in dust and ashes. It was the present encounter with the proclamation that called forth the confession. The ancient story of Adam and Eve came to be employed more as a retroactive interpretation of the confession than as the occasion or cause for it. The first Adam is understood only in the light of the second. We confess to being in Adam only because of being in Christ. It is what we do to Christ and what Christ in turn does for us that finally convicts us of original sin, not the story of Adam as such nor deductions from it. We no doubt have some inklings and indications of sins apart from the confrontation with Christ and the proclamation, but probably not of what the tradition has meant by original sin.

There is one point at which the historicity of the fall becomes theologically important: on the question of necessity. If the fall (our entrapment in original sin) is not a historical event (something that happens in time), then it is necessary (that is, built into the creation). It is of the very essence of the confession of sin, however, that we admit it was not necessary. In being confronted with the proclamation, we take responsibility for it. We confess that things could have been otherwise, that whatever temptations we may have faced, we were ultimately controlled by no necessity external to us, that it was our fault. If we confess to being in Adam, then it is not to some unavoidable fate that we confess, but to something we do "with a will."

Original Sin and Human Responsibility

Some comment on the problem of responsibility is in order here. The complaint is often made that the view of original sin and especially the view of bondage espoused here destroys human responsibility. The point, however, is that we take responsibility for sin, even original sin, in the light of the proclaimed liberation from it, and such taking of responsibility is the highest act of freedom. We become responsible through the hearing of the gospel; we are not "naturally" so. God would not have come in Christ if we were responsible. God came because we are not, and intends to make us so. We are tricked by the word "responsibility" (which, incidentally, is not biblical and never appears there). We treat it as though it were a something, an abstract "ability," we somehow possess. That is surely a mistake. We respond when the gift is given. The gift drags it out of us. We need to be set free to respond. Being set free in this instance we see the depths of the bondage out of which we have been rescued. We recognize that we actually do not want God to be God, the "I" does not want it. The sinner is precisely the "I," not "my lower nature," or "the flesh" and its lusts, but "me." We realize that there is something profoundly wrong and that "I" will it so. Only when that occurs do "I" take responsibility. Otherwise there is only posturing and dissembling.

Indeed, modern ideas of freedom and autonomy have fostered not the responsibility they set out to promote, but its opposite. There is a fatal flaw in the understanding of freedom. Since freedom is defined as reason's or the self's ability to transcent "lower" impulses, drives, animal instincts, and natural laws, it has fought a losing battle against a rising tide of scientific determinisms—biological, psychological, sociological, environmental. The result is that confession of active responsibility for sin is rare. Sin is largely associated with forces and actions of others which are all beyond our control. It is mainly expressed in passive terms: we are "oppressed," "alienated," "exploited," "victimized," "violated." How could we be responsible if we had a bad relationship with our parents, or were victims of a bad environment? As such, we are not responsible or guilty, just ill or disturbed. Meanwhile, the dreadful, unspecified feeling that it is somehow our fault continues to gnaw away at our support system. Ironically, the very assertion of free will has put responsibility in great jeopardy. The great and true theologians of the church have known that all along. Remember again what Augustine said, "Wishing to make men free, he [Cicero] makes them sacrilegious."

By taking responsibility for sin we confess that it was not necessary—it could have been otherwise. But that means we can only understand the entry of sin into the world as a historical event, something that was not built into the creation by the Creator. Yet even if historical, the entry of sin into the creation could not have been such as to force sin upon us. That is the kernel of negative truth in the argument for "free will": we are not forced into sin. The argument is overstated when the positive conclusion is drawn that we have "free will" and that sin is the act of such a will. Sin is not an act of freedom, it is precisely the loss of freedom. It is selling out, being seduced by rebellion, captured, captivated. We are not forced into it, but at the same time it is not an act of a "free will." Sin is like hatred. It is not forced upon us, we do it "with a will." As such it is bondage, not freedom. We are caught in its clutches, possessed by it, driven by it. Worst of all, we perversely enjoy it.

But if sin enters historically and is not necessary, then we need to confess both that creation is good and that we are bound by cords we will not break. Since sin is such power it is there before us. We did not create it but were captivated by it, seduced by it, at our very origin. It precedes us, and as such is the work of the divine adversary Satan. It is, so to speak, there waiting for us. We are born into a world where it awaits us. We are born into a world that is cut off from God. We are born in Adam.

Orthodox Christian tradition tried to express this by the doctrine of inherited sin. But there is danger of misunderstanding if not overstatement in that doctrine which might tilt the matter once again in the direction of necessity. The doctrine may have been serviceable in a prescientific age when heredity was a mystery controlled by the gods, but it is no doubt best avoided in an age that thinks of heredity in terms of genes and DNA. Such talk might lead us to think that genetic engineering could discover and remove original sin. In any case, it makes the mistake of offering a biological answer to a theological question.

Since sin is original—there before us, yet historical in origin and so not necessary, and at the same time does not force but seduces so completely we do not will to escape it—it is hardly possible to encompass all this in a neat and coherent doctrine. Without entering into all the arguments about historicity, nature of myth, saga, metaphor, it would seem that the ancient story of Adam and Eve interpreted in the light of the proclamation of Christ still provides the best vehicle for telling the story of sin. Finding ourselves "in Christ" and consequently bound to him, we see and confess ourselves to be "in Adam." The story of Adam and Eve is our story. We confess to that when our lives are transected by the story of Christ. The liberation exposes the bondage. Sin is recognized and confessed in the moment of its overcoming. Thus both the power and the ultimate powerlessness of sin are simultaneously exposed.

The notion of the upward fall could also more neatly avoid the criticism launched from the side of contemporary science and views of evolution. The downward fall is criticized because it seems to imply that humans fell from a beginning state of perfection to a lower state. Evolutionary theory, however, suggests that humans evolve from a lower animal state toward perfection. Theologians who have a stake in the doctrine of the downward fall because it enables them to retain the idea of free will and the theodicies based thereon (for instance, John Hick, in *Evil and the God of Love*) attempt a modification of the downward fall by invoking what has been termed the Irenaean view: the creature begins in a state of "dreaming innocence" rather than perfection, and is intended to "evolve" toward perfection by the proper exercise of freedom. However, the creature succumbs to the tempter and "falls" to a lower place on the scale. While there may be some merit in such views as attempts to accommodate scientific criticism, they fail to avoid theological criticism—they tend only to diminish the seriousness of the fall and to mistake the nature of bondage. Consequently a theological explanation is substituted for proclamation.

The understanding of the fall as an upward rebellion is better able to meet the theological criteria demanded by proclamation as well as to accommodate current scientific views. It enables one to say that when the creature arrives at the point where self-consciousness appears, the fundamental problem of being human appears. At least three possibilities present themselves: (1) the creature can refuse the human task, sink back into the vitalities of nature and continue to be driven by instinct; (2) the creature could refuse the human task by attempting to overreach itself and become "as gods," what we have called the upward fall; (3) the creature could be human and image God in caring for the creation. This possibility remains somewhat ill defined since the fall obliterated it and since we are given only glimpses of it in the promised redemption. In any case, the concept of an upward fall more easily accommodates modern scientific views without betraying theological concerns.

This concludes what we have to say about sin as the presupposition of the proclamation. To whom is the proclamation addressed?

To bound sinners, those who are not only bound but think they are free. Thus no explanation will bring us to confess. Only the proclamation will do.

The Shape of the Proclamation

Before turning to the proclamation itself, exactly what the presuppositions about the hearer mean for the shape of the proclamation should be indicated. The hearer is afflicted with the bondage of the will, which consists, paradoxically, in the hearer's very claim to free choice. That claim is the hearer's defense mechanism against God and the proclamation. These very presuppositions flow from the confession made in the light of the proclamation and as such are the highest act of freedom. So there is one more all-important presupposition that flows from the hearing of the proclamation: though the will is bound, it can be changed.[10] The very fact of the proclamation is evidence to this. The proclamation takes place because there are those who have been set free to say it, those who "were dead through trespasses and sins" and have been "made alive" (Eph. 2:1). The change that takes place, however, fits none of our known schemes of human transformation, smooth or violent. The Scriptures speak of it as a dying and being raised through proclamation of Christ. It means that we can be reached by one who comes "from without," something "no eye has seen, nor ear heard" (1 Cor. 2:9) in this age. The act of proclaiming proceeds on the hope that the hearer can be "gotten at" from without, that the proclamation in Word and sacrament is the means of grace, the "sword of the Spirit" which cuts through the bondage and sets the captives free.

The proclamation is therefore shaped by the fact that the bound are to be set free. This means that the proclamation cannot be an appeal to free choice. Whatever freedom the bound hearer may claim is in fact a defense mechanism against God. The hearer in this state is interested only in keeping God at arm's length, so to speak, using God to fulfill his or her own desires, to bolster the self in its conceits. So the proclamation is not an appeal to "decide for Jesus" in the fashion of much current "evangelicalism," nor is it an attempt to persuade one to make Jesus one's example, moral guide, or paradigm for possibility thinking. Whatever the theological difference among such appeals, since they rest on the premise of free choice they turn out in the end to be more or less the same: Jesus is used as a religious enforcer to back up the particular mores or "life-styles" or politics that the preacher has decided to push. The pulpit becomes a platform.

The proclamation must be shaped by the realization that God does not work that way. God does not come hat in hand begging, "Won't somebody please believe in me?" God does not come in ways that pander to our so-called freedom of choice. God comes to invade the house of the "strong man armed" who aims to keep his goods in peace. God comes to challenge the adversary to battle for the life of the captive.

The human problem is a desperate one. Since the captives believe themselves free, and since this belief is actually their captivity, God cannot come directly. God cannot come as the great and glorious One, the almighty One of all the magnificent abstractions. That is what holds the captives in bondage in the first place. God can only come as one who is just the opposite—the negation—of what we might choose. "Since . . . the world did not know God through wisdom, it pleased God through the folly of what we preach to save those who believe" (1 Cor. 1:21). God comes as the rejected one, beaten, spat upon, crowned with thorns, and wasted. We are on the way up, seeking to be gods; God is on the way down, becoming human. Will our paths cross? Or will they only pass like ships in the night? The proclamation is the place where they meet. And the proclamation can only be shaped by the cross. For in the last analysis, the bound sinner cannot be saved directly. The bound sinner will never choose the crucified God. Jesus said as much: "You did not choose me, but I chose you and appointed you . . ." (John 15:16). The sinner must die to be raised to newness of life. The proclamation is shaped by that realization. It administers death in order to call to life.

3

The Preacher

For Jews demand signs and Greeks seek wisdom, but we preach Christ crucified, a stumbling block to Jews and folly to Gentiles, but to those who are called, both Jews and Greeks, Christ the power of God and the wisdom of God. For the foolishness of God is wiser than men, and the weakness of God is stronger than men.

(1 Cor. 1:22-25)

*H*erein lies the heart of the matter: Jesus and his proclamation—the proclamation both by him and of him. There is risk in using the present chapter title. Traditional dogmatics and systematics would prefer a title such as "Christology," or "The Person and Work of Christ." I have no particular quarrel with those titles, nor do I intend by speaking of "The Preacher" to question or undermine traditional belief in Jesus Christ as true God and true man. I affirm that belief completely and hope rather to enhance it by this treatment.

To carry through a systematic that drives to the proclamation, it seems useful to talk about Jesus the preacher, the role in which he is first presented to us in the Gospels. John the baptizer was the last and greatest of his line, but was just a voice in the wilderness crying "Prepare the way!" (Mark 1:3). Jesus came preaching. Jesus announced and gave what John could only prepare for. He said, "The time is up! The kingdom of God is at hand; repent and believe in the gospel" (Mark 1:15; my own translation).

What happened to Jesus the preacher is the stuff of Christology. This has become more apparent recently, especially due to historical investigation of the Scriptures. The crucial question has been: How did the Jesus who preached become the Jesus who was and is preached in the church? How is the move from Jesus the preacher to Jesus preached as Lord and Christ, the very Son of God, our Savior, warranted? At the deepest level, this is the question about the authority of the proclamation. If there is no legitimacy in the move from the Jesus who came preaching to the Jesus who is preached, then there is no authorization for the proclamation as a present-tense, "I say unto you" (first- to second-person) declaration. The claim that proclamation is the actual doing of the deed of God in the present—the electing itself—would not be warranted. If Jesus and what happened to him gives no backing for the proclamation, then all is in vain. The christological question is at bottom the question of the legitimacy of the proclamation. The question of the preacher is the question of how any human being, including Jesus, can claim to speak for God. In other words, in what ways can the claims made for the proclamation be justified? How could one be so presumptuous as to take up this task? Indeed, more precisely, how could one be emboldened, even driven to say such strange words as "Necessity is laid upon me. Woe to me if I do not preach the gospel!" (1 Cor. 9:16).

The Stone the Builders Rejected

Jesus came preaching. According to the Gospel writers, he said: "The time is up! The kingdom of God is at hand. Repent and believe the good news!" But his words did not do him any good; they only got him killed. It is vain for us to rummage around in our systematics or sift through the literary remains in order to construct or discover a Jesus we would not have killed had we been there. If only he had said or done the right things! So our complaints always go. But it is too late. The time is up. The cock has crowed. We killed him. God ("whoever out there is messing with us") has turned the tables on us again and done a new thing. God has raised Jesus from the dead and so taken on a new name: the Father of Jesus Christ. So Jesus is now proclaimed as raised from the dead, the true and only-begotten Son of the Father. The stone that the builders rejected has become the head of the corner (Ps. 118:22; Mark 12:10 and parallels; Acts 4:11; 1 Pet. 2:7). Of all the shocking and offensive things God has done to us, this no doubt tops them all! God accepts and vindicates the one whom we reject! This is a stumbling block. Nevertheless, it is not only the impetus, the reason and the authorization for the proclamation, but also its essential content.

We must not forget this heart of the matter when we enter the labyrinth of christological discussion, for the problems we encountered in systematic reflection about God repeat themselves when we come to Christ. We endeavor to construct out of the ruin of our misdeed a Christ who is amenable to us: a Christ we would never have crucified had we been there, a Christ who would be approved by reasonable and free beings, a Jesus who is the perfect earthly exemplification of our "Christ principle." Just as we try to make God "nice" by our theologizing, so also are we inclined to make Jesus into a "gospel" suitable to our taste. Thus we return to our old tricks and substitute our systematics for proclamation. We forget that we killed him, and that God, not theology, raised him up.

If Jesus, the one we crucified and God raised, is Lord and Christ, then he is in the first place the end of us as old beings, the end of our upward rebellion. He is, of course, also the new beginning. But he can be that only as he is first the end of the old. As we shall insist throughout, it is a matter of the death of the old and the resurrection of the new. Our very lives are to be conformed to that of the crucified and resurrected one. Therefore Jesus must be preached as the absolute crisis, the bitter end, of us as would-be Gods. (What else could it mean to call him—the rejected one—Lord?)

One searches almost in vain through the mountains of New Testament research—old or new, fundamentalist, conservative or liberal—for recognition of that fact. Could it be that our historical research, no matter what its presuppositions, is already a sell-out? Might the researchers be like the lawyers who comb the records for evidence in order to construct a case for the defense? Perhaps a reasonable argument can be mounted to shift the blame to someone else—maybe the Romans. Such constructions, however, serve only to tame Jesus, and if Jesus is turned into a domesticated house pet, it makes little difference from the perspective here what sort he turns out to be: orthodox, fundagelical, conservative, liberal, leftist, rightist, or middle-of-the-road. In any case, he is no real crisis or death threat for old beings. He becomes one we might be persuaded to choose if sufficiently cajoled. Bonhoeffer was right in saying, "Christ is still betrayed by the kiss. Wishing to be done with him means always to fall down with the mockers and say, 'Greetings Master!' There are only two ways possible of encountering Jesus: man must die or he must put Jesus to death."[1]

Preaching Jesus as the End

Jesus cannot be proclaimed as the One who comes pandering to our religious conceits. He cannot be preached as though he were the object of our choice. He must be preached as Lord, as the one who comes to dispose of our case, to decide the matter. He must be preached as the end of us, for only then can he also be a new beginning. He must be preached, that is, as the death of us before he can be new life. The encounter with him as proclaimed Lord is not such that we simply go on as continuously existing subjects making our "religious preferences" felt, but rather that we are put to death to be made new. The proclamation brings radical discontinuity into our lives. We are to be turned into those who hear the word gladly—"You have not chosen me, but I have chosen you"—and learn to stammer "Amen, so be it Lord!" We are indeed to be made new, re-created as beings who can finally speak the truth about God: "O Lord, open thou my lips, and my mouth shall show forth thy praise" (Ps. 51:15).

The christological question, therefore, is not merely that of how the Jesus who preached became the one who was preached, but much more critically, *how this Jesus is now to be preached.* What does it mean to say that he must be preached as the end, as the death of the old, and the beginning of the new? How does one proclaim such discontinuity? What sort of Christology does this entail? What sort of death and resurrection are we talking about here? And how does one move from systematic to proclamation when one aims to put the old to death so as to raise up the new? These are the questions with which a systematic that intends to foster proclamation will have to concern itself.

Discontinuity: Its Root and Purpose

How did the Jesus who preached become the Jesus who is preached as Lord and Christ? Historical investigation of the Scriptures has made that a central question for Christology and certainly therefore for authoritative proclamation today. Traditional Christologies generally assumed that there was no real discontinuity between Jesus' preaching, and self-designation and the church's preaching about Jesus. That assumption was based mostly on the Jesus of the Gospel of John. Since, it was thought, Jesus himself accepted and even used christological titles, it could be assumed that the Christology later taught by the church began with Jesus. There is direct continuity between Jesus' self-understanding and the Christology of the church. Jesus himself is the source of the church's Christology.

More careful study of the Gospels, however, led to serious questioning of this assumption. It became evident that the Gospel of John differs in literary type from the Synoptics, and that the Jesus of the Synoptics is much more reticent about accepting or publicizing the titles his followers wish to give him. A definite discontinuity appears between the Jesus who preached and the Jesus who was preached in the New Testament. That is quite clear even without critical historical study. The discontinuity is most obvious in the Synoptic Gospels, but as we shall see, it is also evident in the writings of St. Paul, the earliest and most prolific New Testament author. Historical criticism of the Gospels, particularly form criticism, did not invent the discontinuity; it has served only to make this discontinuity inescapable for systematic theology. In whatever manner one may seek to settle the endless debates about Jesus' historical self-understanding, systematic theology has to reckon with the probability that the "historical Jesus" did not, at least openly and explicitly, apply titles of divine majesty like Christ and Lord to himself. The application was made explicitly in the subsequent proclamation of the postresurrection church. So a discontinuity between the Jesus who preached and the Jesus who is preached has become inescapable.

It is vital for the proclamation to come to grips with this discontinuity. A systematic theology concerned with the proclamation needs to understand both the roots of this discontinuity and its purpose. If the move from the Jesus who preached to the Jesus who is preached is improperly made, the proclamation of the gospel loses its authority and descends to a peddling of Jesus as an ideal. Modern theology demonstrates that failure to attend to the problem of discontinuity leads inevitably to the collapse of proclamation with a vital christological and soteriological core.

Why the discontinuity? Is it perhaps an embarrassing historical fact that one must seek to gloss over to cover up? So it would seem, judging by the ever renewed efforts to establish unbroken continuity with the historical Jesus. On the other hand, at least two facts support the idea that the discontinuity is not just an intrusion from without, but rather lies in the very nature of the case itself. The first is primarily formal, having to do with the mechanics of proclamation, of turning to another to speak of Jesus. The second is primarily material, having to do with the discontinuity in the life of Jesus—the cross and resurrection itself—and how that impinges on the lives of those grasped by it. We shall look at these two reasons in what follows.

Who Do You Say That I Am?

There is a formal discontinuity in turning to proclaim to others simply because we cannot hand on what Jesus said as though the words were ours. Willi Marxsen has pointed this out in his essay on the beginnings of New Testament Christology,[2] an analysis of what confessing and turning to others to speak involves. Marxsen's analysis is vital for understanding proclamation.

The critical passage in the Gospels for getting at the mechanics of confessing and proclaiming Christ is Mark 8:27-38. After asking who others say he is, Jesus puts the question squarely to his disciples: "Who do you say that I am?" Now they are caught in the situation of having to speak, and penetrating exchange about the prospect and peril of such speaking follows. The disciples are formally asked to give Jesus a name or a title. Whoever answers will be put on the spot to speak for himself or herself. It is a question Jesus cannot answer for us. There are some things one cannot say about oneself. One can only be acclaimed as Christ and/or Son of God, since, traditionally, titles cannot be self-designations. Further, Jesus cannot answer for us since it is out of the heart and from the lips that the words must come (Rom. 10:9). Christology is our problem, not Jesus'. It would be comforting perhaps to be prompted by Jesus, to have assurances of a continuity that would eliminate all risk, but the Scriptures deny us that. Jesus does not use the words. He does not speak of himself openly and directly as Christ or Son of God. Those words must be spoken by others, even if by Jesus' enemies.

"Me and My Words." The closing passage of the section lays bare the systematic of confession and proclamation: "For whoever is ashamed of me and of my words in this adulterous and sinful generation, of him will the Son of man also be ashamed, when he comes in the glory of his Father with the holy angels" (Mark 8:38). What is involved here? The passage exhibits a "tri-polar" relationship. One pole is the "historical Jesus" ("me and my words"), the second is the hearer ("whoever is ashamed"), and the third is the expectation of an eschatological future—at present held open by Jesus' enigmatic self-designation as the "Son of man" who will come "in the glory of the Father with the holy angels."

> The current state of New Testament scholarship on the Son of man is far too fluid to assure the kind of christological claim Marxsen himself desires to make. Some, with Marxsen, take Son of man to be a title with more or less specific apocalyptic content. Others understand it to be simply a rather enigmatic self-designation on Jesus' part which leaves the christological question open: "You shall see. . . ." In any case, the systematic argument here does not depend on the outcome of this historical/exegetical debate. What I have called the tri-polar relationship holds even if one were to change the specific title of the third pole to, for instance, "the Christ." The third pole is the eschatological future opened by what happens in the man Jesus. While this awaits final vindication and appropriate naming, I will designate it here in a generic sense as the eschatological title.

Note in the passage that Jesus makes no explicit christological claim. However, the passage does claim that the eschatological issue is being decided in the present by one's relationship to Jesus. Whoever is ashamed of the actual Jesus, "me and my words," will not stand the final test. This apocalyptic or eschatological element is, as Marxsen rightly says, the primal datum of Christology. Jesus is important because of his relation to the eschatological future, the question of the end (*finis*), and goal (*telos*) of all things. So, as current scholarship expresses it, there is an implied christological claim: to stand in the end one must be properly related to Jesus here and now (not be ashamed of "me and my words").

Thus there is a tri-polar relation: Jesus to hearer; Jesus to the eschatological title; and the hearer to the title. One can indicate it by the diagram on p. 64:

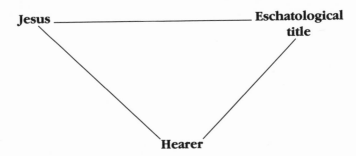

Marxsen points out that the whole complex, the entire tri-polar re-lation, is Christology: Jesus; the hearer; and the eschatological future indicated by the title. In Jesus' own preaching the hearer would be put into an immediate crisis, a situation of promise or judgment by virtue of the relationship to Jesus and the implied claim. The hearer's participation in the claim is to be settled by whether the hearer is ashamed of Jesus, the concrete "me and my words."

The Necessity of Titles.   The formal problem for proclamation aris-es, however, when one who has heard and been grasped by Jesus' proclamation turns to speak to others. Then one needs to shift from the more immediate relationship to the Jesus who preached to preach-ing Jesus. One must make explicit the claim implicit in the immediate encounter with Jesus. But the subsequent proclaimers cannot simply repeat the words of Jesus. We cannot repeat Jesus' words as our own— "Whoever is ashamed of me and my words . . . of him will the Son of man be ashamed"—because that is not true. We and our words are not that important. What we say in the first instance is that Jesus said these words, and in the second instance we claim that if one wants to avoid the judgment "when he comes," one had better not now be ashamed of Jesus and his words.

But then comes the inevitable question: Who is Jesus? Why is he so important? So the question comes back to us again: Who do you say that I am? Why bother to speak of Jesus to others? In other words, when we turn to speak to others, we have to make the move from the implicit claim of Jesus' own preaching to explicit confession and proclamation of him. There is, then, on the formal level, a necessary discontinuity between Jesus' own preaching and our preaching of him.

We are called upon to make explicit what was implicit in him. We cannot simply repeat his words as though they were ours. Christology is our problem, not his. That is why there is a tri-polar relation. We must make our confession.

So the proclaimer is left with the question: Who do you say that I am? What happens when the question is answered, when we move to confess or proclaim him? What happens formally is that the third pole of the relation, the title and its pregnant consequence, gets explicit interpretation. A great variety of titles have been spawned through the years. Since no one outside of first-century Judaism is likely to understand or be grasped by all that is involved in titles like "Messiah," one might use others like "Son of God," or "Lord," or "Logos," or "Master," or even "Man for others," and so on endlessly. But that step is fraught with peril. The Markan passage bears eloquent testimony to this. Every new title brings with it its own world of meaning, its own story. Inevitably pressure is exerted in countless subtle ways to rewrite the story to fit the title, to redo the "me and my words." Perhaps that is why the Jesus of the Gospels either refuses the titles or wants them kept secret. The story is not yet over and all the fine titles press toward a different end. The actual "me and my words" would get swallowed up in some grand christological project, which would obscure what in fact happens to Jesus.

The Markan passage itself is a prime indication of the peril in the titles. Jesus asks "Who do you say that I am?" Peter answers boldly with what appears to be an appropriate title: "You are the Christ." But when Jesus turns to tell them the end of the story—that he must suffer, be rejected, killed and raised after three days—Peter is offended or perhaps "ashamed." The story does not fit the title and so he rebukes Jesus. "The Christ" is not supposed to suffer and die. The title exerts pressure to end the story differently. But Jesus sees this precisely as the work of the tempter: "Get behind me Satan! For you are not on the side of God, but of men." Thus is the peril revealed. Seeking to flatter Jesus with high-sounding titles, one can unwittingly fall into the clutches of the adversary. Satan is very interested in titles that obscure the cross. Jesus is always betrayed by a flattering kiss.

Proclamation as explicit Christology, therefore, involves the interpretation of the third pole, usually by supplying titles or meanings and their consequences for our ultimate destiny. The move is perilous because of the temptation to put too much of ourselves into the title, to seek subtly to control our destinies by means of the title. Yet it is a move we must make if we are to proclaim. How then shall we proceed? The passage itself indicates that we can do so only if we move carefully within the tri-polar relation. In the first place, the title must be transformed to fit the story, not vice versa. We see this when Jesus turns to teach his disciples: he must be rejected, crucified, and on the third day raised. The title and all it involves must be transformed in the light of the "me and my words," of what actually happens to Jesus. We can legitimately proceed only in this fashion. That is why the oft-repeated attempt to construct a Christology by rummaging around for the meaning of all the titles in the New Testament is usually a blind alley. The titles as such tell as little and determine the christological content even less. The story interprets the title.

The Place of the Hearer.   But now we have spoken only of two poles in the relation, the "me and my words," and the title. The third is the hearer, the "whoever is ashamed." The christological problem is more than an abstract or objective one of argument about sources and proper interpretation. It is not only that the title conforms to the story, but also that the hearer and eventual proclaimer is drawn into the story as well. The question "Who do you say that I am?" cannot be answered without consequence. The hearer also is at risk and is redone in terms of the story. The "me and my words" puts an end to the hearer's story both negatively and positively. It stops the old story by giving it a new end. Whoever would follow after Jesus must take up the cross. The old life ends, the new begins. The hearer's story is transected by the "me and my words."

The hearer, it should be realized, has a stake in the giving of titles. The title represents dreams and hopes: the final ratification of our aspirations; a judge who will finally give evildoers their come-uppance; a Messiah, a Christ who will finally do in all the enemies; a Son of God who will be a universal ruler; a liberator; a man for others; one in whom God-consciousness reaches its zenith. Our ability to apply titles pleasing and convenient to Jesus is almost unbounded. We would like nothing better than that all our dreams, without alteration, should be realized in him. We would like not to be ashamed of him.

So we too are drawn into the relationship and cannot be abstracted from it. We face a crisis in reinterpretation, the question about the end of our story. After rebuking Peter for his self-serving flattery, and insisting that he must suffer rejection and crucifixion, Jesus goes into the well-known peroration about the third party in this relation:

> If any man would come after me, let him deny himself and take up his cross and follow me. For whoever would save his life will lose it; and whoever loses his life for my sake and the gospel's will save it. For what does it profit a man, to gain the whole world and forfeit his life? For what can a man give in return for his life?
>
> (Mark 8:34-37)

It is no simple matter to speak the truth about Jesus. If the title is to be transformed by the story, so are we. To answer Jesus' question aright is to be drawn into his story. If everything about Jesus and what we say of him is transformed into the Word of the cross, then this means that our stories too can only be radically transected by that word. Jesus must be preached as the absolute crisis of the old, the end of bondage, the end of our upward rebellion. This is borne out dramatically by the Markan text.

So the discontinuity involved in turning to proclaim draws the proclaimer into that very discontinuity because the proclaimer cannot continue "as is." Proclamation occurs, in other words, when the hearer is drawn into the picture, into the story. "No one can say 'Jesus is Lord' except by the Holy Spirit" (1 Cor. 12:3). Thus the triad is completed. To confess and to proclaim Christ involves becoming a theologian of the cross. It is not that one must have a theology of the cross (whatever that might be), but that one is to become a theologian of the cross. Much of our talk about a theology of the cross goes awry in this regard. It is difficult if not finally impossible to isolate or write a theology of the cross. Rather, what the designation invites us to is a way of being a theologian, a mode of operating. That is manifest in our passage. There is a direct connection between the death of Jesus and our death. As Paul puts it, "I have been crucified with Christ; it is no longer I who live, but Christ who lives in me; and the life I now live in the flesh I live by faith in the Son of God, who loved me and gave himself for me" (Gal. 2:20). That means at the very least that we lose whatever stake we might have had in those props we had hoped would support us: titles, ideologies, philosophies, theologies. For what can one give in return for one's life? There is nothing left to do but proclaim, to attempt the risky business of speaking the truth concerning Jesus.

The Cross and Resurrection

The formal problem draws us more deeply on into the material problem. On the purely formal level we have seen that the discontinuity is not an embarrassing historical lacuna, but belongs to the very nature of the case, the move to proclamation. Whenever one turns to speak of one's encounter with Jesus to another, one faces the question, "Who do you say that I am?" The proclaimer cannot repeat the preaching of Jesus because Jesus' preaching is inextricably bound up with his person. The proclaimer must launch out on the perilous journey for himself or herself, and this fact draws us into more than formal considerations. We can undertake the journey of proclamation only at the risk of becoming theologians of the cross, only by being divested of the stake we might have in the titles and their like so that they might be used to give glory to the Jesus who actually came and walked among us, the "me and my words" just as they are.

> From this perspective one might well ask why there is so much religious fury directed at historical criticism. Will we be ashamed of the one we find thereby? To be sure, the historical critical method is not theologically neutral; ambiguity surrounds its usage. It is highly questionable when used to establish continuity with "the real Jesus" who is supposed no longer to be an offense or a threat. But resistance to the method can also be due to the stake we have in the titles that similarly protect from that offense. The controversy is about titles: "Who do you say that I am?" The inclination of both sides in the debate is to seek titles that will protect them from the "me and my words." Being a theologian of the cross is the only way to escape both errors and to use the historical critical method properly. Historical critical investigation uncovers a discontinuity that prevents every move but the drive to proclamation. The Scriptures cannot be used as protection from the word of the cross and its consequences.

In other words, we can proceed only under the sign of the cross and the resurrection. When we are put to death as old beings and are raised to the new life of faith in Jesus, we can do nothing other than proclaim. "For necessity is laid upon me. Woe to me if I do not preach the gospel!" (1 Cor. 9:16).

This means that we are drawn automatically into a deeper and more material reason for the discontinuity between the Jesus who preached and the Jesus who is preached: the cross and resurrection itself. One cannot encounter Jesus and remain the same. Discussion of this material reason will bring us more directly into the problematics of Christology proper.

The Stone the Builders Accepted? The problem with most christologies, conservative or liberal, right or left, is that they depend upon a continuity that undercuts the proclamation and substitutes a lecture about Christ for the preaching of him. Usually they look to the historical Jesus to substantiate the titles they seek to attribute to him. One may call these "Christologies of continuity." A Christology of continuity is one that attempts to root itself directly in the deeds, the preaching, and the teaching of the historical Jesus, more or less ignoring the cross and resurrection. I say "more or less" because cross and resurrection, even though accepted and taught, do not play a decisive role in the understanding of who Christ is. Indeed, Christologies of continuity are usually constructed as a detour around the folly of the cross and the shock of the resurrection. Continuity is established by going back to a Jesus either prior to or at least relatively untouched by the cross.

Christologies of continuity throw Jesus' question back at him: Who do you say that you are? As at his trial, Jesus is expected to tell us plainly who he is, to relieve us of the risk of an answer. Then we can judge him and, like Pilate, wash our hands of the matter.

The freedom of choice is the counterpart in theological anthropology to continuity in Christology. Since the cross and resurrection pose no serious discontinuity in the story of Jesus, there is no serious disruption in our lives either. One can simply look at the life of Jesus and, if one is pleased by it or satisfied that Jesus is divine enough to meet with our approval, make one's choice. In other words, the hearer, the third pole in the triad, does not get drawn into the story, but remains more or less "above it all," expecting to retain control of the matter. There is neither consciousness of bondage nor release from captivity. There is only a demand for a Jesus who "meets our religious needs." The fundamental paradigm for Christologies of continuity is free choice, not death and resurrection.

Conservative Christologies. Using the labels broadly, both conservative, two-natures Christologies and liberal Christologies fall into the trap of such continuity. Conservative Christology seeks to trace explicit "proof" for the "divinity" of Jesus directly back to the teaching of an inerrant scripture. There is direct continuity between the Christology of Jesus thus uncovered and their own. Today such a Christology can maintain itself only by ignoring the development of careful historical investigation of the Scripture and the problematics that gave rise to that historical work.[3]

Failure to deal seriously with historical criticism and the problem of discontinuity seems somehow to take its toll nonetheless. If Christ is at all the subject of the preaching, a vital proclamation of him is rare. Instead, the exercise turns into a lecture about Christ, his "saving activity" and moral precepts, with appropriate exhortations to choose and follow him. Where that is done, systematics (usually bad at that) once again displaces the proclamation. For the most part, however, serious Christology is on the wane and even preachers whose theology may be quite traditional and orthodox preach a sentimental Jesusology from the pulpit.

Liberal Christologies. Strangely enough, more liberal Christologies are also Christologies of continuity, even though they generally accept the judgments of historical criticism. They mostly use the historical investigation negatively to tear down the continuities supporting conservative claims to the divinity of Christ, while they at the same time depend on their own positive variety of continuity with the alleged, quite human Jesus. Thus they will often reject the traditional "proof" for the incarnation and the divinity of Christ, for example, but then turn about and root their own views of the religious value of Jesus in supposed continuity with the "historical Jesus." Here continuity with the teachings of the "real" Jesus is claimed. Instead of an inerrant Scripture, here historical research is insulated against the crisis of discontinuity. Extravagant claims are then made about the supreme religious worth, the sublime teaching, the transforming power, the overwhelming and vibrant God-consciousness, the tremendous ability to challenge and change people, and the contagious spirituality of Jesus. Such claims, however, have even less historical backing than the older orthodox claims.[4] After reading such romantic pap, one wonders why anyone would have bothered to crucify Jesus. Such Christologies try to explain the existence of Christianity apart from the discontinuity and shock of cross and resurrection and so end by making highly inflated claims about the "human" Jesus. Claiming to establish continuity with the "real" Jesus, they usually just substitute adjectival divinity for substantial divinity. So they tend to promote a Jesus who was "simply divine," and rue the fact that he got into all that trouble in Jerusalem.

Ironically, as far as proclamation is concerned, matters turn out pretty much as before. The sermon turns into a lecture about the supreme wisdom and virtue of Jesus, which, held before us as examples, ends only by being a rather tiresome business, occasions for us to exercise our free choice and test our moral fiber—if we are foolish enough to take such outrageous pulpit oratory seriously. Mostly we nod appreciatively at the splendid eulogy for Jesus, sigh regretfully at the impracticality of it all, and then go home and forget it.

The Problem of Conservative and Liberal Christologies. Between conservative and liberal, right and left, Christology is in a bad way today. But discovering what is wrong seems a difficult task. The conservative, on the one hand, will accuse the liberal of preaching a Jesus who is not good news because he is all too human and so cannot save us. The liberal, on the other hand, will accuse the conservative of preaching a Jesus so divine that he cannot reach us, a Jesus who is heteronomous, a dogmatic affront to moderns. We get to the nub of the problem only when we consider the move to proclamation. Then it becomes clear that both conservative and liberal Christologies of continuity amount to about the same thing. There is little practical difference between a superdivine Jesus and a superhuman Jesus. In both cases the systematic tries to establish too much because it does not see the move to the proclamation as the crucial issue. Instead, it crowds out the proclamation once again.

What happened in the doctrine of God is thus repeated in the Christology. Just as the systematic tries to make God so nice that there is no room for or purpose in the preaching, so here the search for continuity with the "real Jesus" reveals an attempt to recast him in the role of one we would be most likely to accept had we been there and had our wits about us. Jesus is made over into the stone the builders accepted and celebrated. The general result is the same. Just as the systematic attempt to make God over results in a bowdlerization, so also the attempt to make Jesus over produces a legalistic or sentimentalized Jesus hardly worth bothering about. We forget that he was, after all, despised and rejected, and that we crucified him.

We might begin to discover what is wrong here if we at last recognize that Jesus is the one we all crucified, the stone the builders rejected, and that precisely as such he is the absolute crisis, the end of our ways in this age. Systematics goes wrong when it produces a Jesus who only bears and exemplifies the titles that keep us in business. The current trend toward Christologies of identification are no improvement. We look, supposedly, for a Jesus who identifies with us, or with whom we can identify. That backfires, for example, when feminists find it impossible to identify with a male Jesus and start casting about for female divinities. But that is symptomatic of the difficulty with all Christologies of identification. We forget or ignore the fact that Jesus was one with whom no one identified in the end. Even his disciples forsook him and fled. The women who wept in sympathy with him (identified with him?) were told to weep for themselves and their children (Luke 23:28). We forget that though we did not choose him, he nevertheless chose us.

The basic paradigm for Christologies of continuity is freedom of choice. Jesus is made over into the One who "meets our needs," whether they be high-sounding religious needs or more mundane psychological, moral, or social needs. Such a Jesus should then be attractive to the "free choice" of old beings. But the facts belie the fantasy. Jesus did not meet anyone's needs. He was of no use to anyone here. He was wasted.

Rather, Jesus was of use only to God, who raised him up. Systematic theology is useless if it does not recognize this and drive to the proclamation of the one God raised up in spite of our universal rejection. The cross itself is the discontinuity planted in our way. There is no detour around it; there can only be a way through it to the resurrection hope. Only a proclamation that puts the old to death and calls the new to life will get us there.

Christ and Him Crucified

The cross and the resurrection put an entirely different light on the life and work of Jesus the preacher. For the fact is—and none of his followers could ignore it—that his preaching, teaching, miracles, and whatever claim he made or implied about himself led only to the cross. All his followers forsook him and fled. In one way or another they were all implicated. One of their own had betrayed him. One of their own had denied him. All seemed ignorant or confused about who he was or what it was all about. Yet in the resurrection God had simply cancelled out the rejection, done a new thing, brought life out of death. The stone that the builders rejected had become the head of the corner.

This meant from the beginning that the teachings and deeds of Jesus could be viewed properly only in the light of the cross. They were not important as detachable, timeless truths, but rather as the words and deeds that got Jesus into trouble and incited the people of this age to crucify him. God alone vindicates him, not his deeds or his teachings. The historical Jesus has no disciples. They forsook him and fled. Modern disciples do the same in one way or another. We need to be confronted by the reality that the teachings, the wonder-working, the apocalyptic preaching—all of it—went down with him to the grave. He was "crucified, dead and buried." And a great stone was rolled over the door to the tomb. He had no disciples left to carry on his teachings. When he was dead and buried, his followers did not get together in a little liberal clique and comfort themselves with the fact that they still had his teachings. It was over. Mostly his disciples seemed afraid that they might share his fate! Little did they know how well-founded their fears were! Mark's Gospel ends (16:8) with the women at the tomb being so overcome by this fear that "they said nothing to anyone."

It was apparent, therefore, that when God raised Jesus from the dead, the preaching and teaching of Jesus could only be handed on as the Word of the cross.

> For Jesus' preaching of the kingdom could not be handed on unaltered, since it had an essential link with his person and could never be separated from it; and it had to be transformed, since with the death and resurrection of Jesus the *eschaton* had begun, and no disciple could ignore this event when he spoke of Jesus. The historical and hermeneutic question, how Jesus who preached became the Christ who is preached, is therefore basically the christological question, how the dead Jesus became the living, the crucified, the resurrected, and the humiliated the exalted.[5]

The question they faced was what God was up to in Jesus, what God meant by it all. Why should God drive this Jesus to the cross and ultimately raise him up? Jesus' teaching, wonderworking, and preaching could not be handed on unaltered as a formula for religious achievement. It had to be transformed and could finally only be proclaimed as the Word of the cross.

A sketch of the basic contours of the New Testament story will provide a sense of the "logic" at work here. We begin with the earliest preacher who has left a written record, the apostle Paul. The question behind his magnum opus, Romans, was that of the righteousness of God. When would God do justly by Israel and vindicate its ancient cause? The people had hopes that the kingdom would be restored to its ancient glory and that God would keep his promises in order to be seen and acknowledged by all. Apparently there were those who believed that if they reformed and kept the law God gave, then God would show his arm and vindicate his cause and theirs. Thus arose the phenomenon of Judaism and later its various sects, each claiming the best way. But history was cruel. One hope after another was crushed until finally Rome brutally held them in chains. Was there no hope? Final hopes and dreams took varied and diffuse shape in what has come to be called apocalypticism. Perhaps there would be no vindication in this age as such, but there would be a final cataclysmic destruction of this age and the advent of a new age in which all evil would be destroyed. Many thought that the just could hope for final vindication in the resurrection. The kingdom or reign of God would be an apocalyptic triumph of the righteousness of God. In it God would be vindicated and would establish the right to be God over all.

This put tremendous pressure on being just, on living according to the letter of the law. The sects debated about just what and how much was to be done. This led, in turn, to a basic split between the "righteous" and "sinners."

Jesus the Scandal

Into this scene came Jesus. He too preached the kingdom of God. But the trouble was that he did not fit anyone's model for righteousness. On the one hand, he attacked the casuistic attempts on the part of the teachers and the sects to make compliance with the law possible, even if difficult. On the other hand, to the consternation of the "righteous," he associated with "sinners": whores, tax-collectors, collaborators with the enemy, the sick, the lame, the beggars, riffraff of all sorts. He ignored the fundamental distinction between the righteous and sinners. Furthermore, he simply forgave sins—even the sins of really wicked people. He preached the kingdom to them! He claimed, on occasion, that the kingdom of God was more like a banquet where everyone would be filled with good things, than a moral rearmament movement. When there was complaint, he brushed it aside by saying that he had come to call sinners, not the righteous to repentance, and that he had come to seek and save the lost. Publicans, sinners, and whores would enter the kingdom before the righteous, he claimed, because the first would be last and the last first. Madness!

The outcome of such conduct is predictable. He was ruining "the cause." He could only be judged as a blasphemer, an outlaw, a rebel. He was wasted—betrayed, judged, beaten, spat upon, mocked, crucified, dead and buried. But he was raised from the dead and his followers were emboldened to continue the mischief he had started by proclaiming that God was behind it all and had now begun a new thing. What was it all about?

Enter Saul of Tarsus

Saul was zealously on his way to Damascus to put a stop to the mischief there, and was struck down. He encountered the risen Lord Jesus. "Saul, Saul," he was told, "You are going the wrong way. What are you up to? Don't you see? It's all over!" According to the story it took him awhile to see, but Saul the persecutor subsequently became better known as Paul the preacher. There was a startling discontinuity. The old life came to an end. A new one began.

It is crucial for our purposes to grasp this discontinuity and the proclamation necessitated by it—how Paul proclaimed the Jesus who had confronted him. The discontinuity between the Jesus who preached and the Christ who is preached comes to its sharpest focus in what Paul has to say. What happened to him on the Damascus road? Discontinuity—but that is too abstract a word. He put it more radically and concretely: I died there. I was crucified. Everything I was, was wiped out. But I was also given a new beginning in faith and hope. I was made a new creature in Christ by this shocking act of God. I was, after all, the best of Israelites, and had every reason for confidence in the flesh. He was supported, one might say, by all the continuity one could possibly have or want: "circumcised on the eighth day, of the people of Israel, of the tribe of Benjamin, a Hebrew born of Hebrews; as to the law a Pharisee, as to zeal a persecutor of the church, as to righteousness under the law blameless" (Phil. 3:5-6). But he got shot down like a bird in flight. So now what was it worth? Nothing. Indeed, worse than nothing: *skubala* as the Greek has it, translated politely as animal excrement and euphemistically as refuse, loss. But not only is the religious continuity gone, everything is counted as loss.

> Indeed I count everything as loss because of the surpassing worth of knowing Christ Jesus my Lord. For his sake I have suffered the loss of all things, and count them as refuse, in order that I may gain Christ and be found in him, not having a righteousness of my own, based on law, but that which is through faith in Christ, the righteousness from God that depends on faith; that I may know him and the power of his resurrection, and may share his sufferings, becoming like him in his death, that if possible I may attain the resurrection from the dead.
>
> (Phil. 3:8-11)

In other words, Paul confesses himself to be drawn into the tripolar relation. Since the crucified Jesus has been raised, Saul, the one righteous and blameless under the law that killed Jesus, has died and Paul the apostle has been born in faith.

Out of the discontinuity came Paul the proclaimer, the apostle of Jesus Christ. What does he proclaim? What does the cross and resurrection of Jesus have to say about God's self-vindication, God's righteousness? That is what the major Epistles of Paul are about, especially Romans and Galatians. The death and resurrection of Jesus means the very self-vindication of God. Now the righteousness of God, the justice and power of God, has been revealed in the gospel, quite apart from the law, because this righteousness comes through faith. This is the vindication of God, the revelation of divine righteousness, because precisely in the cross, in Jesus' execution under the law and the subsequent triumph in resurrection, God is proven to be God of all. The distinction between Jews and Gentiles, between righteous and sinners, between bond and free, male and female, is cancelled out. The law is but a historical interlude, a political necessity. It is not a means whereby one could bargain with or vaunt oneself individually or collectively before God. The law is not a remedy for sin. Where it is so understood it only makes sin worse. Therefore, all—Jews and Gentiles—have been shut up under disobedience so that God might have mercy on all. God has simply shot everyone out of the saddle by choosing to have mercy. God is the God of all as the God of mercy. Thus the vindication of God has been carried out by God alone. A new age has dawned in Jesus Christ.

God's Self-vindication in Jesus

How could so much depend on the cross and resurrection of Jesus? Because the law—indeed the very law of God—attacked Jesus and was broken by the resurrection. Jesus was born "under the law" and "became a curse for us." He was quite justly condemned by the law. Indeed, we were driven to do it by the law. But God reversed the sentence and brought the law to an end in the resurrection of Christ, ushering in the new age to faith.

In all of that the very godness of God comes to light. God establishes the right to be God. This is God's "righteousness," God's self-vindication, indeed, the propitiation that God puts forward through the spilling of Jesus' blood under the law. God cancels all bets and lays claim to all by simply having mercy on all through the raising of Jesus. Faith in God is possible now. What we are blind to is not the law of God, but the glory of God—calling into being that which is from that which is not. The essence of sin is to fall short of the glory of God, to attempt to bargain with God on the basis of the law, and thus to refuse to let God be God. In forbearance, God had overlooked or passed over such sin. God did not immediately exert the claim to be God. As in the days of the great flood, such exertion would have wiped us out. But no longer. All that is now over. In Jesus God has reclaimed the right to be God here and now in the living present.

> For there is no distinction; since all have sinned and fall short of the glory of God, they are justified by his grace as a gift, through the redemption which is in Christ Jesus, whom God put forward as an expiation by his blood, to be received by faith. This was to show God's righteousness, because in his divine forbearance he had passed over former sins; it was to prove at the present time that he himself is righteous and that he justifies him who has faith in Jesus.
>
> (Rom. 3:22-26)

God's self-vindication in the cross and resurrection of Jesus, however, confronts us with a radical discontinuity. Living "under the law" we simply cannot fathom, accept, or trust an act of sheer mercy. When we come up against the godness of God in any form our bondage becomes evident. We cannot give up. It does not seem safe to us. We hang onto the law because it appears to offer us a way to control our own destiny, our future. It seems to promise us the continuity we think we need. It was just such a promise that was grasped at as the heart and soul of the faith among God's people.

But now God had shattered everything. God shut up everything, even the keepers of the law, under disobedience by raising the crucified Jesus from the dead. All the old continuity was gone. Now they had lost whatever advantage they supposedly had over others in the law. There was no longer any distinction. Law could no longer be an excuse for separation. But this brings in a shocking state of affairs for those who live under the law. "What then is the use of the law? Who then will be good?" We protest in offended disbelief. Paul, of course, rings all the changes on the arguments about the law and poses all the questions more radically than we would dare. Was the law a bad thing? No, it is holy, just, and good. But it has to be seen in the light of what actually happened. The law did not stop sin but only made sin worse. In so doing the law showed sin to be exceedingly sinful. The law exposed the depth of sin by showing it to be ineradicable by human power. Indeed, the law increased sin so as to bring it into confrontation with its sole remedy: that where sin abounded grace might much more abound. But such logic only brings us to even more dangerous consequences. In the first place, if our unrighteousness just becomes the occasion for God to be a God of mercy, if the game is "rigged," why does God still find fault? Does this not just turn everything on its head? Should not God compliment us in our unrighteousness for providing occasion for the demonstration of mercy? In the second place, if more sin only brings more grace, why not sin so more grace may abound?

These questions are the agonized protest of the old being who can think only in terms of continuity. They make sense only if one assumes continuity under the law. They arise out of blindness to the glory of God manifest in the new being called to life by faith in the resurrected Christ. Such blindness declares God unjust for finding fault in us when our unrighteousness becomes the occasion for the demonstration of God's righteousness, or that we should do evil that good may come, or sin more that grace may abound. Such declarations are based in thinking according to law, in terms of the old. The old does not see the glory of God in Jesus. Paul can quite summarily dismiss with them with the judgment, "Their condemnation is just" (Rom. 3:8).

Without hesitating, Paul answers the questions from the other side of the discontinuity, from the point of the new being raised with Christ in faith. "Are we to continue in sin that grace may abound?" (Rom. 6:1). No way! But why not? Because the law is still in effect? Because there is continuity with life under the law? Not at all. Death, not laws, puts an end to sin. Rather, it is because in Christ believers have died and live in the hope of the resurrection.

> For if we have been united with him in a death like his, we shall certainly be united with him in a resurrection like his. We know that our old self was crucified with him so that the sinful body might be destroyed, and we might no longer be enslaved to sin. For he who has died is freed from sin. But if we have died with Christ, we believe that we shall also live with him. For we know that Christ being raised from the dead will never die again; death no longer has dominion over him. The death he died he died to sin, once for all, but the life he lives he lives to God. So you also must consider yourselves dead to sin and alive to God in Christ Jesus.
>
> (Rom. 6:5-11)

Thinking from the point of view of this faith and hope leads to a quite different answer to impious suggestion that we should sin the more so that grace can abound. One who in faith catches a glimpse of the glory of God in Jesus simply cannot think that way: "How can you who have died to sin still live in it?" The relationship is by its very nature irreversible. If sin is at its root bondage, mistrust, unbelief, one really cannot sin the more that grace may abound. One cannot turn off the trust, so to speak, to have the joy of discovering it again. One cannot go back into bondage only to have the joy of escaping it again. That would be like a lover who turns off love to have the rapture of falling into it again. That would be quite impossible and rather silly. In actuality we do sin, fall away, and lose trust so that we do need the gospel again and again. But that could never be a deliberate practice to "get more grace." If it were, Paul's dictum—"Their condemnation is just"—would apply. For it would simply be a matter of the old being attempting cynically to parlay sin into personal advantage.

Newness Means Discontinuity

The discontinuity is involved in the very nature of the case. It is a new thing that God has done by raising Jesus from the dead. Indeed, God does this *to us*, putting to death the old and raising up the new. This all pertains to God's self-vindication, the establishment of God's justice and righteousness. It was impossible for this to be done under the old: the law could establish the righteousness neither of God nor of humans. But now God is vindicated and righteousness established in the sheer gift of the new.

> For God has done what the law, weakened by the flesh, could not do: sending his own Son in the likeness of sinful flesh and for sin, he condemned sin in the flesh, in order that the just requirement of the law might be fulfilled in us, who walk not according to the flesh but according to the Spirit.
>
> (Rom. 8:3-4)

That is the way Paul fosters the proclamation of Christ. What Paul proposes we preach is simply the folly of the cross, the sheer offense that brings the old to its end and creates hope in the resurrection of the new. The discontinuity between the Jesus who preached and the Jesus who is preached is of the essence of the matter. Indeed, in Paul's understanding of the madness and folly of the cross, the very discontinuity is done to us in the Word of the cross.

> When Paul speaks of the "folly" of the message of the crucified Jesus, he is therefore not speaking riddles or using an abstract cipher. . . . The reason why in his letters he talks about the cross above all in a polemical context is that he deliberately wants to provoke his opponents, who are attempting to water down the offence caused by the cross. Thus in a way "the word of the cross" is the spearhead of his message. And because Paul still understands the cross as the real, cruel instrument of execution, as the instrument of the bloody execution of Jesus, it is impossible to dissociate talk of the atoning death of Jesus or the blood of Jesus from this "word of the cross." The spearhead cannot be broken off the spear. Rather, the complex of the death of Jesus is a single entity for the apostle, in which he never forgets the fact that Jesus did not die a gentle death like Socrates, with his cup of hemlock, much less passing on "old and full of years" like the Patriarchs of the Old Testament. Rather he died like a slave or a common criminal, in torment, on the tree of shame. Paul's Jesus did not just die any death; he was "given up for us all" on the cross, in a cruel and contemptible way.[6]

Indeed, one can say that Paul is so anxious to drive home the discontinuity here through the folly of the Word of the cross that he seems to have little interest in the historical Jesus at all. At least in his extant writings, he says nothing of Jesus' teachings, miracles, or life history. He even says that whereas once we regarded Christ "from a human point of view, we regard him thus no longer" (2 Cor. 5:16). The question of Paul's attitude toward the historical Jesus is a much debated one among scholars. It is clear that Paul was neither a Gnostic who thought Jesus revealed heavenly secrets nor a docetic who thought Jesus was a heavenly being who only seemed to be a human. Paul was convinced of the historical reality of Jesus' life, death on the cross, and resurrection, but is not concerned merely with relating such information. Paul is concerned with proclaiming Christ and him crucified so that the crisis comes home to his hearers. He does not confront us with comfortable continuity between the historical Jesus and the subsequent teaching of the church. Indeed, his very apostolate was challenged in Galatia by those who claimed authenticity for their preaching and teaching in their association with the historical Jesus. Paul turns back the challenge because he knows that such "Judaizers," like their modern-day counterparts, only used the historical Jesus as an excuse for reimposing the law. Direct and unbroken continuity always turns out to be law.

Discontinuity is of the essence here because only the Jesus who dies and is raised can be gospel for us. Jesus did not come to add one last legalistic straw to the camel's back; he came to die for us and to bring new life in the resurrection. We do not have to believe Jesus or his teachings because he is divine or sent from God. That would make him only a new Moses. Jesus is our Savior. Belief is not a matter of "have to." Jesus is not a law-giver. He is the one who comes to set us free so that we will want to believe. So he comes to die under the law to redeem those who are under the law. The fact that we no longer regard Christ from a human point of view is immediately followed by the declaration,

> Therefore, if any one is in Christ, he is a new creation; the old has passed away, behold, the new has come.
>
> (2 Cor. 5:17)

This drives immediately to proclamation:

> All this is from God, who through Christ reconciled us to himself and
> gave us the ministry of reconciliation; that is, God was in Christ rec-
> onciling the world to himself, not counting their trespasses against them,
> and entrusting to us the message of reconciliation. So we are ambassadors
> for Christ, God making his appeal through us.
>
> (2 Cor. 2:18-20)

The discontinuity has to do with the advent of the new creation
and that can only be proclaimed, announced by its ambassadors to
faith. The righteousness of God is revealed in the gospel, from faith
to faith (Rom. 1:17).

The Earthly Jesus and the Risen Christ

It can be dangerous to push discontinuity as adamantly as Paul does.
The danger is that one might destroy or ignore all connection between
the earthly Jesus and the crucified, risen Christ. One could be tempted
to conclude from what Paul says that since one is now living the new
life of faith in Christ, one need pay no attention to the earthly Jesus
and what happened to him. The "new life" could become a kind of
mystical fancy talked about theologically with no concrete existence.
Or one might take Paul's past-tense language that since Christ died for
all, therefore all have died, to mean that one is already living the
resurrection life and so can do what one wishes and will never die.
In other words, one can attempt to turn Paul's theology of the cross
into a premature theology of glory.

Paul encountered this kind of theology in Corinth. Insistence on
discontinuity may even have led to a polemic against the Jesus of
history, the "Jesus be cursed!" referred to in 2 Cor. 12:3. Since they
belonged to the resurrected Christ, they had already "made it" and so
could do what they pleased in complete disregard of and even disdain
for the historical Jesus. Paul's response to this "resurrection enthusiasm" is an even more adamant proclamation of the cross. "I decided
to know nothing among you except Jesus Christ and him crucified"
(1 Cor. 2:2). Paul does not, that is, invoke the law or even the teachings
of the historical Jesus to cure their enthusiastic philandering. Paul just
returns to the cross. Paul puts the cross to them to remind them that
even though they are crucified with Christ through faith and so looking

forward to the resurrection in hope, they have not actually made it yet.

Paul is reticent to speak about being already raised with Christ. For the time being, the believer lives under the sign of the cross, bearing the suffering, serving in humility and love. For the time being, life is to be conformed to the cross, not marked by premature resurrection enthusiasm. If one boasts, then one is to boast in the Lord, or boast of one's weaknesses, not of one's prowess in spirituality. Christians were to be of the same mind as Christ Jesus who, unlike Adam, did not think equality with God something to be snatched at, but rather emptied himself, took the form of a servant, and became obedient unto death, even the shameful death on the cross (Phil. 2:5-11).

This means that in spite of the discontinuity that breaks in with the death and resurrection, there has to be some connection with the life of the earthly Jesus. Paul insists that the death must be that of the earthly Jesus, the human person "born of a woman, born under the law." Without the earthly Jesus the cross is not real, and if the cross is not real, the resurrection is a sham as well. That is, the discontinuity cannot be of a metaphysical sort, like the discontinuity between the real and the ideal, the many and the one, the sensible and the intelligible, or even the mortal and immortal. That is the discontinuity that Gnostics and other docetists both ancient and modern impose on the story. It can only mean that the earthly life is in one way or another not real. It is a front for some heavenly idealism. The discontinuity preached by Paul had to be the actual, bitter, offensive, discontinuity in the life of the man Jesus. It is the end of all idealisms, the death of heaven-stormers.

Paul saw the cross as the necessary connection between the earthly Jesus and the risen Christ. That is, there is a dialectic between continuity and discontinuity. The discontinuity can be real only if it is a rupture in the story of the human Jesus, a story that is nevertheless continued, but only by God. The earthly Jesus must actually come to a full stop, must die, in order to be raised. But it is through the death and resurrection of the earthly Jesus that God does God to us. The continuity consists in the fact that it is in the life story of this one person that the discontinuity occurs. God, that is, continues the story in spite of the discontinuity. That means that God alone is the carrier of whatever continuity there is, both in the story of Jesus and consequently in our stories as well. Continuity in the face of discontinuity is rooted ultimately in the fact that God is triune.

It is this dialectic of discontinuity and continuity that drives to the writing of the Gospels and to the recasting of the life and teaching of the historical Jesus as the Word of the cross. The Gospels had to be written to maintain the dialectic, to show and proclaim what God was up to in the story of Jesus. There were from the start those who would dissolve it on one side or the other. On the side of continuity were those whose heresy has gone down in history as Ebionitism, descended from early Jewish Christianity, who looked upon Jesus as an eschatological prophet, a reformer and heightener of the law. That was an attempt to take his work as an earthly being seriously and to see what happened in the cross as validation for his teaching. But such continuity only places his followers under the law all the more securely.

On the side of discontinuity were the Gnostic and docetic heresies. The earthly Jesus was an embarrassment to them, so they promulgated the idea that the human Jesus was only the temporary garment for the Gnostic redeemer from another realm. He only seemed to be human (docetism). The gnostic redeemer was sent to release or awaken spirits in prison by imparting secret knowledge. But that would, of course, bypass the cross and resurrection. Some Gnostics even held that Jesus changed places with Simon of Cyrene who carried the cross and so was not crucified at all. The Gnostic, in general, opts for a metaphysical discontinuity between the historical Jesus and the divine redeemer which renders the earthly Jesus irrelevant and so, in turn, also ends on the side of law. The "secret gnosis" brought by the heavenly Redeemer turns out to be some species of rule promising escape by detaching oneself from earthly existence.

The curious thing is that when one falls off on one side or the other, one ends only with the law. That is a vital theological lesson to learn. Without the earthly, human Jesus who actually dies—comes to his end—under the law, and is nevertheless raised to new life by God, the law reigns supreme.

The Gospels had to be written to tell the truth about Jesus in the light of the cross and the resurrection. They had to be written to preserve the delicate dialectic between continuity and discontinuity. We may indeed argue as to the relative success each of the Gospels achieves in this sensitive enterprise, but it is essential for proclamation today to understand this if one is going to preach significantly on the Gospels. On the one hand, the life and teachings are of no significance apart from the death and resurrection. Indeed, they had to be transformed in the light of the cross and resurrection. This fact is usually the most difficult, especially for the literalists among us. We must reckon with the fact that the words and teachings of the earthly Jesus in all probability could not have been handed on as he gave them even if those very words had been preserved. The death and resurrection had intervened and it would be untrue to what God was doing to hand on anything about Jesus apart from that fact.

On the other hand, it is likewise necessary to maintain that the death and resurrection are of no significance unless they happened to the man Jesus who came preaching—thus the Gospels. The whole can be designated in shorthand fashion as the Word of the cross. The subject of this Word of the cross is Jesus Christ, the earthly Jesus who is also Lord and Christ. The name and the titles belong indissolubly together for they hold the continuity and the discontinuity in delicate balance. Precisely so must he be preached. But how shall we do this? How shall we answer his searching question, "Who do you say that I am?" How shall we shape our reflection so as to drive to appropriate proclamation? Such questions lead us into more direct reflection on the explicit Christology of the church and its problems.

4
The Preached God

Since therefore the children share in flesh and blood, he himself likewise partook of the same nature, that through death he might destroy him who has the power of death, that is, the devil, and deliver all those who through fear of death were subject to lifelong bondage.

(Heb. 2:14)

C hristology is reflection on the Jesus who has been proclaimed to us in the church so that we will return once again to the proclamation. In the terms of the three poles set forth (Jesus to hearer, Jesus to eschatological title, hearer to the title), Christology is the interpretation of that third pole. What was implicit in Jesus and his preaching is made explicit through other titles and attributions, most of which he himself probably did not use. The purpose of the titles and attributions is to foster proper proclamation of Jesus and so to evoke proper praise of God and his work among us—in settings and contexts quite other than those in which Jesus originally appeared and worked. Christological reflection is to guide us on our way from yesterday's to today's proclamation. As such, it is a constructive task. Those who have been grasped by the proclamation measure past reflection critically so as to propose ways present reflection might once again foster vital proclamation.

Toward Reconstruction in Christology

Today we must begin by taking account of the fact that the traditional Christology of the church has been under heavy attack for a long time now. It began in the sixteenth century with the anti-trinitarians and the Socinians, and culminates in various contemporary skepticisms and relativisms. In the light of this constant and withering attack, it should be apparent by now that something is amiss. There has been, on the one hand, no want of affection for Jesus, but on the other hand, considerable antipathy to Christology. Even present traditionalists display this erosion when they shelve their official Christology to preach a Jesusology: Jesus is important religiously for us because he is such a nice and impressive person, or perhaps someone with whom we can "identify" and not because he is the Son of God who was crucified and yet raised. Passing reference might be made to the idea that Jesus is the "Christ," but mostly in incidental fashion (*sotto voce*), and with little explication of what that is supposed to mean or do for us. Both the direct attacks on traditional Christology and the more subtle erosions among traditionalists themselves indicate the need for a renewed attempt at reconstruction.

The project of this chapter is to work out what Christology might look like when systematic theology is for proclamation. We shall be concerned more directly with what the tradition has called the person and the work of Christ, explicit interpretation of the "third pole" in the tri-polar relation. Since the entire tri-polar relation is Christology, however, interpretation of the third pole cannot be carried out in isolation from the other two. We shall find it necessary, therefore, to make constant reference to the other two poles in the relation, the "me and my words" of Jesus and the stance of the hearer who stands under the danger of being "ashamed."

It should be evident from the previous chapters that a systematic theology concerned with proclamation needs to be sensitive to the ways in which faulty moves in christological reflection can subvert the preaching of the church. Even Christologies most revered by the tradition will come under critical scrutiny. Indeed, the barrage of criticism leveled at the traditional two-natures Christology of the church in recent centuries and the general collapse of vital proclamation of Christ because of that barrage indicate that this is the point at which we need to enter.

Problems in the Tradition

We will specify, for the sake of proclamation today, where the traditional reflection seems no longer to foster vital proclamation. The problem is not that the traditional Christology is materially wrong. The confession that Jesus Christ is true God and true man belongs to the indisputable and unalterable credo of the Christian church. To deny this creed is to no longer remain Christian. The problem arises when one moves to the "two natures" and attempts to put them together in systematic fashion. The temptation is to think in substantialist terms so that Christology becomes the business of putting the two natures together into an appropriate synthesis.

The aim is laudable and correct enough: to convey the truth that in and through Jesus Christ we are rescued from sin, death, and the power of the devil. But substantialist language tends to convey the idea that Jesus rescues us *because* he is a synthesis, that he is made up of undying substance joined in some way with dying substance. The danger thus lies near at hand that the actual story of the suffering and dying one will be altered, becoming either an unreal appearance or an afterthought. The true miracle in substantialist terms is the joining of the two substances or natures. It is, we might say, a "systematic" miracle, not a real one. All too often what is born from it is a bastard child called incarnational theology with attendant sophistries. So impressive, it seems, is the systematic miracle of joining the natures that this becomes the center of everything. Theological focus shifts to the miracle of the beginning—the virgin mother and the birth of Jesus—away from the One he called his Father and the miracle he wrought in the death and resurrection. As a consequence, one does not proclaim but rather practices "incarnational ministry." One just puts in an appearance in a turned-around collar as though that were some sort of repetition of the original systematic miracle.

The result of such misuse of the two-natures doctrine is that the proclamation—the actual doing of the story to the hearers—gets crowded out by another sort of enterprise: the lecture, the demonstration, and the proof that Jesus is actually the person claimed by the synthesis. The Christology does not lead or drive unerringly to proclamation; it can all too easily subvert it. And the most subtle problem, in terms of the tri-polar relation, is that we have a stake in such subversion. For if Jesus does not die, we do not have to die either. The peroration in Mark 8 about losing one's life for Jesus' sake in order to find it is not really true. Perhaps, as the saying goes these days, it is "only a metaphor," supposedly the universal solvent of all hard sayings and offensive claims.

The difficulty dogging christological discussion and criticism is that the disputants rarely put their finger on what is wrong. The critics of traditional Christology were right in sensing that as doctrine it was not really very good news. Christology became a doctrine about an undying Christ who once upon a time visited earth in human form, performed some miracles, left a number of very difficult laws, escaped our universal fate, and eventually absconded never to be seen or heard from again, leaving the church behind as the authoritative purveyor of this dubious legacy. The critics of such views thought the trouble was in the idea of God in human form so they attempted to dismantle it and replace it with a human Jesus, one who perhaps just taught eternal and divine truths—the same sort of thing any good philosopher would do. They failed to see that our real problem was in the question of the death, Jesus' death and ours. If the divine nature of the tradition protected Jesus from death, so do the divine teachings of the human Jesus. Jesus does not really die, he lives on in his teachings. No doubt we have a stake in an undying Jesus because as old beings we seek self-preservation. In terms of the tri-polar relation, by preserving Jesus' continuity we preserve our own. No one wanted to think that it was only through death we could be saved. It was not realized clearly that if Jesus does not die for us, we are still under the law of sin and death. To be saved the old must die in Christ. But that is done only through the proclamation and the sacraments. Without that the law holds sway eternally.

Here we come to the root of the problem in Christology. A God-man, either orthodox or liberal, who does not truly die and is not truly raised cannot save us. That is the ultimate reason why after brief initial acclamation the Christology of the tradition is experienced as a threat, a heteronomy. An undying God-man is just another Moses and all too easily takes the form of the magnificent almighty Christ (*Christus Pantocrator*) enthroned in the apse of the churches. Someone has to put us out of our misery! Since that was not understood, the Christology more modern critics in turn proposed was just a variety of the same thing, only worse because now one had only the virtue of one's immortal soul on which to rely.

The problem seems still to be that the substantialist and essentialist language gets in the way of the story, especially the death of Jesus. This has, of course, been sensed from the first. Indeed, Arius, the arch-heretic in these matters, apparently started with just that complaint. If the incarnate Logos suffers and dies in Jesus, then that Logos cannot be of one substance with the eternal God. But like most moderns, Arius only tried to solve the dilemma by making the divine Logos who became incarnate in Jesus something less than God: like God perhaps, God's first deed and emanation, but nevertheless a creation of God and so something less than God. But that destroys the possibility for proclamation. It turns the Word into a lecture, reinforces the religion of so-called free choice, enables us to avoid the death of the old, and leaves us still under the law. If Jesus is the incarnation of a Logos who is only "like God," we, like those nineteenth-century pundits who found a "divinity" amenable to human autonomy in Jesus, already know God in some way and so can recognize Jesus to be like God. We can "see through" Jesus. The Word incarnate in Jesus is enough like God, you might say, to be recognizable to us "God specialists." So then we can exercise our freedom to choose him. He is not the despised one "from whom we hid our faces." We approve of Jesus because he is so "God-like." Once again the old being escapes. But then we are still in our sins. Christianity has been transformed into a Greek religion.

It is understandable that the church fathers ultimately took refuge in substantialist language to plug up this loophole. The Word confronting us in the crucified and resurrected Jesus is not "like God" (*homoiousious*), not, as some are wont to say today, a parable or metaphor for God, a front or stand-in for God through which we with our sharp religious sensibilities can see. No, Jesus is the incarnation of the Word who from the beginning was with God and is God (John 1:1). If Jesus is to be proclaimed as the crisis of our lives, the one we cannot see through or get around, the one before whom we can only say, "I repent, you are the Lord," then no escape can be allowed.

So it was natural and even appropriate that the great Councils at Nicaea (325) and Constantinople (381) after furious and acrimonious debate countered the Arian threat by saying that the Word incarnate in Jesus is "of one substance" (*homoousios*) with the Father—the divinity confronting us in Jesus is not merely adjectival but "substantive." There are, nevertheless, indications that for various reasons they were not particularly happy with the language. It had been used previously in unfavorable circumstances,[1] and it was not biblical. But it certainly plugged the loophole and aggravated the Arian opponents. Quite probably it came to be favored for just such reason. So after considerable argument, theological clarification, and politico-ecclesiastical maneuvering, the "of one substance with the Father" established itself in the creed as the canon of orthodoxy.

But the substantialist language (the *homoousion*) was in most ways effective more for what it excluded than what it included. It effectively excluded Arianism, at least as long as people had any appreciation for the language! But what did it import positively into the faith? Here we must state unhesitatingly today that it was *the* basic Christian doctrine of the triune God. It was the first and most fundamental step in the battle against the gods of religion. The "God-story" itself is modified by the Jesus story. It provided at least a beginning grammar for clarifying the threefold-ness of God proclaimed in the New Testament, and a language for engaging the mind of the times.

It is perhaps difficult for us today who have lost a feel for the language to grasp what was at stake. It is also true that the language was originally much more plastic and conveyed more sense of action and movement than does subsequent hardening, materialization, and fixing by a set of dictionary meanings. This will be important for us later in our reconstruction. Words like "essence" (*ousia* and especially *essentia*) are, after all, verbs made into nouns. They probably meant something like "is-er," or "is-es," instead of "basic stuff" or what we today speak of as "substance." One's essence is one's "is-er," that which operates or drives one. The language sounds odd to us but probably approaches what they meant. To say that the Word confronting us in Jesus is of one substance with the Father meant they were of the same is-er, the same operation.

The relation of the Father to the Son is therefore not that of static "stuff" or even that conveyed by the more physical images used by philosophers, such as "overflow" and "emanation." The Father eternally begets the Son, and so is revealed to be the eternal begetter, the Father of this only Son in that eternal begetting. Both the Father and the Son are established in precise self-definition through this relation. The Son is the only-begotten of the Father and so only through the Son is the

Father known. "No one has ever seen God; the only Son, who is in the bosom of the Father, he has made him known" (John 1:18). The Father and the Son are not to be defined, therefore, by analogy from human fatherhood and sonship, a point seemingly difficult to get across these days. The Father is unlike all human fathers at least in that he has never been and will never be a son. He is *the* father. The Son, likewise, is unlike human sons in that he will never be a father.[2] The Spirit "proceeds" from this unique relation of the Father and the Son as creative, life-giving and liberating power. The unity of the Trinity was therefore to be understood finally as a unity of operations, not a problem in mathematics. It was, so to speak one, "is-er" who "is-es" in three, and only three, ways. The true God really proves to be one by repeating the God operation three times over: Father, Son, and Holy Spirit.

This is absolutely essential for proclamation. Proclamation as present-tense Word of God spoken by a human being is possible only under the aegis of this divine self-repetition. Only so can the Word we proclaim today be the Word of God. One proclaims the only Son of the Father in the Spirit and so "does God" to the hearers.

The exclusion of the Arian heresy is not, however, the end of the matter. The fact that the Word incarnate in Jesus was declared to be substantially one with the Father only postponed the problem and shifted it from the level of the doctrine of God to the level of Christology. The problem of mediation between the timeless realm of eternal abstractions and the world of change, suffering, and death had to be confronted all over again. The Logos, the eternal Word, was not a halfway house. But then how could a Word substantially one with the Father possibly also be one with the suffering and dying Jesus? Two-natures Christology is the outcome of theological wrestling with this problem. In Jesus there is a union of the divine nature, the eternal Word, and the human, the man Jesus, in one person. The furious debates leading up to the Council of Chalcedon (451) had to do with the nature of the union and the kind of person produced by such a union.

What we do need to do is look at the history of the debate with a view to what it means for proclamation. Within the middle Platonic thought-world of the time there were, broadly speaking, two ways one might think of the union between the divine and the human. One was oriented more toward categories of being, and the other more toward becoming. The two ways begot two different schools of christological thought, Alexandria and Antioch, and fired debate issuing finally in the Chalcedonian decree. The Alexandrians tended to think more in terms of being. The union between the divine and the human had to be conceived as one of being, a "physical" union (*henosis physike*) of divine and human being. The eternal Logos assumed human flesh, so vivifying it as ultimately to conquer the death to which such flesh is fated since the fall. Antioch tended to think more in terms of becoming. The union between the divine and the human is more of a "moral" oneness, a conjunction (synapheia). The Logos is so intimately conjoined with the man Jesus that he becomes the one in whom sin and death are conquered.

It is inevitable that the two schools are at each other's throats. Antioch charged Alexandria with a mixture or confusion of divine and human which truncated the humanity and threatened to make the real life of Jesus irrelevant. Small wonder that the Antiochene school tends to be the darling of most contemporary christologians. Alexandria, on the other hand, charged Antioch with a separation and division, positing "two sons," two acting subjects in the person, which made salvation dubious. At the Council of Chalcedon the disputants tried to forge a compromise largely by denying the charges each made of the other. So the guts of the decree are contained in the famous exclusions: "One and the same Christ, Son, Lord, only Begotten," is "made known in two natures" which exist "without mixture, without change, without division, without separation."

Critical estimates as to the success or failure of Chalcedon are predictably varied.[3] We need not trouble ourselves with such variations here since they usually depend on the set of abstractions to which one is most sympathetic. We need to probe a little deeper to get at the problems affecting proclamation. The problem is that neither christological school is able in the end to foster unambiguously a viable proclamation. The reason is that neither school is finally able adequately to handle the root issues of freedom, bondage, and death.

The middle Platonism that influenced the two schools was ambiguous on just such issues.[4] The questions revolved around the soul and its relation to the world of sense. They believed, like the neo-Platonists, that the soul is by nature immaterial, intellectual, impassible, belonging to that world of eternal abstractions. Yet the soul finds itself in the world of sense, caught in change, decay, and death. They had a difficult time explaining how and to what purpose the soul came to "fall," to be enslaved, in such a world. If the "fall" was involuntary it would mean that the impassible soul could be acted on from without, that it was subject to some cosmic fate that cancels its freedom. But that is logically impossible. On the other hand, if the "fall" was voluntary, it would mean that the impassible soul has the capacity for self-alienation. That too is unthinkable. So they settled on a compromise of sorts: the idea of the mixed nature of the soul. The soul is caught betwixt and between, forever aspiring to the world of the intellect, the world of eternal, impassible abstractions, and yet forever turned toward the world of sense, decay, and death. This meant that they finally could not decide whether the soul's true element and destiny was freedom from the world of sense, decay, and death, or whether the soul was really made for embodiment and was to work out its destiny by exercising its freedom of moral choice in the world of sense.

This basic indecision is reflected in two different Christologies and likewise two different soteriologies. The Alexandrians held that the divine logos-soul so vivified the flesh in the person of Jesus as ultimately to bring freedom from change, decay, and death. For this to work there must, of course, be a real "physical" union between the divine Logos-soul and the human flesh (*sarx*). Therefore the degree to which the human side in Jesus survives the union tends always to be problematic for the Alexandrians. Or, even if the human nature intended for union is complete, does it survive after the union (Eutyches and the Monophysites)? For the soteriology to work, the flesh must, so to speak, be swallowed up by the divine life, dissolved as some Alexandrians could say, "like a drop of vinegar in the ocean." By participation, for the most part sacramentally conceived, in the mystery of this divinely vivified life, we too can be "divinized," freed from change, decay, and death.

Curious things happen when this middle Platonic tendency is thus Christianized, most of them having to do with the question of death and, ultimately, resurrection. On the one hand, it is clear that if the tendency were driven to its logical conclusion, it would lead to salvation by absorption in the divine, complete extinction of the flesh, of human individuality. Now if it is true that we can be saved only by dying, only by losing our lives for Jesus' sake, then there is something right about this. The problem, of course, that the "death" proposed is not that of the crucified One which leads to the hope of resurrection, but rather the extinction of the individual, the body, and its particular story, for the sake of the abstraction, the "soul." No theologian, furthermore, could drive the system to such a logical conclusion and still be considered Christian. The Christology forbade it, to say nothing of the view of creation. To adapt the scheme for christological use, therefore, the Alexandrians had to put a more or less arbitrary limit on the absorption and extinction logically demanded. Only so could they preserve the human. But that simply means that for all its tantalizing suggestiveness, the Alexandrian system is deeply divided within itself. It rightly knows that salvation comes only through death, but at the same time has to protect the subject from the "death" the system imposes in order to remain Christian. It has to protect itself from the logic of its own soteriology.

But that in turn has the consequence that under the cover of such protection the old being finally escapes. Protected from "death" by absorption or extinction, the old being tends finally not to be confronted by death at all, but only with the promise of escape from it. The upshot of all this is that in the end proclamation is not fostered. There is no Word that slays the old and makes the new alive. Rather, the emphasis falls on participation in the divine mysteries through which one becomes immortal. The "death" one dies tends, so to speak, to be a "mystical" death. One is purged of individuality and particularity to become a kind of living abstraction.

There is, however, one more highly significant christological consequence of the Alexandrian scheme, perhaps in the final analysis the most important of all. Precisely because they insisted on a physical union between Logos and flesh in which the flesh has no independent acting subject other than the Logos (often falsely called an "impersonal human nature"), and because they insisted, against the Gnostics, on the reality of the death of Christ, they could not avoid the conclusion that the Logos somehow suffered the consequences of death. Curiously, while all along being suspected of ignoring the human life of Jesus because it was simply absorbed or overridden by the divine, that same absorption brought the suffering and death of Jesus home to the Logos, to a member of the Trinity. It is as though the shocking story of a real death suddenly intrudes upon a polite theoretical discussion. But this startling development seems to burst upon the scene like a strange comet that cannot really be charted on the known celestial maps. Just as ancient astrologers wondered about the meaning of such comets, so its real import tends to remain obscure. Nevertheless, this tantalizing and suggestive circling around the question of death makes Alexandrian Christology finally more significant for the development of a theology interested in proclamation than that of Antioch.

The Antiochenes tended toward the other option present in middle Platonism, the belief that the soul, quite contrary to the spirit of Platonism, was intended for embodiment and was to exercise its free moral choice in that state. So in their Christology the Logos entered into a conjunction with the human being Jesus, body and soul, so intimate as to enable Jesus to conquer sin and death. But this introduces quite another set of problems. For the soteriology to work, the union cannot be so close as to override the soul of the man Jesus and his freedom. Consequently the real nature of the union is always problematic for the Antiochene. If there are two natures even after the union, does this not mean that there are really two acting subjects in the person? Who is in charge here? Is Mary really the bearer of God or is she not rather the bearer of the child who is, or becomes, the Christ? Once begun, will this "Doppelgaenger" act not have to be played out to the logical end and say that there are two wills in the God-man? And so on.

Once again the system becomes divided against itself when it is put to christological and soteriological use. The scheme proposes that the "salvation" of the soul is to be realized by aiding the moral will in its struggle for freedom. Were the scheme taken to its logical conclusion this would mean that the more one succeeds in the struggle, the less aid one would need until one would be independent of God altogether. The only one in the history of the church who actually dared to assert something like that to my knowledge is Julian of Eclanum, the arch-Pelagian of them all. But that is, in effect, the apotheosis of the human. God is as good as dead. If the logical end of the Alexandria scheme is the extinction of the human, then the logical end of the antiochene scheme is the extinction of God!

Again, one could not drive the system to its logical conclusion and still remain in the orthodox Christian fold. The Christology, at least, forbade it. But again that only meant that the Antiochenes had to set arbitrary limits to the logic to keep the scheme Christian. The Logos does indeed enter into a union with the man Jesus, but it cannot be such as actually to extinguish or override Jesus' moral freedom. There is a perfect "conjunction" of the two in one human phenomenon (*prosopon*). There is indeed a union, but it is difficult to avoid the suspicion that the divine has to be held at arm's length to give human freedom room to operate. The old dilemma of the relation between divine omnipotence and human freedom plays itself out christologically in the standoff of two natures.

So in the final analysis the Christology that leans on the language of becoming fares no better than that which uses the language of being. If anything, matters only get worse. There is, of course, something quite right about it. Its concern to protect the human from being swallowed up by the divine abstraction is quite legitimate. One could even say that in its protection of freedom it presages the idea broached earlier (see chap. 1) that somehow we have to get God off our backs. Even the hint that this somehow entails the death of God is not entirely off base.

But it is, of course, all curiously wrong. The language of becoming, at least in this version, shows itself to be only a variation on the language of being. Again the death proposed is not the real death of the man Jesus, but theoretical death imposed by the system. God dies a systematic death, so to speak, to make way for human freedom. In the very attempt to give full import to the human life of Jesus, the Antiochenes nevertheless lost the real contact between that human life and God. If the Alexandrian insistence on physical union did a curious flip at the last and brought the suffering and death directly to bear on at least one of the Trinity, the Antiochene insistence on giving the human life and suffering validity likewise does a turnabout at the end which has just the opposite effect: it protects the Logos from the consequences of too close a union with the human. The system has to intervene, so to speak, to "save" the Logos. Since there is only a "conjunction" or moral union between the natures, they could assign the alleged ignominies of being enclosed in the womb—the agonies of life and eventual suffering and death—to the human nature. The divine is saved by transcending such messy business. Western Christology, which has been mostly Antiochene, has been dogged by this docetic tendency ever since.

But this means once again that proclamation is undercut. The sermon would tend to become not a word that proclaims the absolute crisis of the death of our gods but a recitation of the accomplishments of the human Jesus albeit, of course, with the divine hovering in the background to render aid. Old beings are not put to death with such patter but only called upon to cut their moral wisdom teeth on the example of Jesus and sue for his aid. It is no wonder that Pelagius found succor later among such christologians. Nor is it a wonder that in the wake of the search for the historical Jesus modern christologians find Antioch more amenable to their tastes than Alexandria. But mostly that just indicates the penchant for turning away from proclamation to pious moral discourse.

Jesus: The Man in Whom God Does God

The attempt to enclose and to preach Jesus in the language of being and its variation in the language of becoming falters when it comes to the cross and so does not drive unerringly to proclamation. The language seems bound always to protect Jesus, and covertly us, from the consequences of actual suffering and death. As suggested all along, we have a stake in such language. If it is true that our fall is an upward one, that we aspire to be "as gods," then it is likely that the divinity being covertly protected from suffering and death in Jesus is not really his divinity but ours. If something in this synthetic Jesus survives death, either by being or becoming, then perhaps something in us will, too. We are reluctant to surrender the comfort of such language. Indeed, we are *bound* not to. The situation is exactly that described by Ernest Becker in *The Denial of Death*.[5] Christology is turned into a death-denying self-centered *causa sui* project. Jesus is not the one who puts the old to death, but the one who enables us to deny death. The supreme irony, of course, is that death-denying projects destroy us. We are drawn like moths to the flame. The divine abstractions that are supposed to sustain us only destroy our humanity. They deal a death from which there is no promise of resurrection. It is true, of course, that the abstractions do not die or change. But it is rarely noticed that they do not give life either. They are abstractions from life, what is left after all particularity and individuality have been shorn away. Attempting to draw life from them is similar to a man trying to stick to a prescribed diet of fruit in order to survive. He does not find

"fruit," only apples, oranges, peaches, strawberries, and plums, and so
he dies. "Fruit," of course, has the advantage that it does not decay or
die. But it does not give life, either. The problem is that religiously
we are like that man. "In the day you eat thereof you shall surely die."

Systematic theology as secondary discourse is problematic in
that it consists of abstractions that can neither be avoided nor removed.
It is crucial to realize, however, that they have an end, a limit (a *telos*).
The situation here is similar to the persistent problem of the relation
of law and gospel. It is a mistake, indeed a heresy (antinomianism),
to think one can erase the law in this age. Nevertheless, "Christ is the
end of the law [to those who have faith]" (Rom. 10:4). There is an
end and *telos*: Christ and faith. As one is in Christ one is free from the
law. But that end occurs only through the proclamation. The law is
limited to this age, and only where faith grasps that will the law be
accorded its proper place. Otherwise we shall always take steps to
end it ourselves in one way or another. But it can never work. The
law, like the masks of God, only changes form, and in the end administers a death from which there is no resurrection.

Abstractions in theology are like the law. But instead of shaping
the moral life, they give shape to the life of the mind. We can not get
along without them. The problem of the man looking for fruit, of
course, was that he mistook the purpose or end of the abstraction.
Only an actual apple could be the end of the abstraction and the
beginning of life. So it must be that the proclamation and the sacrament
that give Christ is the end of abstraction, the deed that breaks the hold
of the "dead letter" and imparts the Spirit that gives life.

For reconstruction in Christology this means that over against a
use of the language of being and becoming which ends with itself we
shall have to set the language of acting, more precisely a language that
fosters and drives to the concrete act itself. This is the import of the
grammatically barbaric heading to this section: Jesus is the One in
whom God does God to us, the true human in whom God does God
to us. The point is that we can move forward here only if we realize
that in and through the human, suffering, dying, and resurrected Jesus
we come up against God. God does himself to us in Jesus. The proclamation is the concrete event in which that occurs for us. Systematic
theology must promote that occurrence. To do so, reconstruction in

Christology must move to a language that drives to the act of proclamation as the doing of the deed.

Movement to the language of act, however, is treacherous. The
danger seems always to be that deserting the language of being and
substance will leave us with a Christ who is something less than God.
The Arian heresy always awaits. Perhaps the language of substance
functions permanently, at least in this age, as a guardian against such
lapses. But perhaps also, like the law, it must have an end. If not, it
tends to obscure the act of God in the suffering and dying Jesus. Perhaps
the matter here is similar to that of the magnificent abstractions in
our speaking of God. Removing them is a futile exercise that only leads
to bowdlerization. They can be ended only by the concrete proclamation. So we must speak carefully here, perhaps not of the outright
removal of the language of substance, but rather of a setting over
against it a language that drives to the act, the proclamation itself. That
is the burden of the reconstruction that follows.

First, we consider Jesus' divinity, Jesus as true God. How can we
safely move from the language of being to act? It seems clear from
what we have found so far that we can do this only if we confront the
question of death and its power manifest in our bondage and sin. What
was it the ancient Christology sought when it attributed divinity to
Jesus? It was salvation from the death wrought by sin. In the language
of being this tended to mean that Jesus survives death because he is
union of the immortal and the mortal in which mortality is ultimately
cancelled or overcome. We are then to be saved by participation in
this triumphant immortality. The problem is that such salvation tends
to dissolve the human, the body and its particularity, its story, both in
Jesus and subsequently in us. Ironically it intends life, but deals a death
from which there is finally no hope for "resurrection of the body." In
a sense, it does anticipate the idea that we can be saved only through
death, but it goes awry because the death inflicted is that imposed by
abstraction. The body is shucked off. The abstraction, the immortal
soul, survives.

The move to the language of act can be made in such a way as
to avoid the charge that Jesus is something less than the true God only
if we face the question of death, sin, and bondage more squarely and
fully than heretofore. Jesus was not immune to death because of being
united with an immortal divine nature; he came truly to die for us.

He partook of our nature "that through death he might overcome him who has the power of death, that is, the devil, and deliver all those who through fear of death were subject to life-long bondage." In the language of act, the divinity of Jesus does not consist in the fact that he successfully avoids death on our behalf, but it is hidden precisely in the fact that he dies for us and so conquers death. That is, we do not see through the humanity to an abstraction called divinity hidden somewhere behind the scenes. It is in and through the humanity, the suffering and the dying, that we come up against what his divinity means. He does not come to protect us from death, he comes to do it to us. He brings death home to us. He does old beings to death. The suffering and dying Jesus is therefore the one in whom we meet our end, the eschatological end of our existence in bondage to sin and death. He is the end of the old being who vainly constructs death-denying projects, who thinks that abstractions such as divinity and immortality can save. He puts an end to our story negatively and positively. He is the end (*finis*) of the old, and the goal (*telos*) of the new. The old is put to death so that the new can be resurrected in faith and hope to look to the last day in confidence.

In the language of act the divinity of Jesus consists in the fact that precisely through his suffering, death, and resurrection, he does God to us. As John's Gospel has it, in the instance where Jesus gets into trouble for breaking the old order by healing on the Sabbath, the Son does what he sees the Father doing. Their unity is a unity of doing.[6] "Truly, truly, I say to you, the Son can do nothing of his own accord, but only what he sees the Father doing; for whatever he does, that the Son does likewise" (John 5:19). He was, of course, killed for that, killed by the likes of us who did not want the old to end because we thought we could bring it to a better end ourselves. But even in his dying, he does only what "he sees the Father doing" to the end. As the one who actually dies, unprotected, rejected, forsaken, even by God, he is "the end of us" as beings who thought divinity was a protection. The crucifixion of Jesus is the end of us. We cannot see through it. There is nothing "godlike" here for old beings to recognize. It is simply the end. God is through with us as old beings. There can be no survivors, no spectators. The only way forward is through faith in the resurrection.

Thus Jesus is the repetition of God to us, because in the first place he is the absolute end of the old, the chaos of darkness, bondage, and sin. He is the end of all the old being's hopes, dreams, and fantasies. He shatters our godlike pretensions, even the possibility of finding them reinforced in his divinity.

And Jesus finally exposes why it is we have such difficulty surrendering the language of being and its surrogates. Like the law, it is our last hope as old beings, our final defense as gods, against having to die. Like Peter's "confession," it is our last line of defense against God. If we could align Jesus on our side as the warranty for our divinity, then we would not have to say with Paul those shocking words, "For [Christ's] sake I have suffered the loss of all things, and count them as refuse (*skubala*), in order that I may gain Christ and be found in him, not having a righteousness of my own, based on law, but that which is through faith in Christ, . . . that I may know him and the power of his resurrection (Phil. 3: 8-10).

Jesus is the end of the old (the absolute *finis*). There is nothing left of us as old beings when he is through with us. There is only him now. Through the death of Jesus we die to all the abstractions, we are reborn concretely as historical beings, creatures, who have no Savior but him. The only hope now is to be found in him, that we may know him and the power of his resurrection. Now those words of Paul begin to find their place—"For to me to live is Christ and to die is gain" (Phil. 1:21)—even though we can hardly say them without a shudder.

Jesus is thus the repetition of God to us. It is a repetition, in the first place, because we have encountered this end before, though we have run away from it. God not proclaimed, the absolute God (*deus ipse*) of the magnificent abstractions, we have said, is the end of us, the death of us. For God not proclaimed leaves us no room, no freedom, no future. In terror and bondage we flee that God, succumbing to the temptation to take matters into our own hands, to be as gods ourselves. But we are not gods, and so we have no end (no *telos*). We wonder what "fate" or "destiny" or "chance" will bring, or what "history" will say about us. We thought to escape fate or chance by claiming freedom, but we only placed ourselves in its hands. Having no end, we are subject to concupiscence, endless desire, driven by a law which says only, "No end in sight." Jesus ends all that. Jesus finds us in our endless flight. He finds us out. Jesus repeats, we might say, "the God experience" by dying for us. He is the one in whom the God crisis confronts us again concretely, the end of everything, the end of our godlike pretensions, the end of the law, the end of the age, and—dare we say it?—the end of God? Certainly the end of God as wrath! He dies the death we refuse to die. "It is finished."

But Jesus is the repetition of God, in the second place, because he is not only end but new beginning (not only *finis* but *telos*). He brings life from death. He creates faith. He does God by calling into being that which is from that which is not *(ex nihilo)*. He is not simply the end of us, he is the beginning. Indeed, he can be the end, the death of us, only because he is the beginning, the one who gives us life. We need not flee him in terror precisely because he dies for us. Even though he is, in the cross, the culmination of the wrath of God against us as old beings, he is through that very fact the warranty for the proclamation of the love of God. As the proclaimed God, he is the end of wrath. Precisely because he is the end of our flight from God he is the love of God for us. The point here is that only in the concrete proclamation "for you" does the new creation break in. As crucified and risen, Jesus makes such proclamation possible. As we have seen repeatedly, God cannot be for us in general. God cannot be for us as old beings without being first against us. New life comes only through death. Jesus is God proclaimed as God for you. So he is the one who finally wrings the truth from us. For there is only one appropriate response to the proclamation. In the Spirit, we can only say, "I repent, you are the Lord."

A systematic theology for fostering proclamation must consequently warn of the difference between dogmatic assertions about the divinity of Jesus couched in the language of being, and an effective proclamation of Jesus. "Who do you say that I am?" Merely saying dogmatically that Jesus is the divine Son of God will likely accomplish nothing more than a Judas kiss if it is not employed to drive to a doing to us of the divinity that occurred in Jesus. Without such proclamation the divinity will be understood as something adjectival, something somehow added to the man Jesus which "peeks out" now and then when he does a miracle or says something "nice" that really pleases us, something "simply divine" we can recognize and affirm. We are led to look exactly in the wrong place for the "proofs" of Jesus' divinity.

"The Jews demand signs, and the Greeks seek wisdom, but we preach Christ crucified, a stumbling block . . . and folly."

The shock, the stumbling block, and the folly consist in the fact that this man whom we judge exactly to be not divine is nevertheless raised by God. "*This* is my beloved Son!" If he is raised by God and thus attested to be Lord and Christ, then a death and life antithesis between our idea of divinity and God's appears in him. Had he remained in the tomb we would have been right. Since he has been raised he is vindicated and we are wrong. That is the end of us. The fruitless search for fruit is embarrassingly exposed and ended. Any proclaiming of the divinity of Jesus must drive that home. Divinity is not adjectival, not something pasted onto a sorry and messy human tragedy. The divinity comes only through the humanity, not by somehow bypassing it. It is the crucified man who does God to us. Any proclamation of this man must therefore seek to do it again. Systematic theology must leave us in the spot where there is nothing left to do but such proclamation. It must unceasingly remind us that all attributions of divinity not shattered by the cross are, like Peter's confession, mere flattery that deserve only the ultimate rebuke, "Get behind me Satan, you are not on the side of God but of men."

All of which is to say that successful movement in Christology from a language of substance to the language of act can be made only when it drives to a proclamation that does the act of God to us. Christ cannot merely be talked about, he must finally be done to us. Christ has been explained to us endlessly, dressed and redressed in everybody's clothes, painted in everybody's color and likeness, fashioned and refashioned into everybody's hero. The explanations never seem to stick. If he is to be our Lord and Christ he must finally be proclaimed so as to do us in and make us new.

Under the Opposite Form

Jesus, the *proclaimed* God, is God done to us under the form of opposites (*sub contrario*), that is, just the opposite from what we might expect or desire.[7] The divine does not come to us somehow outside of or in addition to the human Jesus, but rather is done to us in and through the suffering and dying humanity. This fits with what we have said about the nature of bondage. Since our presumed freedom to choose what is right for us is really a bondage to ourselves and a defense mechanism against God, God does not come to us as one whom we would choose. He comes to us as one whom we in fact reject and waste. As such he is the end of us, and the doing of God to us. But we must dwell a bit more on the significance of the form of opposites as the way God is done to us in Jesus.

There has been too great an inflation in the concept of revelation in current theology since at least the time of Hegel. Jesus is touted as the "self-revelation" of God. The idea seems to be that we more or less directly "see through" Jesus to God, that Jesus' life is perhaps transparently "god-like," a "parable" of God or some such. The idea of revelation involved is more or less Platonic or perhaps Neoplatonic. The universal (God) is at least partially reflected in the particular (Jesus), and since our minds participate to some degree in the universal mind we can "see" God through Jesus. We know a God when we see one! Like is known by like. But that only puts us back to square one. We try to find a God to our liking in Jesus. We try by hook or by crook to spy out God not proclaimed.

The contrary form simply shuts down all such ideas of revelation. We have to do not with seeing but with faith. It is therefore risky to speak loosely about God being "revealed" under the form of opposites. God is not "revealed" as such, but hidden from those who think they can see. Our problem is not that we know so little about God, but that we know so much that we think we can see through the masks. And Jesus comes, supposedly, to ratify and augment what we already know. The contrary form actively shuts down the whole knowledge-of-God enterprise understood as such seeing. "No one has ever seen God," says John's Gospel (1:18). Only the Jesus who washes his disciples' feet and is about to be glorified in crucifixion can say, "He who has seen me has seen the Father" (14:9). All there is to see now is the suffering and dying Jesus. But it is only through the proclamation of this suffering and dying Jesus that the seeing God enterprise comes undone. The blind see but those who can see are blinded. "As one from whom men hide their faces he was despised . . ." (Isa. 53:3). Jesus is God under the opposite: "This is God for you." Precisely so is he done to us as the end, even the end of our seeing. Only faith can proceed here. Faith grasps and is grasped by the God under the form of opposites, the suffering and dying one. A faith that frees us from our fatal attraction to the abstractions must replace sight. Indeed, faith is precisely the flight from God not proclaimed to God proclaimed under the opposite. The classic passage in Luther sets just this contrast between faith and sight.

> Faith's object is things not seen. That there may be room for faith, therefore, all that is believed must be hidden. Yet it is not hidden more deeply than under a contrary appearance (*sub contrario*) of sight, sense and experience. Thus when God quickens, He does so by killing; when He justifies, He does so by pronouncing guilty; when He carries up to heaven, He does so by bringing down to hell. As Scripture says in I Kings 2, "The Lord killeth and maketh alive; He bringeth down to the grave and bringeth up." ... Thus God conceals His eternal mercy and loving kindness beneath eternal wrath, His righteousness beneath unrighteousness.[8]

The form of opposites is not an explanation of God. It is a statement about how God must be proclaimed to bound sinners. If one attempts to explain God under the opposite, one always encounters foolish questions about how one can see God in a Jesus who is just the opposite. Then one is off and running again trying to get a peek at God not proclaimed through the agony of Jesus. One will likely end with Hegelian high jinks about a "speculative Good Friday" or some such. It is as though we might stand before the cross all decked out in liturgical regalia and say, "Ah yes, God, I see what you're up to!" The danger of displacing faith with sight lies in wait even for so fine an exposition of the matter as this one. One might say, "Ah yes, now I understand the form of opposites. Perhaps nothing is more blasphemous than to claim to see through the agony of Jesus, to have a pat and patronizing answer to his final, despairing "Why?" The point is that systematic theology must aim to shut down sight by driving to a proclamation that actually puts an end to us, truly drives us to our knees to confess "I repent, you are my Lord."

Jesus is therefore the repetition of God to us under the form of opposites. The divine attributes, you might say, are repeated under the form of opposites. One cannot see, one can only believe in life out of death: strength and almightiness under the form of weakness; impassibility under the form of suffering; wisdom under foolishness; love under wrath; presence made inescapable through one consigned to oblivion; justice and righteousness under supreme injustice. Eternity in time. Changelessness under the form of the greatest change of all: death. God is done to us in the proclamation under the form of opposites.

The True Human

But what shall we say of the humanity of Jesus when we move thus to a language that promotes the act of proclamation? We have, of course, already been speaking of humanity in the insistence that God is done to us through the entirely human suffering and dying of Jesus. Indeed, in the language of act it is virtually impossible to speak of the divinity apart from the humanity. As a matter of fact we are already well on the way toward realizing, perhaps in new fashion, the Chalcedonian insistence that the divine and human natures are "without division, without separation." One might at this point suspect our attempted reconstruction of leaning toward an Alexandrian type of "mixture" however. So we must try to show how the divine and the human, though undivided and inseparable, are nevertheless "without confusion" and "without change." To do this we speak briefly about the humanity of Christ.

Jesus Christ is the true human in whom God does God to us. How shall we think of that true humanity? First, it is important to emphasize that he is the true human. Thus to resort to substantialist language again, he is of one substance (*homoousious*) with us just as he is with the Father; nevertheless he differs from us in one crucial point: sin. Thus he is *true* human and we are not. The manner in which we understand sin and the fall plays a decisive role in understanding this. If we understand sin in terms of the "downward fall" we tend to look on it as certain acts stemming perhaps from the shadowy condition of original sin, but which really ought to be avoided. A true human, no doubt, would be one who does not do any sins. Thinking in this fashion always raises fruitless question about whether Jesus did not actually show tell-tale signs that call into question his "sinlessness," or whether he could really be tempted or actually could have sinned had he wanted to. If he could not, it is usually averred, he is not really human like us. We tend to forget that since he is true and we are not, it is not possible simply to understand his humanity through direct analogy with ours.

Thinking in terms of the "upward fall" affords us more help once again. If sin is not merely acts stemming from a corrupted source, but upward rebellion, a succumbing to the temptation to be as gods, and subsequent bondage to that project, then the true humanity and sinlessness of Jesus take on quite a different cast. He is unlike us in that he goes in exactly the opposite direction. We seek to ascend to divinity, he is on his way into humanity. He is true to the human quest all the way to the end; we abandoned it before it even got started.

> Have this mind among yourselves, which you have in Christ Jesus, who though he was in the form of God, did not count equality with God a thing to be grasped, but emptied himself, taking the form of a servant, being born in the likeness of man. And being found in human form he humbled himself and became obedient unto death, even death on a cross.
>
> (Phil. 2:5)

Unlike us, Jesus did not snatch at divinity, but went just the other way into humanity, suffering even death on a cross. His trueness, his sinlessness, does not consist in the absence of acts that look like sin to us, but in his persistence in pursuing his way without swerving aside even to death on the cross. His "sinlessness" is not something we would have seen or even applauded. Quite the contrary, we judged him to be guilty of the greatest of all sins, blasphemy. So we killed him. That was our judgment and it is too late to reverse it now. God vindicates him in the resurrection, not in our judgments. The sinlessness of Jesus is a theological judgment, a confession, arising from the cross and resurrection, not a conclusion drawn from evidence presented in courts where we sit in judgment.

Jesus is truly human, we are not. The trueness of his humanity and his sinlessness comes to light through the resurrection as vindication of his unswerving obedience to the way of the cross. But that means that he shows what being human means. So we have the paradoxical fact that the one whom we confess to be divine discloses the truly human, and vice versa that it is through this truly human one that the divine is done to us! This no doubt appears confusing to ordinary systematic thought. But it is not so strange for a thinking that has a proclamation that is to bring an end and new beginning as its aim. For it is through death that we are saved, not through systematic demonstration. Through the death of this truly human one we come to our end and just so come up against God. Precisely by being "not God" but truly human, Jesus is the one in whom God is done to us. To put it most dramatically, the situation is one in which we have killed someone, someone perhaps who offered no resistance at all, and so have come to an absolute end of our ways and are thrown on the mercy of a higher court. By simply being obedient unto death, by being, in this case, truly human, the Jesus whom we kill brings us to our end, brings us up against the God question. He does God to us through his true humanity. "The Son of man came not to be served but to serve and to give his life as a ransom for many" (Mark 10:45).

From this perspective we can now also ratify the Chalcedonian decree's assertion that the natures are "without change, without mixture." It is by being "not God," by not changing or mixing, by making the difference between divine and human quite clear to beings who in their attempt to be gods reject the difference, that Jesus does God to us. He becomes truly human in a way we never would or could. He comes into this world of would-be gods and takes the pain of our bitterness and hatred upon himself all the way to the end. As Moltmann put it:

> God did not become man according to our conceptions of being a man. He became the kind of man we do not want to be: an outcast, accursed, crucified. *Ecce homo!* Behold the Man! is not a statement which arises from the confirmation of our humanity and is made on the basis of "like is known by like"; it is a confession of faith which recognizes God's humanity in the dehumanized Christ on the cross. At the same time the confession says *Ecce deus!* Behold God on the cross! Thus God's incarnation "even unto death on the cross" is not in the last resort a matter of concealment; this is his utter humiliation, in which he is completely with himself and completely with the other, the man who is dehumanized. Humiliation to the point of death on the cross corresponds to God's nature in the contradiction of abandonment. When the crucified Jesus is called the "image of the invisible God," the meaning is that this is God, and God is like this. God is not greater than he is in this humiliation. God is not more glorious than he is in this self-surrender. God is not more powerful than he is in this helplessness. God is not more divine than he is in this humanity.[9]

It is precisely in the difference that the unity becomes evident. Maximus the Confessor noted this long ago. The closer the unity, he said, the more one is aware of the difference. "The unity of the divine and the human is not simply opposed to the difference between the two, rather increasing differentiation (and above all increasing consciousness of such differentiation) is a condition for increasingly intensive community and unity." [10] Precisely by being not God the Father, Jesus demonstrates his personal unity with the Father. By being precisely the truly human one he shows who the Father is. Thus in obedience to the Father the Johannine Jesus can rightly say, "I [as one who is not the Father] and the Father are one" (John 10:30). As the human he is, he is perfectly in accord with the will of God. "My food is to do the will of him who sent me, and to accomplish his work" (John 4:34).

To illustrate this we might look at a couple of passages that have been troublesome for traditional Christology. The first is the famous passage from Mark 10:17ff, in which Jesus is asked, "Good teacher, what must I do to inherit eternal life?" Jesus prefaces his answer by saying, "Why do you call me good? No one is good but God alone." This kind of reply from Jesus has generally put a strain on orthodox and perhaps even liberal Christology. The Arians used such passages to demonstrate that Jesus as incarnate Logos was something less than the Father. The orthodox response was most often to invoke the two-natures doctrine and say that here Jesus was speaking more strictly according to the human nature whereas elsewhere he would speak or act according to his divine nature. But both the Arians and the orthodox tend to miss the point. What sort of person would make the response Jesus made? We as aspiring gods would be flattered by being called "good." We might demur outwardly, perhaps, in false humility, but could hardly escape being inwardly pleased and quite in agreement with the judgment. Jesus is quite different. Precisely by refusing the flattery, by insisting on being not God but human, he demonstrates his unity with God. For our part, we can only be left with the question, "What manner of man is this, after all?" Precisely in not claiming anything for himself he brings us up against God. The Arians were mistaken to think the passage shows Jesus to be less than God, just as the orthodox missed the point by saying he speaks or acts here according to the human nature only. It is only through the humanity that we encounter the divinity. It is the truly human one who refuses to be called good who does God to us.

The second passage that has always been an embarrassment to traditional Christology is the cry of dereliction from the cross, "My God, My God, why have you forsaken me?" Again, the usual move is to say that Jesus here speaks according to his human nature, not the divine. A more contemporary and perhaps liberal variation might be to say that Jesus was simply quoting Psalm 22, which has a happy outcome in the end. Hence the cry is not really one of dereliction, but of faith and hope even in the blackest of hours. It is as though Jesus in his dying agony was really just meditating aloud from the cross for the benefit of those assembled. Thus do our systematics and exegesis seek to protect us to the end.

Most everyone—conservative, orthodox, or liberal—seems to have trouble thinking the cry could be real. It seems as though having dispatched him to a humiliating, cruel, and agonizing death, we are surprised and shocked that he should find it all that bad. We just can not give up on making him our religious hero, desperately seeking in him the last spark of divinity, the courage, the faith, that will somehow see him through and thus enable us to avoid facing the end. There must be some way for him to transcend the fate to which we have dispatched him. It is as though by crucifying him we had merely provided the occasion for him to exercise his divinity, or as though as his murderers we hope that our crime was all a bad dream. For if he goes into the blackness of death forsaken even by God, what chance do we have?

But that is, of course, precisely the point. We have no chance. He comes to die for us, to enter into the blackness, the nothingness of death alone. Thus he goes the road of being human to the end. But it is even more than that. He took our place. He took our nature, being born under the law. He was made a curse for us, and he followed the course to death on the cross. In the end he cries out in an agony that Mark concentrates into the totally human question, "Why?" And there is no answer. Beyond the "Why?" there is only God. We are, once again, simply brought up against God. God is done to us. The true human can only wait on God here. "Father, into your hands I commend my spirit." The human Jesus brings us to that end. This is his self-emptying (*kenosis*). Not that he divests himself temporarily of some divine prerogatives, but that he pours himself out into that last desolate cry.

Only by so pouring himself out can he finally be for us. Were he to hold something back or somehow to be protected from the stark reality of the death, he would be our lawgiver but not our Savior. His dying words to us would be some sort of admonition to stop our perfidy, shape up, and perhaps take him down from the cross before it all goes too far. His dying would be perhaps just the supreme example of how to die, and so the most strenuous law of all. That, one might say, is the theological way of taking him down from the cross. Only by truly dying does he put an end to us as old beings so that we can be made new. Only so do we come up against the one who calls into being that which is from that which is not.

So, once again, it is by following the course of humanity to the end that Jesus does God to us. When we think in terms of a language that drives to the act of proclamation, the cry of dereliction is not just an embarrassment to the system. It is the end of the system. And so it signals the end of us as old beings. And just so it must be preached. (But now we are already well into the doctrine of atonement and more explicit treatment of that is reserved for a later section.)

Just a remark or two about Jesus' self-consciousness to conclude this section on the truly human. Does Jesus' divinity mean that he transcended the limits of strictly human consciousness somehow? Should it mean that he understood himself to be what later titles such as Messiah and Son of God ascribed to him? Could he see into people's hearts and into the future with divine perspicacity? First of all, it is important to realize that it is virtually impossible now to discover by historical investigation of the sources exactly what Jesus thought of himself. For the most part I expect the writers of the gospels were not really interested in that sort of question. Fascination with one's inner life and "self-consciousness" is a modern affliction. Once God has been banished from the public world "out there" one seeks answers in the "inner life." But the Gospel writers were more interested in what God was up to and accomplishing in the public life and death of the man Jesus and what that life as a totality "says" to us, indeed proclaims to us, in the light of the biblical witness to God's mighty deeds. They were interested in Jesus as "public person," not in what went on in the privacy of his psyche.

It is best to practice considerable reserve on this question. Otherwise, one might allow the titles or even the rejection of them and/

or conclusions drawn from them to obscure the actual story and undercut the proclamation. This can happen most obviously if Jesus' self-consciousness is so conceived as to protect him from the actual catastrophe of the cross. If, for instance, Jesus is portrayed as going to the cross in full confidence that it is simply a temporary discomfort and that the resurrection will put all irons out of the fire, the death takes on a docetic hue—Jesus only seems to die. Or if one parcels out the agony and suffering to the "human nature," leaving the divine nature in unruffled serenity, one destroys the unity of the person. In every such instance, one undercuts the proclamation. One does not then preach a word that crucifies the old with Christ, but rather delivers a lecture that appeals to our "free choice," our aspirations for divinity.

But the proclamation can be undercut also if one attempts in more liberal fashion to enhance the human self-consciousness of Jesus so that the crucifixion becomes, if anything, merely the last act in his "supreme religious achievement." The cross becomes the occasion for him to demonstrate a religious heroism that transcends death and can thus be an inspiration to us all. In such a view something survives the death even if one is dubious about resurrection. And so too we, if we are so inclined, can be inspired by Jesus and in some way "leave a legacy" to posterity. But such eulogizing is hardly proclamation of good news. It is the same old story again. Seeking to get rid of the heteronomy of the divine Jesus it only falls into the same trap. It is just that the "divinity" that was once safely off in a distant heaven has now moved in on us in the form of a romantic idealism. Jesus is only adjectivally divine and as such is just another lawyer.

Currently there is more of a move toward the opposite side of the argument, that is, to say that in order for Jesus really to do his mission it would be necessary for him not to know who he was. Thus Pannenberg can say that Jesus' not knowing is precisely the ground for his unity with the Father.[11] And Paul Althaus could say that "Jesus was who he is before he knew it."[12] The idea here is that if the Father's will was to send Jesus to die a totally human death, then in order to be totally at one with the Father Jesus could not possess a knowledge that would make that death something of a sham. While such arguments could likely lead to a proclamation more effective than that which uses divine self-knowledge to protect Jesus, they succumb to the same temptation as the older systems, that of trying to determine the answer to the historical question by systematic necessity. Whereas once "divinity" was thought to mean Jesus must have known, here unity with the Father is taken to dictate that he could not have known. In either case one risks forcing the story too much to fit the systematic necessity.

So it is best to refrain from dogmatic judgments in that regard. One could, for instance, give an account of Jesus' self-consciousness in terms of possibility and actuality, which would be amenable to the proclamation. Jesus could no doubt have reckoned with the possibility of his death, but that is no protection from the agony and desolation of its actuality. Indeed, consciousness of his mission might heighten the apprehension. No doubt the account of the bloody sweat and desperate prayer in the Garden of Gethsemane intends to get that across to us. We all in some way reckon with the possibility of death, but its actuality is another matter. "Death" is an abstraction. Expiration itself, particularly when accompanied by suffering, is something we know nothing of until it occurs. One does not have to deny a certain self-consciousness to Jesus, it would seem, to support the proclamation. What is necessary is that it not be so construed as to deny the reality of the end, the death on the cross, the fact that Jesus was "crucified, dead, and buried." Only the resurrection rescues the dead Jesus. Not the titles, not exegesis, not systematics, not our pious hopes, but God. For one crucified with Christ, the God question hangs entirely on the resurrection. If there is no resurrection, then faith is in vain.

It is hardly possible to recover now what Jesus thought of himself, but the public Jesus tells a story. He appears and is crucified as a Messianic pretender. Pilate put the charge up for the public to see: "Jesus of Nazareth, King of the Jews." In that sense, Pilate was the initiator of Christology. Whatever the state of his self-consciousness, Jesus impressed the public as a messianic figure, and when the time came for judgment, he would not back down. True, this does not require divine perspicacity, but nevertheless he must have had, it would seem, a consciousness of a messianic mission strong enough to take him to the cross and all the way to the final agonizing "Why?" The resurrection was the only answer to that "Why?" The question turns back on us again: "Who do you say that I am?"

The End of God

Now we must examine atonement directly to close out the chapter on Christology.[13] If we approach the doctrine of atonement from the perspective of proclamation, we find here a problem of the same sort as we have found elsewhere. Our dogmatic and systematic theology tends to develop theories that purport to explain how God is mollified by what happens in Jesus so as to be reconciled to a lost world. Proclamation becomes the promulgation of the explanation. The paradigm for appropriation of such proclamation is free choice. If we explain it clearly and persuasively enough, people will opt for it (with a little prompting from the Spirit, of course).

Such a procedure does not bring about atonement, that is, genuine reconciliation with God. It does not actually end the wrath of God or get God off our backs. It is not the "end of God." That phrase signifies two things. When genuine atonement occurs, God both ends as the God against us, and reaches the goal (*telos*) God intends. We might say God ends as God against us and begins as God for us. But the theories do not deliver that, precisely because they pretend to explain things to old beings and so keep them alive. They do not realize that God can reach the intended goal only in the concrete act of the proclamation which ends the old and begins the new. When the explanation is promulgated on the presupposition of free choice the old being remains alive and well. But then there is no reconciliation. God can only be a God of wrath over against old beings. The explanation, however clever, will turn on us in the end, usually in the form of a demand of some sort to believe the metaphysics, the "behind-the-scenes" logic of the explanation. In this regard it makes little difference what theory is espoused or touted. Where there is no recognition of the necessity for the move to a proclamation that "ends the matter" and as such is the concluding step in the atoning act, systematic theology aborts itself at the most crucial juncture of all.

The problem we must deal with is this: If God is free then we are dead; if we are free then God is dead. There is no way to reconcile these two opposing claimants to freedom in the abstract. Atonement can occur only when they meet concretely in the event of Jesus Christ. We in our "freedom" move to eradicate God's freedom to be God in Jesus Christ. God dies at our hands in Christ. But God is free even over death, so the claim of Jesus is vindicated in the resurrection. We also die. Atonement comes only through the death and resurrection of Christ. God dies for us in Christ, and so puts us to death as old beings. God's freedom and our freedom are reconciled in Christ.

Through the resurrection God establishes a new creation of faith and freedom in Christ. In faith we are reconciled to God.

We have already seen that if God is free, then we are dead; the God of the magnificent abstractions leaves us no room, no freedom, no life. God, the almighty, immutable, timeless, omnipresent, omnipotent One, absconding behind the masks, simply snuffs us out. We cry out in indignation at the loss of our very life and freedom, "We aren't puppets, are we?" This just means that we are not reconciled to God.

In the face of this death sentence passed on us by the freedom of God we are bound to insist on our own freedom, especially in "those things which are above"—matters having to do with our ultimate destiny. But our claim to freedom is the death of God. We are at the real seat of power. There is no point in trying to mask the fact, for we are not quite so clever at masks as God. We attempt various compromises in which we modestly claim some freedom and leave the rest to God, but it is only a deception. Whatever we claim, no matter how little, negates the freedom of God. We may say, for instance, that God does all the work, that the grace offered is absolutely free, and so on, but that all we have to do is add our little bit, make our choice, accept acceptance, or however we may put it. That means that God in the final analysis does not act, but just offers a constant fund on which we can draw. So when everything then depends on us, when our destiny remains in our hands, God is dead. Nietzsche was right in announcing that. It was not immediately obvious, because we think we have given God so big a share of the business. God, after all, makes the "offer" of grace. But over the years this gradually erodes and disappears. People wonder more and more whether it is really relevant to their needs. And so it is today. We have listened to the voice of the tempter saying, "You shall be as gods." And if we are God, there can be no other.

The upshot is that God, if remaining in our scheme of things at all, is there largely to ratify and assist us in our projects. As Feuerbach insisted, God is the projection of our needs. But a God who is there merely to ratify our causes does not bring reconciliation. Such a God eventually just gets blamed for the inevitable distortion, misdirection, and failure of our projects. That is obvious in the contemporary disenchantment with our gods and in the largely futile attempts at theodicy.

So it is not strange that the problem of evil is widely regarded as a paramount cause of contemporary unbelief. A predictable inversion has taken place. We claim freedom in things "above," where we have none, and then blame God for the sorry outcome of things "below," where we have been mandated to take care. We are incensed if anyone asserts that God alone is in charge of things above, of eternal destinies. We seem quite assured that we have such matters well in hand. "All religions lead to the same place," we tell ourselves. Surely everyone in the end will be saved. Meanwhile we abdicate from the freedom we have in things below and wonder why God does such a poor job at it. God is blamed for our failures and we remain unreconciled.

We are confronted with a problem that is insoluble on the abstract level. We are actually separated, put off by the masks, alienated from God. And yet at the same time we are locked into the seemingly inescapable fate of contending and contesting with God. We know no other God on our own than the God of the abstractions, and we are at once attracted and repelled by that God. We seem fated to try our hand at solving matters on the abstract level. It is, no doubt, a matter of self-defense, freedom's move to maintain itself. So we are constantly about the business of redoing, removing, redefining, trying to see through the abstractions, the masks. But matters only become worse. We go out of the frying pan into the fire. We live inexorably under the wrath of God.

Neither God nor we can do anything about that in the abstract. God cannot call off such wrath by some sort of abstract fiat. God might, perhaps, thunderously announce from heaven a resolution to be love rather than wrath but that would do no good. If anything it would likely have an opposite effect from what was intended. We would be frightened to death, and be charged with mistaken thinking. Or God might try through a mighty prophet to tell us that wrath is over, or through a famous theologian that wrath is an idea mistakenly attributed to God. We will still be left charged with faulty thinking and bad theology. There is no cure in the abstract for the broken relationship, the alienation, the being blocked off, the bondage, the absence. The only cure for absence is presence.

If God can do nothing about it in the abstract, we may try our hand at it. We may seek by sentiment, projection, and theological or philosophical speculation arbitrarily to change God's image. We may try to insist that we are not under wrath because God is, after all, love, love, love. But love in the abstract is as frightening as wrath: it turns on us. "God is love," one may maintain, as does the Bible. But then questions come back on us: Why then are you such unloving creatures? If God is love, why is there so much evil in the world? If anything God becomes more threatening and suspect. Wrath is not ended by love-in-the-abstract. The reality continues no matter what words one uses.

Atonement Theories

That is why theological theories about atonement do not bring about actual reconciliation. A construct, for instance, like vicarious satisfaction, taken to mean that God in the abstract is somehow moved objectively to change from an attitude of wrath to one of mercy or love by the sacrifice of Jesus on the cross, always creates more problems than it solves. On the one hand, it has difficulty avoiding the implication that God could or had to be bought off. The theory generally fails in the attempt to reconcile us to God. Favor that is paid for is not really mercy. God looks like one who will not be gracious unless proper payment is made. On the other hand, one is faced with the difficult task of believing the questionable celestial bookkeeping of the theory in order to reap its benefits. Everything important takes place "behind the scenes," in the realm of universals. Such things as payment and satisfaction are not immediately evident in looking at the cross. They are constructs that hope to lend it some kind of universal meaning, an attempt to translate the "accidental truth of history" into a "universal truth of reason" and make it more accessible to reason's cohort, free choice. But it does not work. Reason itself will not buy it. Rationalism in particular rejected the view of God projected by the theory.

In fact, all the theories of atonement, though containing and reflecting something of the truth in varying degrees, tend to suffer from the same drawback. Neglecting the move to proclamation, they tend to deal in and draw one into the abstractions, a behind-the-scenes theology, a construct which gives no assurance and little comfort. The wrath of God does not end for us in reality. At best it only changes form.

If vicarious satisfaction does not end wrath by proposing an "objective" change in God, a "subjective" view, the idea that we rather than God are to be changed by the attractiveness of Jesus' exemplary life and death fares no better. Not only are we left with the arduous business of following Jesus' example with little more than a theological pep talk to help us, but the picture of God is hardly improved. Even in the sixteenth century orthodox Protestant theologians maintained against the Socinians that a God who would subject his Son to such a cruel fate merely to provide us with an example of what we already know is not so loving as the theory purports to establish. The agonizing "Why?" of the cross cannot be answered with such sophistries.

The classic or victory view of atonement comes closer to concreteness by looking on the crucifixion as a battle against demonic forces, issuing in an entirely new situation through the power of the resurrection. The cross and resurrection are proclaimed to us as a victory over demonic forces threatening to dominate and destroy us. Atonement is not just a repair job on the old, but the breaking in of the eschatologically new. The basic systematic structure of such a view is a vast improvement. Resurrection and eschatology gain a proper place.

Nevertheless, a degree of abstraction remains. The demonic forces tend too readily to become abstract mythological beings too removed from what actually occurs. It was, after all, human beings who actually killed Jesus. We did it. To be sure, we may have been acting at the behest of demonic forces, but we cannot be abstracted out of the picture. As a matter of fact, one of the reasons atonement theories remain abstract is that in the very move to give the death of Jesus universal meaning the actual participants tend to drop out of the picture. Atonement becomes a transaction among or even a battle between abstractions: wrath versus love, justice versus mercy, vice versus virtue, divine versus demonic forces, and so on. To be sure, all these must find their place in the final picture. But theology must not lose sight of what actually happened.

A common characteristic of the various theories of atonement is just that: a tendency to forget that it was actually a murder and that we did it. We seem in such haste systematically to explain why it had to happen that we become exonerated from our part in it. We say perhaps that it was necessary to satisfy God or to provide an inspiring example or to defeat the demons. To be sure, we will want to say that the ultimate reason for the death of Jesus lies in God. But we must take care lest our part in the matter and the blame accruing thereto disappear in the thin air of too much transcendent metaphysical necessity. If fingers are pointed at all it will usually be to discredit those we do not like. We can say "they" did it. Usually the Jews have been blamed or of course Judas. More lately, under the pressure of protest, the blame has been shifted to the Romans. Since there are none of them left to protest, that is where such effort to fix the blame on others is likely to rest. If systematic theology is to drive to viable proclamation of the cross all this must cease. If our thinking is to drive toward an actual reconciliation, it has to avoid constructions that abstract the real alienated parties out of the drama.

Actual Atonement

Atonement thinking has to proceed from the actual story of Jesus and his way to the cross. Perhaps the fact most conspicuous in its absence from our theories of atonement is the fact that we killed him. He was despised and rejected and we esteemed him not. Jesus came among us exercising the freedom of God, declaring the reign of God through repentance and the forgiveness of sins, and we would not have it. The trouble was that he forgave really wicked people. He said that sinners and whores and traitors and riffraff of every sort would enter the kingdom before the righteous and the pious.

The problem with forgiveness is that it simply does not fit in this world. Naturally so, for it brings the kingdom of God! Forgiveness full and free is therefore the most subversive rebellion against the powers of this age there can be. It is not simply a matter of whether we feel "guilty" enough to bother ourselves to opt for it or seek it out. It is the end of the age. It spells the end of our upward rebellion, our attempt to be gods. It means that ultimate control of our destiny and so of our kingdom is being wrested from us absolutely. How can we control things if God is simply going to forgive? Surely no one can even dare to claim such authority here. So to protect ourselves and our kingdom we must kill him. To quote Bonhoeffer again: "There are only two ways possible of encountering Jesus: man must die or he must put Jesus to death."[14] So we kill him. It is a matter of self-defense.

If there is to be a proclamation of an atonement today which actually brings reconciliation we must drive this point home. Whatever we want subsequently to say about God's action transcendent to it all, or whatever we want to say about the demons and demonic forces, we must not obscure the fact that we did it. We did not choose Jesus, we rejected him. In the end no one stood with God. Whether it was out of religious incredulity, defensiveness, disappointment, antipathy, cowardice, fear, avarice, lust for power, or even just the sentimental pity of "the daughters of Jerusalem" makes little difference in the end. Jesus was one "from whom we hid our faces." God died alone.

Thus did he "bear our sins in his body." We would do well to think of this concretely before we resort to metaphysical mystification, constructing ideas of how our sins as some kind of abstract whole were transferred to Jesus. He bears all our sin, our ambition to be as gods, our attempt to protect our kingdom in his body in actuality. He is beaten, his kingship is mocked, he is crowned with thorns and subjected to the most cruel and degrading death possible, simply cast out of our world onto a cross. Thus does he become a curse for us, for cursed is everyone who hangs on a cross. He not only bears our sins but becomes sin for us though he knew no sin. He does not protest at the charge of being a sinner of the worst sort, a blasphemer. The One who forgives sin here is the biggest sinner against the order of the age and its gods. He has nothing with which to defend himself in this age because there is no defense. He can only look to God and a "kingdom not of this world" for vindication. He enters no disclaimer at being found among sinners. He pours himself out into the human situation just as it now is. "Being found in human form he humbled himself and became obedient unto death, even death on a cross" (Phil. 2:8). There was nothing to do but die.

Jesus came preaching the forgiveness of sins in God's name and we killed him for it. How can it be said that we did it? We were not there. It is important for the proclamation to encompass this because the universal claim of the cross to be for us all depends on it. Older theories tried to assert the universal significance of the cross by translating what happened into a universal: Jesus' death was universal because it was of a worth so infinite as to pay for the sins of the whole world or it was an example of universal significance. It is more apropos to what actually occurred to say that the universality arises out of the fact that all are brought under judgment by the cross and resurrection because all rejected him, and consequently his resurrection is a triumph and vindication over against all. Paul put it this way: "For God has consigned all men to disobedience that he may have mercy upon all" (Rom. 11:32). But this is difficult to establish in the abstract. It can be accomplished only through a proclamation that brings everyone to repentance and confession. The theological claim that all killed him and that therefore he is vindicated over against us all is simply the mandate that cross and resurrection are to be proclaimed universally. The Spirit is to convince of sin. How? Not by means of an argument from universal principles but because of failure to believe in Jesus (John 16:9). It is not likely that all those to whom Peter preached on the first Pentecost (Acts 2) had something to do directly with the crucifixion of Jesus. Yet the proclamation was that God had made this Jesus whom "you" crucified both Lord and Christ by raising him from the dead. And it was such that they could not respond "What shall we do?" There was no way out. The universal claim of the death and resurrection of Jesus comes through the proclamation that puts all under the charge of sin in order that all might obtain mercy. Indeed, one is not likely to confess to being implicated in the cross unless one is grasped by the mercy. It is characteristic of unbelief to put the blame on anyone and anything rather than on oneself. Confessing one's implication in the cross is concisely stated in Luther's "Meditation on Christ's Passion":

> You must get this thought through you head and not doubt that you are the one who is torturing Christ thus, for your sins have surely wrought this. In Acts 2 [:36-37] St. Peter frightened the Jews like a peal of thunder when he said to all of them, "You crucified him." Consequently three thousand alarmed and terrified Jews asked the apostles on that one day, "O dear brethren, what shall we do now?" Therefore, when you see the nails piercing Christ's hands, you can be certain that it is your work. When you behold his crown of thorns, you may rest assured that these are your evil thoughts, etc.[15]

Mention of the Jews here no doubt jars and rankles, but one should not miss the point. It is not the fact that one is a Jew that brings one under the judgment, but that the proclamation strikes home. The immediate move, therefore, is not to use the Jews to exonerate oneself, but rather to a proclamation and consequent confession that "you" did it. It is through the proclamation fired and authorized through this concrete meeting with God in Jesus Christ that atonement, reconciliation occurs. That is, what happened in the death and resurrection of Jesus Christ reaches its goal in the present event of the proclamation itself. Systematic reflection must recognize, foster, and aim for that. Reconciliation cannot happen in the abstract. If systematic theology veers off into the realm of the magnificent abstractions it only makes the move to proclamation more difficult and frustrates the actual reconciliation.

The problem both with respect to God and with respect to the human predicament must be dealt with concretely. The problem with respect to God is that there is no end to wrath in the abstract. God's problem, so to speak, is how actually to have mercy on those who will not have it. The problem is not that God is not in the divine depths loving or merciful. The favor of God does not have to be purchased by the suffering and death of Jesus. God cannot and does not need to be bought, even by Jesus. It is not that Jesus has to die before God can be forgiving. God out of love and mercy sends Jesus to forgive. God's problem is how to get through to us, how to get through to people who aspire to be gods, and who are thus bent on getting rid of God.

Our problem on the other hand is simply that we cannot let God be God, and certainly not a God of absolute mercy and forgiveness. We are bound to reject a God "above" us. Of the prerogatives of the God above, absolute mercy and forgiveness is the most godly and so the most disruptive of all for us and for our projects. There we are put to the real test of God-ness.

But the matter cannot be resolved in the abstract. It comes down to the actual meeting. God sends Jesus to forgive. We will not have it so we kill him. But God will not change in his determination to be a God of mercy, for God is immutable. So Jesus will do nothing to stop our attempts to banish the ultimate Word of God, and insist on for-giveness to the absolute end. The concrete meeting can only end in death. He comes to die for us, to give his life as a ransom for many. He will not swerve aside. In the most real sense he cannot. Were he to swerve aside, were he to put up resistance, were he to claim some immunity or injustice, he would not be the bringer of the absolute mercy and forgiveness. He would not be the Son of God. He would be rather a prophet "like unto Moses." So his would-be defenders must put up their swords, and the ear that has been struck off healed. If resistance were the name of the game, he says, "My Father would send legions of angels."

In the cross the two immutables, the two freedoms, meet. Since God is immutable and will not desist in determination to have mercy God (*sub contrario*) dies at our hands. Since we are immutable in our determination to get rid of God and cannot change ourselves there is no other way. God can no more surrender the insistence on having mercy than God can cease to be God. God's right to have "mercy on whom he wills" (Rom. 9:18) is of the very essence of God. To surrender that to humans either wholly or partially is to cease to be God. It is therefore the very immutability of God which drives to God's death. The dying Jesus cries, "Father, forgive them, for they know not what they do!"

It is also our immutability, that of our bound wills which has brought us to this meeting. We cannot surrender to a God who says, "I will have mercy on whom I will have mercy." In one last fury we strike to erase the cry of the dying Jesus from the vocabulary of humankind, to bury it in a tomb, shut it in with a great stone and set soldiers to guard it. Death, the ultimate solution to all our enmities, shall protect us. This is the end of God.

But God cannot just die. God's determination to have mercy cannot waver. God is immutable love. God remains God and vindicates the claim to be God through it all. God raises Jesus the preacher of forgiveness from the dead and so insists that the proclamation go on in his name. Our last move has now been countered. Our ultimate weapon has failed. The end of God against us is the beginning of God for us. Had the matter ended in the cool tombs where all human affairs end, we would have been right and God wrong. But God, in vindicating his claim, authorized and mandated the proclamation of forgiveness, so God is right and we are wrong. But then that is the end of us. So in his death we die. We are through as old beings. We are crucified with Christ, ended as would-be gods. Since one died for all, Paul says, all have died (2 Cor. 5:14). It is an accomplished fact. Nothing can be done about it now. The time is up.

It is vital for a proclamation of the death and resurrection of Jesus that aims at actual atonement to grasp what it means to say that Jesus died for us and that consequently we too have died. How is this so? We breathe, we walk around, we exist, but we have made our last move. It is checkmate. We are dead as old beings, as those who seek to establish and control their own destiny. The God who raised Jesus insists that our destiny can be established only in divine mercy. Since Jesus has died and been raised there is absolutely nothing we can do. We have done everything we can and that resulted only in putting Jesus to death. He goes to that death without giving in to the temptation to be something other than merciful, and he is vindicated. So we have died, and that is forever past tense. Over. And just so the absolution is forever present tense.

We might, of course, attempt one last stratagem. We might try even to turn death into something we can do. We might attempt to set up a process of "mortification" so we can control our destiny by bringing even our dying under our power. But that only means that the old being is still alive and is trying to use even the death of Jesus as a "paradigm" or an "example" to feign death. Any move we could make to control our destiny either by piety or impiety would only be a crucifying of Christ anew. But having died once to sin he dies no more (Rom. 6:9). Death is past tense.

It is essential to see that the death of Jesus is not a way for old beings to traverse. It is not a system or a process to be mastered. It is not something to do. He has died for us. "You *have* died." To die in this regard is to be put in the position vis-à-vis God in which there is finally nothing to do but listen to God, the God who creates by the Word of his power. Everything depends on seeing how absolutely God has succeeded in having mercy through the cross. The old being who is bound to its god projects, insistent on controlling its own destiny, is put to death. There is nothing to do but await the actual and living Word of proclamation summoning to life, to faith in the God who does not stop until indeed carrying through concretely in the proclamation on the promise, "I will have mercy on whom I will have mercy." And now it is for you.

So it is through the death and resurrection of Jesus done to us in the proclamation that we are reconciled with God. In the living present we hear the Word of absolute forgiveness and mercy authorized by the cross and resurrection of Jesus which calls us to life. To be reconciled is in the first instance to hear that Word and begin to whisper amen to it. It is to begin actually to trust God with our destiny, to believe God can actually be trusted with it, to want God to take it over, to let God be God, to allow God freedom in things above, and to be reborn as a creature of God here below. One can be reconciled to God only through a faith that lets God be the God of mercy God has decided to be.

If we can think about atonement as an actual event that roots in what happened once for all to Jesus and is carried into the present and done to us in the Word of the Cross, it should be possible to recover much, if not all, of the traditional vocabulary so it can function in more vital fashion in proclamation. For now it should be clear that the doctrine should not be constructed so as to translate what happens into the kind of universal truth supposedly acceptable to the free choice of old beings, but rather so as to drive to a proclamation that puts to death and makes new.

The Accidental Truth of God

We now can venture an answer to the old question posed by Lessing but modified here somewhat by Kierkegaard: How can accidental truths of history be a point of departure for an eternal consciousness?[16] The answer is brutally simple: when the accident kills you. What happens to Jesus, that is, also happens to us. We are "caught in the act." We are involved in it something like being stopped by an accident that interrupts our lives, indeed, an accident in which we are implicated. It is after all a murder that we perpetrated. It should strike us more directly as something that happens to us to throw everything out of kilter rather than as something filtered down to us through the screen of a universalizing theory that leaves everything the same. It is as though suddenly we find ourselves with the blood of this good man on our hands, or splattered against the front of our machine. When the "accident" happens everything stops. One can only wait for the "outcome," for help, for the verdict. One loses control of one's destiny. It is in the hands of another—someone who transcends the situation.

Such an accident would not in and of itself be the point of departure for an "eternal consciousness," as Kierkegaard put it. Were it simply the event of a death in which we become so implicated we cannot extricate ourselves—we might nevertheless gradually get over it in some way or other. Time heals all wounds, as the saying goes. We could no doubt find some appropriate therapy. We might even be inclined to say it was just an accident, after all. We were only going about our business and got caught in an unfortunate and sticky business. This man suddenly threw himself in our way. We could not really stop and so could do little other than to play our role to the end. So it was, after all, with Pilate, the religious authorities, the disciples, the soldiers, the crowds, everyone. As an accident, it was not really our fault. The grim inertia of all our social institutions and personal agendas could not be expected to abate or alter itself. The world keeps on turning and we will soon forget, we hope. We might even, in Hegelian fashion, come to think it was necessary in the dialectic of history.

So it looks from a human perspective, and would no doubt remain so were it only the matter of the death. But the resurrection ends everything with a new beginning. This man whose blood is on our hands is raised from the dead and comes back to confront us again. Small wonder that the first reactions to this act seem to have been simple terror. According to Mark, the first witnesses fled in trembling and astonishment and said nothing to anyone, "for they were afraid" (Mark 16:8). In Luke the disciples were startled and frightened when Jesus appeared. They thought they had seen a ghost (Luke 24:37), a quite natural reaction for those implicated in his death.

But Jesus returns only to say "peace" (*shalom*). We are then forced to look at the whole event from an entirely different perspective—the scriptural point of view, the vantage point of the new. It has all happened that the Scriptures might be fulfilled. Seen from this vantage point, it is no mere accident. It was God who put this man in our way. God has determined to meet us here. He was delivered up according to the "definite plan and foreknowledge of God" (Acts 2:23). John's Gospel even has Jesus insisting in no uncertain terms that no one takes his life from him, but that he lays it down of his own accord. That gives strongest expression to the fact that Jesus came to die, and no one could alter or dissuade him from his course.

That does not lessen the shock or the offense of it nor our implication in it. It simply means that there is no way we can escape now, no way that time in the old age will heal this wound, nor is it "just one of those things," because it is God who is at work here, who intends to bring us to our end, to put all things "out of joint," and make a new start. It means that everything and everyone stands under the judgment, that God has found a way here, so to speak, to do what he would not quite do in the flood—wipe out everyone and start anew. Here he has found a way to do it so as truly to save and not destroy. There is a new creation in Jesus, the risen one. Because he is risen he is now inescapably present in the Word of promise, in the proclamation, in the sacraments. So it is that the accident becomes the point of departure, not for Lessing's "eternal truths of reason," nor even for Kierkegaard's "eternal consciousness," but for something absolutely new: faith in the God who calls into being that which is from that which is not.

Recovering Traditional Words

When one understands that atonement is actually made through the proclamation it is possible for the traditional vocabulary to be recovered in a more vital sense. The differences between the older use and this newly recovered sense are no doubt subtle and sometimes elusive, but they are vital to the move to proclamation. Jesus' death can indeed be seen as a sacrifice, even a vicarious sacrifice, for us. One might even say that it was a substitutionary act. He died in the place we should have died. But there is a subtle and profound difference in the way in which we construe the "for us." In the tradition at least since the time of Anselm in the West, the matter seems to have become increasingly juridicized. The tendency is to understand the "for us" as "instead of us," that is, that Jesus is sacrificed instead of us to pay the debt we owe to God's honor or justice. Thus God is enabled to become merciful. The vicariousness, the substitution, means that Jesus dies and because of his infinite worth is able to make satisfaction instead of us. The sacrifice is necessary because God's justice and honor are the major obstacles to reconciliation. The presupposition seems to be that God's intention even originally was to relate to us in terms of law and justice, but that this intention was frustrated by sin. The sin subsequently has to be "paid for." Jesus is sacrificed to God instead of us to make such payment.

There is a subtle but profound difference, however, when one understands the "for us" to mean that he was sacrificed to do us to death as old beings and raise us up to newness of life in faith, when one assumes that God's intention all along is to relate to us in terms of love and mercy. Then Jesus dies to vindicate God's determination so to relate to us. Jesus dies because we will not have such a relationship. He comes into a world of sin, that is, a world that will not have a God of mercy. He insists on forgiving sins nevertheless and is wasted for it. He was sacrificed not instead of us but in our stead, not in place of us but in our place. As maintained earlier (p. 108) he goes the way we should have gone, insisting on being truly human to the end. In this world of sin that cannot mean other than death "in our place." He dies, that is, not so that we do not have to face the death, but precisely in order that it be done to us to make us new, to make beings who will live by God's love and mercy. He dies, as it has been said, not instead of us, but ahead of us.

Where this is seen, it should be possible to recover a more vital understanding of Jesus' death as a sacrifice for us. Extreme care should be exercised in venturing opinion about to whom such sacrifice is made lest one slip back into juridical ideas about appeasing God. Instances from more common understandings of sacrifice have been used elsewhere to try to get this across.[17] If a soldier dies in battle it is possible to say it was a sacrifice. It is also possible to say for whom it was made. It was made "for us," for the country. But to whom? If someone is killed in the attempt to rescue a child from disaster or death, one can say it was a sacrifice for the child. But one cannot really say to whom such a sacrifice was made. The question seems beside the point. When the immediate benefit of the sacrifice is evident one does not need to ask to whom it was made.

Jesus died for us, to get us, to save us, not to appease God. The overwhelming evidence of the Scriptures is that God is never the object of the sacrifice, but the subject, the one who sends Jesus to be the propitiation, not the one who has to be propitiated. If we understand the "for us" to mean that we are actually remade, we are more likely to preach a Word that seeks to do that rather than to leave the hearers with theories to opt for or against. In this light it is misleading to say or imply that the sacrifice is necessary before God can become merciful. God in mercy and love sends Jesus to die for us so as actually and concretely to have mercy.

The problem is similar in the case of the wrath of God. We do indeed live under the wrath of God. We have insisted all along that that wrath is real and not to be trifled with. It cannot be removed by theological erasing, penetrating the masks, or redoing our concept of God. But in the light of a proclamation that puts to death the old and raises up the new, we can see that the problem is not that God is not merciful or does not desire to have mercy. The problem arises because we are trapped in bondage and so cannot, will not, desist from seeking to manipulate God according to our own projects. God is indeed love, but we will not have it. Nothing is more threatening than a love or mercy that takes over the destiny of those who want to be gods. The declaration of love—"I will have mercy on whom I will have mercy"— taken in the abstract is the most threatening of all because we do not know upon whom, in particular, God desires to have mercy. Everything turns to wrath and such wrath never ends in this age. God, as we have said repeatedly, simply cannot actually have mercy in the abstract. For God actually to have mercy God must die as abstraction and we must die as would-be gods. So Jesus' death engenders the Word that ends the abstraction, the wrath of God, and ends our lives as would-be gods at once. Jesus dies for us and so is the end of the God of wrath and the beginning of actual love when he is proclaimed and received in faith.

Thus it is quite proper to say with the tradition that Jesus satisfies the wrath of God. But that is true now in a more vital sense. When through the proclamation of Jesus' death and resurrection faith in the concrete Word of promise is created, we are no longer under wrath. When the proclamation creates faith, then God can say, "Now I am satisfied." When such faith is created, God has reached his intended goal. One hears the concrete Word in the here and now. It is "for you," for Christ died and was raised for you. Such faith is always precarious. As long as we live in this age we will face temptation. Wrath always threatens. But we are baptized and the Word has broken in upon us. We shall need to hear it again and again.

Such an understanding breaks the old impasse between a sup-posedly objective and subjective atonement. It is "objective" in the sense that it comes to us entirely from without. In the Word and Sacrament engendered by Jesus' death and resurrection atonement is done to us entirely from without. Since it is a Word that brings death and new life it is not a Word the old subject can generate or speak. No doubt it is only in death that we come up against that which is absolutely and entirely from without. This Word is entirely from with-out because the old subject is not merely altered but rather put to death and a new subject raised to new life. But of course, it is not without what we might want to call "subjective" effect. It reaches its goal only in the creation of faith, for the time being. "I have been crucified with Christ," says Paul, "it is no longer I who live, but Christ who lives in me; and the life I now live in the flesh I live by faith in the Son of God, who loved me and gave himself for me" (Gal. 2:20). This subjective effect does not involve just an alteration in the subject. Faith anticipates the new subject, the new creation, which lives from God and his love and mercy alone.

"Objective" and "subjective" do not prove themselves very helpful categories in reflecting on atonement. When one sees that atonement works death and life a different conceptuality is necessary. Subjective versus objective apply more to an understanding of the self as a continuously existing substance and asks whether what occurs is entirely "outside" the self or more "within" the self. The "objective" view of atonement seeks to avoid any hint or synergism by placing it entirely outside. In actuality only an apparent objectivity is achieved since the theory is worked out according to a scheme of justice and retribution designed to protect the continuous existence of the subject. Jesus pays completely and without help the price we ought to pay for our failure to negotiate the scheme. But that leads to the intricate question of whether Jesus' death effects a change in God. To avoid such difficulty, the "subjective" view takes an opposite tack, the idea that the death of Jesus effects a modification of some sort in the continuously existing subject.

In either case the question of death and life is avoided. The paradigm for both remains that of the free choice of the continuously existing subject. Thus it is always difficult for an entirely "objective" view to avoid the impasse between universalism on the one hand and limited atonement on the other. If it is entirely "objective" and non-synergistic, either the whole world is atoned or atonement is limited to the elect, those God has secretly decided to save. What usually happens is that one mixes in a small bit of synergism nevertheless. Better that than give up the idea of the continuously existing self. Perhaps the "subjective" view is more honest in that it simply admits to a degree of synergism from the outset.

If one has to use the terms, perhaps one can say that the construing of atonement as a death for us rather than somehow for God, a death that is done to us in the proclamation, leads to an actual atonement that is at once entirely "objective" and "subjective." Just because it is a death for us, entirely from without, it at once entirely involves us in the movement of being made new subjects. Because it is entirely objective it is entirely subjective at the same time. That is what it means to say, I expect, that the will, though bound, can be changed. The aim is to be made one in Christ with God. Just so is it an atonement, the raising up of a new being who actually enjoys God. That is the subject of the next chapter.

5

Hearing

So faith comes from what is heard, and what is heard comes by the preaching of Christ.

(Rom. 10:17)

*T*he outcome of everything discussed thus far, the goal of the proclamation, is the hearing of faith. Proclamation, by the nature of the Word itself, is constantly in the position of hearing. The Word of God arising out of the tomb and coming to us from the startling and new future has no home in this old age of sin and death, this "evil and adulterous generation," as Jesus called it. It is the promise of a kingdom "not of this world," the promise of a new age. It is an eschatological Word, a promise. For that reason it is a Word that can only be preached, and can only be received by hearing. As such it is a Word that cuts us off from our rootage in this age and calls upon us simply to stop and listen. If we hear correctly we will know that we shall for the time being never get beyond being hearers, and that the Word will have to be preached again and again and again. The problem is that we cannot believe our ears, as the saying goes. What is said is too good to be true, so we can only listen and pray that the Spirit will open our ears.

Whoever Has Ears

For the Word to be spoken is unheard of in this age, startling and offensive, negating and contradicting everything the age stands for. It is all summed up in the fact that through the death and resurrection of Jesus God has done absolutely everything for the salvation of humankind. It is summed up in the fact that Jesus died for us, and so we have all died. We are through, "washed up" as old beings. It is summed up in the fact that forgiveness of sins is to be preached to all in Jesus' name and for his sake. It is summed up in the fact that there is nothing left to do. What shall we do to be saved? Nothing! He, she, whoever has ears to hear, hear it! Just listen for once!

That Word is most simple and direct, but at the same time it is the hardest thing of all for us to hear. Having eyes we do not see, and having ears we do not hear. Indeed, Christian theology has always maintained that without the Spirit we will not and cannot hear. Why is that? It is simply the fact that God has done it all, that there is nothing to do. That is impossible for us to take as old beings. That is the stone of stumbling, the rock of offense. Our whole being is staked on our god-project, our upward rebellion, our attempt one way or another to take our destiny into our own hands, to do something to establish our being or realize our destiny. The shock of the Word utterly unnerves us and calls everything we are and hope to be into question. The shock of the "nothing to do" is just incredible to us. We sputter and fume because, quite literally, we do not know what to do with it. But the sputtering and fuming is the death rattle of the Old Adam.

One way or another the "nothing to do" spells death. The Old Adam may, of course, think to take advantage of the situation. Since there is forgiveness, since there is nothing to do, we may exchange this liberty for license, try desperately to realize some kind of destiny by a life of self-indulgence. But that only means that the Old Adam has not died to sin and so shall die the death of sin from which there is no return. But that is a depressing business and one does best by spending as little time with it as possible. Paul usually just gives such positions the back of his hand by saying, "Their condemnation is just."

The reason why we cannot take the proclamation of this Word is that here the Old Adam and Eve sense themselves to be under the most radical and final attack. Here the rebellion is countered and checked most totally and directly. As old beings we had hoped to get by with the ruse that our problem was only one of a greater or lesser degree of weakness or lack of resolve and fortitude in carrying out our projects. That is why it is most often precisely in the church where indignation reaches its highest pitch. For old beings repair to the church to look for help when their projects begin to falter or sag or collapse, expecting to be "affirmed" in their quest. It is in the church, as Barth once put it, that the "God sickness" breaks out most virulently.[1] To be met with the announcement that there is nothing to do is the most devastating of all. "We do have to do something, don't we?" comes the incessant and plaintive cry. "Don't we have anything to say about it?" We hope to keep our projects going or even to find more worthy ones. But now our projects are suddenly wiped out. The Old Adam and Eve are themselves directly attacked and wiped out. The rebellion is countered by rendering it pointless. The reason why this is so offensive to us as old beings is because we no doubt sense that there is nothing left now but to be the creatures God made!

And that, of course, is the point. If we can just hear, if all the garbage of our rebellion can somehow be cleared away, what begins to emerge is creation.

Faith

Faith is the state of being grasped and captivated in the Spirit by the proclamation of what God has done in Jesus. The life of faith is the art of living in that light. It is always dangerous to attempt to describe faith or the life of faith too directly or extensively, for at least a couple of reasons. First, it usually turns out to be too much like locker-room bragging about sexual prowess and like exploits. It does little good other than to make the hearers envious or despairing. Nothing like that has ever happened to me nor is it likely to! Second, it leads to the persistent temptation on the part of the preacher to preach a description. That is almost always deadly. It is, as far as I can see from listening to sermons, one of the most persistent temptations. One preaches a description of faith, or the experience of faith, or the nature of the Christian life, or currently, spirituality, in tones stirring and even momentarily inspiring, but which all too often have little or nothing to do with actuality. Few things are so deadly or depressing, Alvin Rogness used to say, as sermons on joy! Preaching descriptions fosters what could be called the magnificent hot-air balloon syndrome. Everyone is expected to talk up and approve the life of piety, to live up to the life of the description. Everyone feels compelled to go along with the game because no one dares object to it. Who can object to pious and righteous talk? Soon the whole enterprise takes off like a magnificent balloon, rising on the strength of its own hot air, with marvelous descriptions of the Christian life, the abundant life, spirituality, and the like. The minister becomes a guru rather than a proclaimer. The balloon rises perhaps until the stratospheric air can no longer support it and so it bursts and falls ignominiously back to earth. Or it is like Andersen's fairy tale about the emperor's new clothes? Everyone feels compelled to go along with the game until the naive little boy blurts out the truth: "But he's naked!" Then all the pretense collapses.

So it is a somewhat risky business to describe faith and its effects. No doubt it is necessary to do so and even we must hazard it here. But the preacher especially must bear in mind the difference between the description and the proclamation that actually intends to deliver and foster what is being described. That is true as well in speaking about the Holy Spirit. We have not said much about the Holy Spirit in this treatise. Actually the Spirit bears very little talking about. The point is to speak *in* the Spirit. That has been the whole burden of this book. It is really an essay on the work of the Spirit. Nowadays some seem to think that one can measure a given theology's enthusiasm for the third person of the Trinity by the amount of talk there is about the Spirit. But talk about the Spirit does not impart the Spirit any more than talk about piety imparts piety. One speaks *in* the Spirit and imparts the Spirit when one speaks the unconditional gospel of Jesus Christ, when one is not afraid to declare the Word that slays and makes alive. Then one wields "the sword of the Spirit." There is no point in talk about the Spirit that does not recognize the move to speak in the Spirit. Faith comes by hearing the gospel, not by describing it.

With that caveat, we will proceed with some caution to try to say something, at least, about the faith aimed at by the proclamation. The proclamation that Christ has died for us, that everything is accomplished, that nothing is to be done to redeem ourselves or establish our destiny, creates faith and reconciles to God. The proclamation that puts an end to the old and begins the new in Christ is precisely what liberates us to believe and trust in God. Just exactly the *nothing* does it, the fact that the old Adam and Eve can do nothing and so are simply killed by the sword of the Spirit. To be liberated here means to be freed in the Spirit actually to want God, to love God, to start over and to receive one's life from God in joy and gratitude. "Where the Spirit of the Lord is there is liberty" (2 Cor. 3:17).

Perhaps we can make this more plain by leaning a bit on Eberhard Jüngel's discussion of God's necessity in his recent book, *God as the Mystery of the World*.[2] In most traditional discussion, God is defined as a necessary being. God is necessary to explain the world. God is necessary to us. We speak of God as necessary to our humanity, necessary for us to be human. Likewise we think of God as necessary for our "salvation," since we cannot quite manage immortality. Faith consequently becomes a matter of necessity. We conceive of ourselves as caught with God, so to speak, in a net of necessity. God is thought of as indispensable to us, and perhaps likewise, we to God. We need God and God needs us. So we picture it.

Jüngel points out that all this has been challenged in the contemporary world. Modern humanity sets for itself the project of getting on without God, of proving the worldly non-necessity of God. The necessary God is conceived of in terms of an omnipotence that threatens the freedom of human thought. As we put it above, if God is free, then we are dead. So the necessary God must be gotten rid of for the sake of human freedom of thought. And if it is possible to will the worldly non-necessity of God, must not humans want to be godless if they can do so without becoming inhuman? Should we not seek to throw off the burden? The worldly or secular non-necessity of God would then mean that one sets oneself the project of being human without God.

Jüngel believes it to be a fundamental task of theology to ask what this thought of the non-necessity of God means for our relationship to God and God's relationship to us. The point is that theology should recognize that rejection of the worldly necessity of God is not merely negative. It is, I think, something akin to what we have talked about as getting God off our backs. The necessary God is the God of the masks, the God of frightening power and thus of law and wrath. The world has caught on to the fact that to be free it must render this God unnecessary to itself.

But what would the worldly non-necessity of God mean for our relationship to God? It could mean that God is less than necessary, not really essential or needed, but maybe nice now and then for ceremonial purposes and such. But if it means that God is less than necessary God is reduced to capriciousness: a God who can be this or that, or who arbitrarily favors some and not others. As usual, matters only get worse. Modern assertion of a merely negative non-necessity founders because, according to Jüngel, it "has not erased the anthropological function which until now had been the function of a God."[3] Getting rid of the necessary God only leaves one in the hands of capricious fate. But if the worldly non-necessity of God is not to lead to capriciousness, then, Jüngel says, it must mean that God is not less than but more than necessary in the world. Necessity is a category that is not really worthy of God; it does not reach as far as God. God is not less than necessary, but more than necessary in the world.

What does this mean for our understanding of faith? Faith means to be freed, liberated by what Jesus has accomplished, to believe and rejoice in God. That God is not merely necessary but more than necessary means that God does not want, so to speak, to be needed as one might need the "necessities" of life. God does not want to be one in whom we have to believe in order to establish our humanity or get what we consider to be "salvation." As a matter of fact, to think of faith as a "have to" is most likely to lose it. The persistent preaching that thunders away at the idea that we "have to believe" or "make our decision for Jesus" or somehow acquire "Jesus as our personal savior" usually defeats the purpose of the gospel altogether. Faith is not something you "have to" do. That is like hollering at single folks that they "have to" fall in love, a mostly futile exercise. You do not "have to" believe. God does not wish to be one in whom you have to believe but rather one in whom you would want to believe. God has acted in Jesus so as to set us free for that. God wants to be desired and enjoyed for his own sake, to be more than just needed or necessary.

There is something deadly and therefore quite unevangelical in our constant talk about "filling people's needs" in the church these days. Need is, of course, a slippery concept. Perhaps there is a sense in which it can be properly used. But one must take care. A relationship built merely on need is likely to be deadly, as in, "You can't leave, I need you!" It may be flattering, perhaps, to feel needed. But it is surely more gratifying and graceful to be more than needed, simply to be enjoyed for your own sake, to be quite "unnecessary" but nevertheless passionately desired.

That is what it means to say that God is not merely necessary, but more than necessary. Faith, says Jüngel, is "joy in God."[4] Joy is an attitude called forth by another, completely uncoerced, spontaneous, gladly realized. This is what the proclamation aims at. Thus the proclamation must be a proclamation that puts an end to the old, tears the net of necessity in which we find ourselves trapped with God and brings the new to light. Proclamation cannot be like exhortation to the single that they have to fall in love. It must rather be the presentation of the sheer beauty and attractiveness of the beloved. Just so must it be a proclamation of what God has done in Jesus, that everything has been accomplished, that nothing can be done now except to listen to the "I love you." Every attempt to use God as a necessary hand up in our projects, however religious, is over. We are saved by faith alone, and faith comes by hearing. To be saved in this sense is truly to be rescued from the net of necessity and law by a spontaneous joy in God. Everything is now raised to a different plane, an absolutely new future opens up. Faith is being grasped by that promise, by that future. Faith is not a "having to," it is a "wanting to," a being set free to, a being grasped by the power that is sheer love, a being raised from the death of the old to the life of the new. Faith is life in the Spirit.

Creation and Sin

Now we can double back and say something more about creation and our rebellion against it than we have said heretofore. The faith that comes from hearing lights up creation and casts the sin that distorts it in darker relief. The usual complaint against a theology that insists as we do here on faith alone is that it tends to lapse into a Manichean denigration of creation. Since sin is so great a corruption that no human cooperation is possible or expected in the quest for salvation, there seems to be no good left in creation at all. But such a view presupposes just that scheme of salvation against which we have been protesting throughout. It presupposes the free-will paradigm, the idea that the subject is a continuously existing being under law who is supposed to be improved through cooperation with grace. Salvation is a repair of the old, not the death of the old and resurrection of the new. When salvation by faith alone (*sola fide*) is proposed, loud protestation is made that the integrity of creation is being denigrated. But that is simply the cry of the disgruntled idealist whose project has been discovered and upset by a salvation by faith alone.

Putting together the pieces we have developed, a quite different picture begins to emerge. There is nothing wrong with creation but the loss of faith. Sin is not merely wrong moral choice, it is faithlessness, unbelief. Sin is simply the lack of joy in God and the creation. Our trouble is that we can never believe that creation is good enough for us. And we should make no mistake about it, this is a desperately serious fault. It points to something profoundly and even innately wrong with us. We have got the directions exactly reversed and we will not change. We are on our way up, out, away, from the creation God gave. We are always on our way somewhere else, to some ideal world, a world abstracted from this world, some place where we can work out our dream of being gods. And so we entirely mistake our plight. Being unable to reach our idealist Valhalla we do indeed usually sense that something might be at least a little amiss. So we might complain of lack of strength and such things. We look, perhaps, even to grace for a little "help." But none of that is serious enough to upset our idealist apple cart. We picture ourselves as potential spiritual athletes, so to speak, just lusting to make God's team, but perhaps having a little trouble with the training rules or not being big enough, strong enough, or gifted enough. But at least our "heart" is in the right place.

This is where the real denigration of creation comes. Lusting to be as gods, we complain about lack of strength and surmise that we must have lost it in the "fall." But we insist that there must be at least a little left to keep the game going. And we call this gratuitous insistence on a "little left" respect for creation! The felony is compounded by the fact that we expect to gain grace by exercising this little bit of ability or strength we supposedly have left. In other words, we expect to gain salvation by doing our little bit. And thus our perfidy is exposed. A little bit is all we planned to do anyway! "We have to do something, don't we?"—that is the pious sounding cry. Rather than face the question of death and life, we hope to get by with a little something! As Luther remarked, this kind of semi-Pelagianism is worse than full-blown Pelagianism. At least the outright Pelagian is honest enough to see that one must throw one's whole life into the balance.[5]

Not only does such a view distort the attitude toward creation, but it also distorts the picture of grace. Grace comes to be understood as a power supplementing the power of "nature." Grace, as the picture has it, perfects nature in the sense that it is an "added gift" (*donum superadditum*). Lost in the fall it is now to be added again through the sacraments of redemption. There is already a hidden denigration of creation in the idea that "nature,"—to be sure a slippery enough concept—needs the added power of grace to perfect it. Perhaps even more seriously, theology becomes a hidden agenda, suggesting a "behind-the-scenes" transaction that nobody really sees. Grace takes on something of a fictional character. The direct power of the open deed of the proclamation in Word and sacrament, which kills and makes alive precisely through its claim that now everything has been accomplished, gets smuggled away behind the scenes as a "secret" or "invisible" grace, a mysterious power, the bestowal of which one can never be quite certain about. One is laid open to the magnificent hot-air balloon syndrome. One talks in marvelous terms of what this grace is to accomplish, but leaves reality behind.

Thus do we sin against God and his creation. We do not believe in it. We are headed in quite the opposite direction. We have fallen short not merely of the law of God but of the glory of God. We sin not merely in our vices, but in our virtues, insofar as they are just attempts to keep the Old Adam in the game. Our idealist piety resents most deeply and attacks most desperately precisely the *sola gratia, sola fide* because it knows that if they hold, it is through. "Wherever God builds a church the devil builds a chapel," says Luther. Here finally we can see the depth and incredible bondage, the blindness, of sin. The cure for sin is not idealism, not better moral choices. The law does not stop sin. It does restrain sin in this age to some extent, but with respect to the age to come it simply increases sin. The only cure for sin is death. Arthur McGill puts it well in commenting on Romans 6:

There is a strong tradition which views sin as moral, as misdirected will. . . . This is not Paul's view. In fact, such an understanding of sin makes nonsense of the passage in Romans 6. If sin is a matter of making a wrong choice, then the overcoming of sin involves us in making a right choice. It involves us in acts of our will—exactly what Paul denies we can do. Paul did not write that through union with Jesus' death we are prompted to give up making sinful choices and begin making righteous choices; thus our sinful self is destroyed and we are no longer slaves to sin. Paul would have nothing to do with the idea that sin is a matter of our willing. Instead, Paul insists that through union with Jesus'

death we die. We are buried with him and we lay dead. Thus our sinful
self is destroyed, and we are no longer slaves of sin. If sin were simply
a matter of wrong choices, it would not require us to die and to lie
dead in order to be free from sin. It would only require us to change
our decisions.[6]

Since sin is contrary to created existence it is only through death
to sin that creation is given back to us as a sheer gift. Grace is not
some secret or mysterious behind-the-scenes power added to an in-
complete or deficient creation. Grace is what happens through the
open proclamation of the death and resurrection of Christ. Grace is
putting a stop to our whole quest to be as gods, the putting down of
the rebellion, the cracking of the bondage, the liberation of creation
to be creation, the sheer gift of God. Nature, I should think we would
want to say, does not lack strength. It is rather more that because of
sin its strength is bent in exactly the wrong direction. Instead of taking
care of the earth and our fellow beings, instead of being content to
be creatures, we are bound to our god-projects and will not let go.

Grace is the breaking of all that, the liberation of creation. In
that sense it could be proper even to say that grace perfects nature.
Not that grace somehow adds to an otherwise imperfect creation, but
that grace puts a stop to our misguided attempts to usurp God's place
and so allows creation to shine forth in all its glory. Grace gives creation
back to us as the sheer gift of God. Through Christ we can believe in
creation. The directional signs are reversed. We receive the world back
as a place in which to live, love, and care, for the time being.

It is thus not a matter of course to look on our world as a
"creation," especially not as a creation out of nothing (*ex nihilo*). The
doctrine of creation has, we should never forget, always been considered a revealed doctrine, not part of our "natural" knowledge. Belief
in creation is a faithful way of receiving and relating to the world. It
is the outcome of the death to sin and the resurrection of the new
being in faith. It is not by any means an ordinary understanding of the
world or how it began. For the most part, the argument about crea-
tionism versus evolution is simply beside the point. It is mostly an
argument about theories of the world's beginning.

One does not come by faith in creation easily. Luther expressed
this in a remarkable passage:

For without doubt the highest article of faith is that in which we say: I
believe in God the Father, almighty creator of heaven and earth, and

whoever rightly believes that is already helped and set right and brought back to that from which Adam fell. But those who come to the point of fully believing that he is the God who creates and makes all things are few, because such a person must be dead to all things, to good and evil, death and life, hell and heaven, and must confess from the heart that he can do nothing out of his own strength.[7]

Faith in God the creator and thus the receiving of creation as sheer gift comes by dying and being raised. It is a new creation out of nothing. Out of the fact that there is nothing to do, the whole creation is made new in the risen Christ. But we should not mistake the fact that in this life such a view is not easily or lightly held. In actuality faith wavers and must be renewed daily. We do not surrender or get over our idealisms readily. They haunt us till we die. Perhaps we could say that to the extent we are grasped by Christ's deed in faith, to that extent we receive the world back as creation. It is important to say that to make it clear that the battle for creation is still being waged very concretely, and we are in the middle of it. Creation is not a static and given reality for us. Faith in creation, as all faith, is held only in the face of temptation.

Corollary to this faith in creation is the much celebrated and denigrated "doctrine of the two kingdoms." Without venturing far into that disputed territory here, it is appropos to remark that there would likely be less trouble with it if one retained something of the more dynamic view of creation just suggested. To the extent that one believes in the realities given by grace alone through the "kingdom on the right," the rule of God established through the gospel, an entirely new realm opens up, the creation as an arena in which to exercise one's God-given gifts. But the two kingdoms are then by no means static entities to be taken for granted. Thinking in terms of two kingdoms is a faithful way of looking at the world. Only because one is a new creature in Christ does one receive the world back again as a new creation. Only then will one turn about to carry out one's vocation in this age and not seek to desert it prematurely.

McGill supplies a helpful indication of what this new creation can mean in his book *Death and Life.*[8] Jesus, McGill says, lived an ecstatic identity. That is to say that the center of Jesus' existence is not within himself but in God and God's future. That is why the miracles, the teachings, Jesus' relationships to others, even his dying and being raised are not regarded as "windows into Jesus' own experience, feelings, insights, and growth."[9] Jesus lives from beyond himself, he knows his reality originates in God. But God is not apprehended by Jesus as an external cause that created once upon a time but as a continually operative cause, a causing. Thus does Jesus live and act as the Son of his Father.

> Such a sense of origin entails a complete reordering of the usual understanding of a person's relation to God. God does not create a person by conferring some reality unto that person. God does not create by so securing a person with being that he or she exists by virtue of a reality which God has imparted. If that were the case, people would know and be themselves simply by taking possession of their own reality, simply by being one with themselves. Then there would be a second and subsequent act in which a person would recognize that this being, which he or she is from God, came from God.[10]

Not so with Jesus. Jesus does not live to himself so that he has to make a second effort to be aware of God. In knowing himself, he knows God. He is never his own being, but continually receiving it from God. One who is remade in his image, therefore, has a radically altered sense of identity. Such a one lives an ecstatic identity, lives as one who is constantly receiving.

This, McGill maintains, is the new kind of identity which comes through the death to sin of Romans 6. It gives rise to the experience of love and the feeling of gratitude: "When we experience ourselves as a gift, as a free, joyful, and continual gift, we are filled with that feeling which Paul placed first of all in the new life—the feeling of gratitude."[11] That is, in Christ one receives creation back again as a sheer gift for which one can only give thanks. In explaining the fourth petition of the Our Father, Luther says that God indeed gives daily bread even to all the wicked without prayer, but that "we pray in this petition that God may make us aware of his gifts and enable us to receive our daily bread with thanksgiving." In other words, God does not need to be reminded of our need by the prayer, but the relationship of gratitude and thanksgiving is all important. It re-establishes us as creatures of God who live in gratitude for the sheer gift of creation. Faith is the joy in God and the divine creation evoked by the proclamation of Jesus Christ.[12]

6

Proclaiming

Of this gospel I was made a minister according to the gift of God's grace . . . , to preach to the Gentiles the unsearchable riches of Christ, and to make all people see what is the plan of the mystery hidden for ages in God who created all things; that through the church the manifold wisdom of God might now be made known . . . This was according to the eternal purpose which he has realized in Christ Jesus our Lord, in whom we have boldness and confidence of access through our faith in him. (Eph. 3:7-12)

*P*roclamation is more like a sacrament than other oral communication such as teaching or informing. The basic presupposition for such oral communication tends to be the freedom of choice. The words provide information about God and Christ which one is expected to appropriate or accept by an act of will. One may, of course, insist that such choosing is aided by grace or the workings of the Spirit and so not only a matter of human caprice. But even so the presupposition remains the same, that of the continuously existing subject making its choice over against a battery of facts.

Such a scheme has the consequence of making grace or the Spirit a mysterious "behind the scenes" influencing of our choices. One is then driven inward upon oneself. If the proper choice does not seem forthcoming, one can draw either of two conclusions. Either one has frustrated grace by one's own failure or God has simply refused to give it. One is usually generous enough not to suspect God of such perfidy and so takes the blame on oneself. But how can one ever know whether one is frustrating the mysterious thing called grace?

The sacraments, however, are quite another story. They presuppose a quite different paradigm. In administering the sacraments we do not merely say something, we do not merely impart information, we do something, we wash in water, we give bread and wine, to those who come. We do not, that is, explain Christ or the gospel or describe faith or give instructions on how to get salvation. We give it, flat out. The paradigm for this is not the continued existence of the supposedly free subject, but the death of the old and the resurrection of the new. We are baptized into the death of Christ to be reborn in the newness of the resurrection life in faith. We eat and drink the body and blood of the crucified and risen One, thereby proclaiming his death until he comes. The subject's continued existence is actually, bodily, interrupted.

This is, of course, terribly disconcerting for our "natural" sensibilities, brought up as we invariably are on the linguistic paradigms presupposing freedom of choice. There tends to be considerable suspicion of sacraments particularly among those who pride themselves in being champions of "the Word." The idea that physical, material acts such as being washed with water or eating bread and wine could have anything to do with salvation is an attack on the entire paradigm of free choice and the idea of spirit that goes with it. So it is not strange that there is a good deal of anxiety, especially among so-called evangelicals, television evangelists and the like, that baptism, for instance, will likely pull the rug out from under their call for decision and morally upright living. It is hardly surprising, therefore, that baptism in particular is under heavy attack primarily among very pious Christians. It does something quite offensive and contrary to most popular and utilitarian Christianity. It comes at us from quite different presuppositions. It does not expect that the ills of humankind will be solved or sin defeated by human resolve. It knows that the only cure is death and life. So it puts to death to raise up. It does not offer old beings a choice, it drowns them to pull new beings out of the water. But the free choice paradigm cannot cope with that.

The result of this conflict in paradigms is an unfortunate competition between Word and sacrament in proclamation. Churches are split between emphasizing one or the other, and within individual churches themselves what is said in the sermon may be quite at odds with what is done in the sacraments. What we offer in the sacraments is often retracted in our sermons; thus we leave people befuddled. We may baptize them but then imply in the sermon that they ought not take the gift too much for granted, or that it is not really what it is alleged to be. People are then cut adrift between Word and sacrament; their allegiance to one or the other is reduced to a matter of preference. One or the other of them is then bound to lose. Churches divide into sacramental and nonsacramental communions and people develop tastes for one type of service or the other. As such, both Word and sacrament will lose out, because the vitality of both depends upon their complementarity and reinforcement of one another in the deed of proclamation.

This book has been pointing in just that direction. The point throughout has been that in proclamation one not only explains the Word but also one does the Word to the hearers. The spoken Word is as much a doing as is the sacrament. Preaching, to Luther, is pouring Christ into our ears, just as in the sacraments we are baptized into him and he is poured into our mouths. Indeed, preaching is as much a physical activity as baptism or the Supper. The proclaimed Word not only explains or informs but it also gives—it ends the old and begins the new, it puts to death and brings to life. Word and sacrament must be brought together in a unity. What usually happens in these matters is that one becomes the primary or even exclusive channel of grace at the expense of the other. But that only spells disaster. It means in the end that both will lose their character as proclamation of an unconditional, killing and life-giving Word.

Without sacramental character, the Word degenerates into information about which the continuously existing old being is supposed to do something. Similarly, without the unconditional promise, sacraments degenerate into conveyors of mysterious power which are supposed to shore up the continuously existing old being's enterprises. Pelagianism threatens in both instances. In short, vital proclamation depends on the unity of Word and Sacrament, the sacramental character of the preached Word.

The Hermeneutics of Proclamation

A sermon does indeed include explaining, exegeting, and informing, but ultimately it must get around to and aim at a doing, an actual pronouncing, declaring, giving of the gift. In proclaiming the Word, our goal is absolution, the doing of the deed that ends the old and begins the new. We must learn to speak a Word that not only explains but does something.

How does one do something with words? "Sticks and stones may break my bones, but words will never hurt me." So goes the old saying. It is not true, of course, since the unkind word is often most damaging of all. But the adage shows a certain attitude or prejudice about the relative futility of words. What can words do? How does one do the Word to the hearers? Actually, the churches of the Reformation tradition have had a good deal to say about that in the tradition of distinguishing between (and preaching) law and gospel. The point in distinguishing between law and gospel is to prepare the hearers for and drive the preacher to that wild kind of speaking unknown to this world: gospel speaking. The point in making the distinction was simply an attempt to sort out and drive to this absolutely new kind of speaking. Those who mock or disdain the attempt should be forewarned that where the distinction is not made and applied there is only one kind of speaking: law speaking.

The distinction was also a proposal for getting the gospel heard in a world that is innately deaf to it. The law was to accuse the sinner and the gospel to absolve. Driven to despair of self, the sinner was to be turned for help and comfort to faith in the gospel. However, this tradition seems largely to have run off into sand. Whether that is entirely good or bad we need not argue at this point. Generally, preachers seem to avoid the old law and gospel method, if it was a "method," because it is held that people no longer are so afflicted with the problem of the anxious conscience as they once were. We have a marvelous cure, but no one has the disease. Accusing people by preaching the law depended, supposedly, on the presence of a sensitive conscience within a universally accepted moral superstructure. Once that is gone, there is no place to begin. One tries to "meet people's needs" or still their anxieties or encourage them in their flagging enterprises. But these procedures are just sentimental surrogates for the old method and only make matters worse. They drive us more deeply than ever into the black hole of the self, turn the pastor into a shrink or a guru and worship into mass therapy.

Now it could probably be demonstrated that most dismissals of the old law-gospel procedure and its dependence on anxious conscience are naive and premature. One is often brought up short, for instance, by the heavy load of guilt-talk one finds in profane circles just when the preachers announce its disappearance. Without some kind of conscience and moral superstructure we are something less than human. As William Hulme put it in a chapel sermon, "Show me a person without guilt and I will show you a sociopath."

All that notwithstanding, there is little point in fighting such rearguard action here. Rather, we need to get at the root problem. The basic difficulty is that the talk of law and gospel has been superimposed on a scheme to which it was originally quite opposed, the same old scheme of the continuously existing subject over against the eternal ladder of the law. The subject is to climb the ladder to arrive at righteousness or heaven or wherever it is supposed to lead. The gospel then comes along to make the law work, to shore up the enterprise when it falters, to provide either power to ascend or pardon for failure and even to offer the promise of the ultimate goal to faith, provided, of course, one lives a decent life afterward. "Sanctification" and the third use of the law is the revenge exacted for too lavish expenditure of the bounty of God. Where old beings are not to be put to death, one must do something to keep them in line. Preachers become moral police. Superimposed on that scheme, preaching law and gospel just goes sour. The gospel is not the end of the law, not the advent of the new, not the act of liberation making its way into our lives, it is just the ratification of the law, which is probably the real reason why there is resistance to the old law/gospel method. Since there is no end, no real gospel, it becomes a species of psychological gimmickry. One tries to scare the Old Adam into becoming Christian. But that will work only so long as the Old Adam is susceptible, for whatever reason, to such fright.

Actually, however, the distinction between law and gospel has its roots in the death/life paradigm rather than that of free choice. It is a particular recension of the old and continuing battle over the meaning and place of letter and spirit in interpreting and applying the Christian message, the battle over "hermeneutics." Since the beginning that battle has raged around the key passage in 2 Cor. 3:6 that the letter, the written code kills, but the spirit gives life. The passage is actually about ministry, but that, unfortunately has not been sufficiently noted.

> Such is the confidence that we have through Christ toward God. Not that we are sufficient of ourselves to claim anything as coming from us; our sufficiency is from God, who has qualified us to be ministers of a new covenant, not in a written code but in the Spirit; for the written code kills, but the Spirit gives life.
>
> (2 Cor. 3:4-6)

The free choice paradigm does not know really what to do with the idea that the letter kills but the spirit gives life. Generally, in accordance with ancient thought, it was interpreted according to the dualism between matter and spirit, sensible and intelligible realms. That the letter kills was taken to mean that the literal message—mere history for the most part in the case of the Bible—belonged to the inferior realm of matter, the sensible. If one remains stuck on that level one will perish in the land of appearances. The letter kills, that is, because it belongs to the realm of the sensible, the perishable, and does not reach the realm of spirit. What is needed is to escape to the realm of spirit.

Letter and Spirit

Nevertheless, the letter, as all appearances, was a kind of pointer to the realm of spirit. The basic hermeneutic was one of signification. The words, the letter, signified things. In the case of biblical words they signified mostly historical events. But these events in turn must be translated into spiritual truth (that is, truths of eternal and universal "significance"). The signification must be extended beyond the mere literal in order to save. In the Christian case, that generally meant that the literal message had to be translated into moral, doctrinal, and eschatological truth according to the threefold exegetical scheme of tropology, allegory, and anagogy. This has come to be referred to as the "allegorical method."

This means that the literal text, especially when it seemed offensive or obscure, could not be taken as directly or eternally meaningful in and of itself. It had to be translated, so to speak, into another story of more universal meaning. It is the ancient version of Lessing's question: How can accidental truths of history be proofs of eternal truths of reason? How can one bridge the time gap between then and now? Of what significance for us today is it that God led the children of Israel out of Egypt? We were neither there nor are we Israelites. So to be made more universal the story could be translated into a story about the exodus from vice to virtue, "the flesh-pots of Egypt" to "the promised land" of morality and piety. Or the story of Moses' journey through the wilderness, the receiving of the law, and the vision of the promised land from the top of Mount Nebo could be translated into the story of the mystical journey of the soul through purgation and illumination toward the ecstatic vision. The literal story is a "front" for a more "spiritual" internal and eternal story. So does one move from letter to spirit, from the mere sensible and temporal history to the intelligible and eternal truth. The move from letter to spirit is therefore an interpretative move. The gap between then and now is bridged, so to speak, by translating the literal history into some kind of eternal "spiritual" truth.

The secret of allegory is that it translates the text into "another" story, a kind of "other-speak." It is the ancient version of making the text "relevant." The text does not interrupt or change our story; rather, it is interpreted to fit our story. And in one way or another that is always the story of what we are to do, the story presupposing the free choice of the continuously existing autonomous subject. That means in turn that there is no real breakthrough to gospel speaking. There is no end, no death to the law. It just goes on and on. To say that the written code, the letter, kills means only that it is inadequate and must be translated into more enlightening "spiritual" truth. To avoid death in the land of appearances one must be apprised of such spiritual truth. It is readily apparent that the system was designed to prolong rather than end the existence of the old subject.

The Reformation, particularly in Luther's case, represented a drastic break with this tradition.[1] Luther took the passage at face value! He saw at long last that the passage was about ministry, not interpretation in the abstract. The passage is not concerned only with what letter and spirit mean, but what they do. The letter kills, and the Spirit gives life. The literal text, the long history of God's struggle with his people culminating in the cross and resurrection is not killing because it is a mere appearance, an inadequate signifier, but because it is deadly for the sinner. The literal history, that is, means one thing for the sinner: death, the end of the way of those who have succumbed to the temptation to be as gods. The purpose of the proclamation is not to present the hearer with one more option, but to put the old to death and to raise up the new in the Spirit. The ultimate purpose of the proclamation is to raise the dead.

When one understands the matter of proclamation against this background of the age-old problem of letter and spirit, the task of preaching can be seen in a new light. This is the proper background and source for distinguishing between and preaching law and gospel. Law and gospel are not to be understood primarily in a narrow moral sense, relative to the moral dilemmas of old beings and questions of guilt or conscience, but rather in terms of the more universal and at the same time concrete question of death and life: the letter that kills and the Spirit that gives life. The "law" as the letter that kills is not just a body of laws, but as Luther could say, the literal works of God in the world (*opera literalia dei*), and most particularly the story, the entire history of God with his people which culminates in cross and resurrection and so ends the story of old beings. The law, the letter, kills. It brings us to an end. And when the letter kills, the Spirit does its life-giving work.

Law and gospel are thus broadened and understood in their functional sense. They do not designate merely aspects or parts of the text but the manner in which the text functions relative to the hearer. It kills and makes alive and is to be so preached. Superficial objections to the use of law and gospel in preaching as well as superficial applications of the same are therewith obviated. The preaching of the law is not dependent upon anxious consciences or ready-made guilt feelings. The preaching of the law is the use of the text to cut in upon and slay old beings. The preaching of the gospel, likewise, not only comforts the conscience-stricken but also raises the dead to new life.

A preaching of the gospel based on justification by faith alone is often criticized today because it is no longer relevant. The criticism is usually superficial, however, because it fails to recognize that such preaching is a two-edged sword. It does indeed comfort the afflicted. It also afflicts the comfortable. The very outcry one hears against the gospel claim is evidence enough of that—"Do you mean to say we are saved by faith *alone?*" As old beings we are under attack. To the comfortable the "gospel" itself functions first and foremost as an attack, as the law that kills. Indeed, the unconditional promise (*sola gratia*) is itself the final crescendo of the "law" as the letter that kills. In this functional sense, the law is, so to speak, simply the cutting edge of the gospel. God kills us, so to speak, with goodness. "Do you not know that God's kindness is meant to lead you to repentance?" (Rom. 2:4). The unconditional promise is not a Word searching merely for those few who somehow "feel the need" for it. It is a Word that goes on the attack to create its hearers out of the nothing of our sin.

Doing the Text

What does this tell us about the move from the text to the proclamation? This move has to be a self-conscious one on the part of the preacher. Observation and experience lead to the perception that such self-consciousness is all too often lacking in preaching. Preachers, that is, do not have enough self-consciousness about what they are doing, or ought to be doing. There is a vague idea that the text ought to be made "relevant," but that is usually done by unwitting reversion to the old allegorical method. The sermon begins with some anecdote, personal or otherwise, which is supposed to introduce or illustrate the text and make it more immediately relevant. There seems virtually to be a dogma these days that that is the way to begin. But usually what happens is that the anecdote takes over center stage, the text is either lost or interpreted allegorically to fit the anecdote, and the whole collapses into a lame moralism or therapy. Nothing is more needed than some self-consciousness on the part of the preacher on what is entailed in the move from text to sermon.

It is here that the hermeneutics of the matter can help us. Proclamation should issue ultimately in what might be called a *doing* of the text to the hearers, a doing of what the text authorizes the preacher to do in the living present. That is to say, proclamation cannot end merely in an allegorical explaining of the text, however clever, so as to provide the hearer with options. Just as in Christology we were impelled to move from the language of being to the language of doing, so also the proclamation must move from explaining to doing the text. The proclaimer should attempt to do once again in the living present what the text once did and so authorizes doing again.

In preparing to do the text, the proclaimer should inquire not only about what the text meant (exegesis). There must be such inquiry, indeed. It is an indispensable step toward the proclamation. There can be no detour around it, and the result of such inquiry should no doubt find its way into the sermon. But exegesis is mostly presupposition for proclamation, not proclamation itself. Nor should one stop or become too preoccupied with the move from what the text meant to what it "means." Of late that has been touted as the decisive move from text to proclamation. But it is too easy for such a move to wander off in the direction of seeking "timeless truths" in the fashion of the old allegorical method.

It is more to the point to inquire what the text did to the hearers and prepare to do that again. That should not prove so difficult. The texts, especially from the Gospels, most often record highly charged dramatic situations and themselves tell us what they did. Forgiveness was announced out of a clear blue sky to a paralytic lying on his pad. What did that have to do with anything? Who can forgive sins but God alone? Blasphemy! Yet an authority is being claimed and vindicated by the healing of that man. And that authority is given to those who follow, and so virtually demands being used. The text impels the reader to use the authority, not just talk about it. The Sabbath rules are broken and lordship over them is claimed. The blind see, the deaf hear, the lame walk, the poor have good news preached to them. The canons and conventions, the works and ways of this age, however pious and godly, are controverted and smashed. The temple itself is cleansed and threatened with destruction. What did that do? The texts do not leave us in the dark. The people were shocked, incensed, amazed, offended, they took up stones to kill. Or they comforted, healed, and gave life. The words drive inexorably to cross and resurrection. Indeed, they are the Word of the cross.

To be true to this Word, the proclaimer must not merely explain, as we have just done, but take the authority granted by the text and do it. Where the text on the healing of the paralytic ends, for instance, with words to the effect that the people were "afraid and glorified God who had given such authority to men" the text virtually insists on what the next move has to be. The proclaimer must exercise the authority so granted. The proclaimer must so announce the forgiveness to those gathered here and now as to amaze them with the audacity of it all. Perhaps they will even glorify God once again. The proclaimer must, on the authority of Jesus, have the guts to do again in the living present what was done once upon a time. The proclaimer must dare to believe that the very moment of the proclamation is the moment planned and counted on by the electing God himself. The proclaimer is there to do the deed authorized, not merely to explain the deeds of the past. In the words of Ephesians used as superscript to this chapter, ministry means that the mystery hidden for ages in God is now to be revealed in the church. The deed is to be done.

In moving from text to sermon, one would do well to look first for the offense, the killing letter of the text, the hard saying, the uncompromising word, and start with that rather than with some cute story. Then one can subsequently turn it over as life-giving Spirit. The word of forgiveness spoken to the paralytic was a blasphemous offense. But the authority claimed was vindicated, so now it is to be used. In the parable of laborers in the vineyard, the keeper's retort, "Can I not do what I want with what is my own?" is tremendously offensive. But it must be so preached precisely as offense to kill the old so that it can be turned over into life-giving spirit. For our only chance is that God can do what God wants with what is his own! And the present moment, the sermons, the sacrament, *is* what God has decided to do! The offense must be done so that the Word can give life.

So the hermeneutics of the Word as killing letter and life-giving Spirit impels the proclaimer to a doing of the Word to the hearer and not merely an explaining of it. The hermeneutics of the matter, that is, once again drives to the point where one can do nothing other than proclaim. One must take the authority and do it again. The move to doing the Word in that fashion involves the recognition that the proclamation must be a Word of the cross. That does not mean only that there is lots of talk about the cross. The point is that the proclamation itself ought to bear the form of the Word of the cross. It is to do the cross to the hearers. The proclamation is to kill and make alive. It purposes to make an end and a new beginning. What makes proclamation the Word of the cross is not the fact that the cross is always the direct subject or the only subject of the address, but that the words themselves have the *form* of the cross, presuppose it, drive inexorably to it, and flow from it. To be a Word of the cross, the proclamation must cut in upon our lives to end the old and begin the new.[2]

All this is to say, of course, that the Word is an eschatological Word, a Word that puts an end to the old and ushers in the new. The doing of the text to the hearers is nothing other than putting an end to our affairs in the double sense already noted above, ending the old and giving an end (a *telos*) to our existence, our world. Proclamation is to be understood and prosecuted in this light. The sacraments sign, seal, and deliver this end in unmistakable fashion. They are the end of the old and the beginning of the new in the midst of our time.

Proclaiming the Sacraments

Sacraments, as eschatological occurrences in the midst of time, are integral to the proclamation. They are embedded in the proclamation. To use Luther's formulation in the Small Catechism, speaking of baptism, they are "comprehended" in God's Word. Baptism is not merely water, but as "water set by God's command and bound with God's Word" *(Wasser in Gottes gebot gefasst und mit Gottes Wort verbunden)*. Since the sacraments are so comprehended in the Word, one cannot have the Word without the sacraments. To hear and be bound by the Word is at the same time to be bound by the sacraments. To sunder the Word and the sacraments would be to be disobedient, to listen to a different word. "Whoever rejects Baptism rejects God's Word, faith, and Christ, who directs us and binds us to Baptism."[3]

But what are sacraments for? They are for salvation. "To put it most simply, the power, effect, benefit, fruit, and purpose of Baptism is to save."[4] Every Christian, Luther avers, ought to have at least some brief elementary instruction concerning sacraments because without them no one can be a Christian.[5] But how is it that sacraments save or make Christians? Do we not have the Word? Do we not have faith? Is it not more important, as some today would like to put it, to have Jesus as "your personal savior," or some such? What is so saving about sacraments?

An External Word

The answer lies in the relation between the internal and the external, the inner and the outer, in the life of faith. We do indeed have the Word, and it is a saving Word. But the Word includes the sacraments precisely to save us. Where an attempt is made to drive a wedge between the Word and the sacraments, disaster waits. The problem arises, we might say, because in the state of sin and bondage, we are all turned inward upon ourselves (*curvatus in se*). Without the sacraments, the words go inside us. They become an internal matter. As we like to say, we "internalize" the words. Once inside we begin to wonder what happened to them. We have an incurable tendency to feed on our own innards. We begin to wonder whether we really have taken the words seriously, whether we are really sincere, or perhaps whether we really have accepted Jesus as our "personal Savior," whatever that is supposed to mean. I may hear the words "Your sins are forgiven," but then wonder whether it could be really me that is meant, or whether it is even relevant to my needs. We become a prey to adverbial theology. Do we really, sincerely, truly, personally, believe? Do we live abundantly, joyously, affirmatively? Do we think positively, praise gratefully, respond generously? What do I do if I just do not see all those marvelous things happening that the preacher is always on about? I get caught in the marvelous hot-air balloon syndrome, dragged along in a game I can only lose. The self is a bottomless pit, a black hole, endlessly sucking everything within and crushing it. The internal self constantly defeats and swallows up the words.

In John Bunyan's *Pilgrim's Progress* this temptation of the inner self is called the Slough of Despond, the first obstacle Christian encounters and falls into on his way to the Celestial City. When the man called Help comes to the rescue, he asks Christian what he is doing in such a place. "Sir," says Christian, "I was bid go this way by a man called Evangelist, who directed me also to yonder gate, that I might escape the wrath to come; and as I was going thither, I fell in here." When Christian asks why the place is not mended, Help gives him an interesting answer.

> This miry slough is such a place as cannot be mended; it is the descent whither the scum and filth that attends conviction for sin doth continually run, and therefore it is called the Slough of Despond; for still as the sinner is awakened about his lost condition, there ariseth in his soul many fears, and doubts, and discouraging apprehensions, which all of them get together, and settle in this place. And this is the reason of the badness of the ground.
>
> It is not the pleasure of the King that this place should remain so bad. His laborers also have by the direction of His Majesty's surveyors, been for above these sixteen hundred years employed about this patch of ground, if perhaps it might have been mended; yea, and to my knowledge, said he, here have been swallowed up at least twenty thousand cart-loads, yea, millions of wholesome instructions, that have been brought from all places of the King's dominions, and they that can tell,

say they are the best materials to make good ground of the place, if so be it might have been mended, but it is the Slough of Despond still, and so will be when they have done what they can.[6]

In spite of all the good words, twenty-thousand cartloads, millions of wholesome instructions (think of all the sermons and all the counseling!), the Slough of Despond remains and Christian cannot get out without Help. The inner self remains just that sort of quagmire.

Sundered from the sacraments, that is, the spoken word can go awry and fail to reach its goal. "Help" must come from the outside, from a more irreducibly external word. Sacraments provide the "Help" that Bunyan, no doubt, would hardly have recognized. They will not let the Word be swallowed up in our internality. They remain always external, from without. They guarantee the character of the Word as what Luther could call an "alien" Word, a Word from without, from out there in the world of things and bodies.

Sacraments save because they save the Word from disappearing into the inner life. They save because they prevent us from understanding grace as some kind of hidden agenda, a behind-the-scenes spiritualism that we are supposed somehow to master or learn the secret of. Sacraments save, that is, because they protect us from the wiles of the devil, the master at turning even the Word of promise into temptation—"Has God said . . . ?" It is quite consequent that Luther could describe the Fall precisely as the enticement of Adam and Eve away from the external word and promise to internal subjectivity, what was then called "enthusiasm." Enthusiasm was taken theologically to mean not just healthy excitement about something, but rather according to its root meaning: "God-withinism." In the Smalcald Articles (Part 3, Art. 8) Luther sketched out a sweeping view of history from Fall to redemption in those terms:

> All this is the old devil and old serpent who made enthusiasts of Adam and Eve. He led them from the external Word of God to spiritualizing and to their own imaginations. . . .
>
> In short, enthusiasm clings to Adam and his descendants from the beginning to the end of the world. It is a poison implanted and inoculated in man by the old dragon, and it is the source, strength, and power of all heresy, including that of the Papacy and Mohamet. Accordingly we should and must constantly maintain that God will not deal with us except through his external Word and Sacrament. Whatever is attributed to the Spirit apart from such Word and Sacrament is of the devil.

The devil, that master of subjectivity, can do nothing about the alien Word, the Word from without, the visible and tangible Word. It has simply happened and nothing can change that. As such it is part and parcel of the proclamation and must be preached against all objection. An amusing incident from the television series "All in the Family" illustrates the point. When Michael protests at Archie's conniving to have the baby baptized, Archie retorts, "What's the matter, you were baptized, weren't you?" "Yes," Michael replies, "but I renounce my baptism." "You can't do that," Archie says, "You can renounce your belly button, but it won't go away!" Archie was a better theologian than most on that point. It has happened. It is a Word from without. It sticks. Nothing can change that. It will not be manipulated by our internality. No doubt that is what rankles us as old beings. It is part of the offense. But the point is that if we can do nothing about it, so also the devil can do nothing about it. In the end it may be our last line of defense. Who knows how we shall die? Demented, raving, despairing? The alien Word will still be there. So Luther, when he was driven to despair by the devil in his tribulation (*Anfechtung*), unable to escape wallowing in his own subjectivity, could at last only cry out "I am baptized!" Precisely so do sacraments save us.

The externality of the Word sealed by the sacraments saves us from the threat of the hidden agenda, the idea that there is some behind-the-scenes operation of the Spirit upon which we can only wait, some secret grace for which we can only hope and pray. Faith must not be so internalized. The fact that we are saved by faith alone must not be taken to mean that we are saved by reliance on our own inner resources alone. As Luther can put it in the Large Catechism:

> Our know-it-alls, the new spirits, assert that faith alone saves and that works and external things contribute nothing to this end. We answer: It is true, nothing that is in us does it but faith. . . . But these leaders of the blind are unwilling to see that faith must have something to believe— something to which it may cling and upon which it may stand. Thus faith clings to the water and believes it to be Baptism in which there is sheer salvation and life, not through the water, as we have sufficiently stated, but through its incorporation with God's Word and ordinance and the joining of his name to it. When I believe this, what else is it but believing in God as the one who has implanted his Word in this external ordinance and offered it to us so that we may grasp the treasure it contains?[7]

Faith must have something to believe, something to which it may cling and upon which it may stand! That pronouncement comes no doubt as something of a shock to us because we tend to understand faith as a strictly internal or more "spiritual" affair. But it is the very concrete externality of the Word and the sacrament embedded in it that calls forth and supports faith. Faith is not centered on itself. Faith is not something we mysteriously get somewhere which subsequently admits us to the sacraments. Faith is called forth by the sacramental Word. Faith is precisely a faith in the God who comes in the sacrament. Faith depends on, clings to, stands on, just this externality. Otherwise it feeds on its own internality.

Indeed, in this view, words are no more or less spiritual than the material signs. The tendency to hold that they are is a prejudice that stems largely from the old free-choice paradigm. Words address us as rational, free, and thus spiritual beings. In our freedom and internality we are called upon to make our choices and to preside over the operation. Sacraments do not fit the paradigm. We fear that our rational freedom is somehow being circumvented. So we try to reduce them to mere signs or symbols of our inner decisions.

But where the Word is understood as the proclamation coming from without that puts to death the old to raise up the new, as attack on the autonomous and continuously existing self, matters are quite different. The Word itself is an external Word, fully as "material" for that matter, as sacramental elements. Faith is precisely the faith that God has encountered us from without in this external Word, that God has showed his hand, that there is no more hidden agenda. What was hidden has been revealed. The new has come. Sacraments embedded in such a Word are one with it. They do exactly what the word does. They attack the old to slay it, to drown it, and so to call forth the new. It is precisely this externality that calls forth faith and upon which faith rests. The object of faith is just this external and sacramental Word.

We worry a great deal these days about "feeling." People complain that they don't "feel" saved. Perhaps the best reply is to ask, "What do you expect to feel? Feel the water! Feel the bread and wine on your lips! That is all you need to feel!" Faith must not be separated from its object. Again Luther in the Large Catechism:

Now, these people [the enthusiasts] are so foolish as to separate faith from the object to which faith is attached and bound on the ground that the object is something external. Yes, it must be external so that it can be perceived and grasped by the senses and thus brought into the heart, just as the entire Gospel is an external, oral proclamation. In short, whatever God effects in us he does through such external ordinances. No matter where he speaks—indeed, no matter for what purpose or by what means he speaks—there faith must look and to it faith must hold.[8]

But now this turn from the internal to the external, the inner to the outer, this claim of the "alien" Word upon us, confronts us in renewed fashion with the age-old problem of the objective efficacy and validity of the sacraments. The stress on the external is not without a certain peril. The peril appears in the medieval idea that sacraments work automatically (*ex opera operato*), just by being done, apart from our subjective participation. The medieval idea was that sacraments "worked" just by being done as long as the individual posed no obstacle to them. The attempt thereby, quite laudable in itself, was to guarantee the objective validity of the sacraments so that they were not dependent on subjective vagaries.

Most Protestants objected that this turned sacraments into a species of ecclesiastical "magic." They tried to solve the problem largely by rejecting the externality and the objectivity, turning sacraments into outward demonstrations or symbols of our inner convictions. But therewith sacraments dropped out of the proclamation in favor of the preached Word. The preached Word, consequently, also lost its sacramental character.

The Lutheran objection to the medieval understanding was quite different, however. Luther did not object to the externality as such, nor certainly to the objectivity. He did not raise the cry of magic; his objection to the automaticity of the sacraments was carefully nuanced. Luther's complaint was that the medieval view did not sufficiently consider or expound the matter of faith in relation to the sacraments. Faith is the only possible aim and receptacle for what sacraments have to give. The point of the sacraments embedded in the proclamation is to create faith, to put the unbeliever to death, and raise up the believer who trusts in that proclamation.

It is useful here to recall the distinction between validity and efficacy. Sacraments are valid in and of themselves. The promise is given, the act done. Nothing can change that. But they are efficacious only when they succeed in creating faith. They work only through faith. They are not magic potions or vitamin pills. Such things work often without our knowing or our contribution, but sacraments do not. We must be grasped by them as proclamation. But this does not mean that they are merely subjectivized or internalized. As external Word they work to create the faith that receives them. The faith in question is not one gotten apart from the sacrament which then makes the sacrament work. The faith here is faith in the sacrament and the sacramental Word. Sacraments work, that is, by creating the faith which receives them.

So does the Word make its way into the "heart." Precisely because it is entirely objective it possesses us subjectively. There is no sundering of the outer and the inner here. It is simply a matter of setting things in proper order. As Luther put it in the words quoted above, "It must be external so that it can be perceived and grasped by the senses *and thus brought into the heart*, just as the entire Gospel is an external, oral proclamation." It is the very externality that grasps us internally.

Sacraments as Attack on Unfaith

Since, then, the sacraments are embedded in the proclamation, they are part and parcel of it and should so be proclaimed. The proclaimed Word and the sacramental Word belong inextricably together. Where they are driven apart both lose their true character and the tie to faith is lost. The sacraments divorced from the proclaimed Word tend to become "magic" in the worst sense, quasi-physical acts which supposedly work automatically. On the other hand, a proclaimed Word without embedded sacrament becomes a merely internal word, a word addressed to one in one's internality which gets lost in the black hole of the self.

Furthermore, the divorce between Word and sacrament can only lead to gross misunderstanding of the sacraments themselves. If there is general ignorance about sacraments and a good deal of superstition surrounding them today, then not only is instruction concerning them needed, but proclamation of them. The tendency abroad in the church today to shore up sacramental understanding by withholding them and introducing more strenuous discipline at this point is not likely to help much. The modern world will only perceive this as a new species of rigorism and moralism. The greatest ally and perhaps the last chance we have in this regard is the proclamation. If people do not know what sacraments are and what benefit they proffer then they must be proclaimed as the alien word that does the same thing as the preached word. They must, that is, find their way into the proclamation itself. They ought to be proclaimed as an act that does the same thing to us as the audible word. In the preaching of the sacraments, that is, the event is to be preached so as to do the same thing as "doing the text" to the hearers does. One must not chicken out and domesticate the alien words, turn them into mere community celebrations, natural rites of passage, and what not.

Like the preached word, the sacraments in the first instance are the letter that kills. They have a cutting edge. The very alienness of the sign makes that evident. So do we complain about a baptism done to us, perhaps, before we have any say in the matter. We forget that the water is after all out first to drown the old Adam, not to coddle his fancies. In a real sense we never have anything to say in the matter. We have had our say and that is just the sickness unto death. The sacraments must be proclaimed without compromise as a Word coming from without, entirely outside our ken, to save us. The very thing the old being finds reprehensible is what is going to save in the end. It is good we have no say. As alien words the sacraments first sound our death knell before they can save. All this must be recognized and driven home in the proclamation. Sacraments kill in order to make alive. The proclamation must make apparent that we are here being saved because our case is taken in hand by the living God.

Where this is realized the troublesome and persistent question of the place of the elements can be given a different theological cast. Where sacraments are understood as a kind of "magic potion," the words become the incantation that is somehow supposed to "change" the elements to make them bearers of divine presence. So the words need not be addressed to the hearers at all. Or where sacraments are understood as sacred analogies or symbolic actions one rummages about in the phenomenology of religion to conjure up the symbolic significance of the proceedings. One talks about the nature of the water, the grinding and mingling of the wheat, the crushing of the grape. Perhaps it is that one tries to ameliorate the alienness, the stubborn otherness of the material by fitting it into another more natural story. It is the sacramental equivalent to allegorizing: the elements are taken out of the story of Jesus and put into a more natural context. But the elements will not disappear into another story. They find their place in the story of Jesus and nowhere else. One is reminded of the old arguments about whether the body and blood of Christ were changed by the human digestive process upon being devoured. Luther, with the Fathers, acidly replied that our bodies, not Christ's, are changed! The elements stay in their story and our lives are being changed by them, not vice versa. The very externality, the materiality is part of the attack on our unfaith. The elements participate in this attack. It is no doubt something of an offense that I, great spiritual being that I am, should have to depend on being washed or eating a bit of bread and drinking a sip of wine for salvation. But so it is and so it must be preached. When they are so preached they hold their place as part and parcel of the eschatological Word.

Baptism

Baptism regenerates. It drowns the old being together with trespasses and sins and raises up the new being in faith. How does it do that? Simply by being done to us as an external Word according to the Word and command of God. If sin is basically unfaith, baptism is the remedy for sin because it creates faith. It gives faith something to believe, to hold to, and so saves from sin. It is a Word of God addressed directly and concretely to us. It has our name on it. There is no mistake about to whom it may be addressed. The sermon is addressed to all those assembled and we may think it addressed to someone else. There is no such mistake possible in baptism. It is concretely and unmistakably "for you." God claims you and you are sealed with the sign of the cross forever. And so it must be proclaimed so that we hear it again and again.

The major controversy surrounding baptism in the history of the church has been about just what baptism accomplishes. The Roman Catholic claim was that baptism removes original sin. The remaining sin and concupiscence were regarded not as sin per se, but rather the seeds of sin, the stuff from which sin arises. The Reformation criticism of this claim was that while it was a laudable attempt to give objective efficacy to baptism, it tended to overshoot the mark. It tended to imply that original sin was somehow mechanically or automatically removed just by the performance of the act. Thus the continuance of sin after baptism became a problem. Where the act does not bring death and new life one always runs afoul of the time problem. If the old subject just continues, what happens afterward? If one discovers that sin also continues (as it no doubt does), what is one to say about the effectiveness of the act? The claims lead more to turmoil of conscience than to comfort.

The Lutheran Reformers wanted to keep the saving efficacy and objectivity of baptism without making exaggerated claims that disturb rather than comfort consciences. Baptism, they said, removed the guilt ✓ of original sin, but did not automatically remove original sin itself. Sin is not a quantum of some sort which can simply be removed in more or less magical fashion. What is missing in such views, once again, is the place of proclamation and faith. Since baptism embedded in the proclamation creates faith, it places sin under radical attack. Thus, though sin is not automatically removed, the Reformers said, it can no longer rule. Baptism, like all the salvific acts of God, does not remove but exposes the depth and persistence of sin, but in so doing dethrones it. Then sin can no longer rule. By faith we recognize that we are at once just and sinner (*simul iustus et peccator*), at once claimed by God at the same time as we see we are sinners. Sin is exposed and so becomes the object of this radical attack from without. Baptism, by being constantly proclaimed and so renewed daily, is a crucial part of this attack.

A Protestantism that presupposes the free-choice paradigm, however, does not know what to make of baptism. For the most part such so-called "evangelical" Protestantism is highly suspicious of baptism and quite often indulges in something of a polemic against it. Because all emphasis is placed on the importance of the will's "decision for Christ," baptism as God's act from without falls out of the proclamation and becomes, indeed, its enemy. "You can't depend on your baptism. You have to make your conscious decision for Jesus." That becomes the burden of the proclamation. Proclamation is allied against the sacrament. But therewith proclamation too loses its character as external Word and becomes mere explanation appealing to choice while the self just sinks back into itself, and so is lost.

But the tendency for baptism to slip out of the proclamation can have disastrous effect even in churches that espouse a high view of

its saving efficacy. Separated from the proclamation baptism gets iso-
lated. Worry grows among the clergy about proper baptismal practice,
especially that of too generous infant baptism. Among the people
meanwhile either custom or superstition takes over. One gets the baby
baptized because it is the thing to do or "just in case." There is movement afoot among some, therefore, to reintroduce a more stringent
baptismal discipline, and to withhold baptism from those who do not
seem qualified or to move more toward adult baptism. While not
wishing to dispute the need for more discipline in the church, it does
seem somewhat perverse to attempt to protect baptism by taking it
away from people. It is unlikely that such moves will engender anything
but resentment today. People will mostly get exactly the wrong message about baptism. It would seem more appropriate to put baptism
back within the proclamation so that it can be preached as the saving
event it indeed is. Proclamation is just about the only weapon left in
our arsenal that has not really been tried in this respect. Whatever
discipline there is can only be effective if it flows spontaneously from
a sacrament firmly embedded in the proclamation of God's unconditional grace. It is the sacrament embedded in the proclamation that
creates faith.

In any case baptism ought not to be performed without proclamation. But how is it to be proclaimed? It ought to be proclaimed
precisely in the teeth of all the objections that arise against it. It ought
to be proclaimed, that is, as the divine yes which counters all our no's.
The objections ought to be seen for what they are, the death rattle,
so to speak, of the old being that knows itself to be under radical
attack. It is the divine yes that intends to drown, to slay the old being
who hopes to continue in control, the divine yes, yes, yes, calling to
us to life out of death. "You are mine," says the Living God, "and I will
never let you go!" All the questions came tumbling out, questions by
which we hope to protect our old way of being. They are to be met
by a confident yes. "Do you mean to say that baptism is enough?" Yes!
It works forgiveness of sins, and where there is forgiveness of sins
there is life and salvation. Believe it, it's yours! "But can it have all
that significance even if I was just a baby and didn't know what was
going on? "Yes, for it is God who speaks that yes and God does not
give up or go back on promises. God is, after all, God."

"Ah, but what about my response?" "Are you saying that I don't have to make my decision?" That, of course, is one of the old being's trickiest questions. But even that has to be met with a confident yes. The old being likes to think of itself as a continuously existing subject who has life under control and therefore disposes over it in terms of what it has or does not have to do. But that is no longer the case. The old being is put to death to raise up a new being. It is no longer a matter of having to but of wanting to. So the answer remains yes; no response is necessary. The question now is rather "What's the matter, don't you want to? It is as though you were given a precious gift, or had won a sweepstakes or a lottery, or fallen in love, and stood agape, as Luther put it, like a cow staring at a new gate, muttering, 'Well, I suppose I have to respond.' " The old self is through, drowned in the gracious water and drawn out to say a joyful yes. Anyone who thinks it is a matter of have-to may just as well forget it! This is the divine yes calling to our yes in the Spirit. "Awake, oh sleeper, and arise from the dead! Come out of your stinking tomb!"

"But do you mean to say I am not free to reject?" Yes, I should hope so! The ability to reject is not freedom but the most desperate sort of bondage. It is precisely the strategy of the old being to call bondage freedom. "We are free to say no, aren't we?" So the protest usually goes. It is the death rattle, a last desperate line of defense for the old being. It is like arriving at the altar to make the wedding vow and protesting "I can say no, can't I?" To which the only adequate reply would be "What are you doing here then?"

"But does not baptism mean that God is taking a great risk? Won't people be likely to abuse it, take it for granted, use it as an excuse for laxity, and so forth?" Yes, no doubt. But who are we to begrudge the goodness of God? God has taken that risk all the way to death and will not turn back. Should God call off his goodness for the sake of the ungodly?

"But you don't mean that grace is irresistible, do you?" Another tricky question. But again the answer can only, in the end, be yes. "Yes, I find it to be so, don't you?" Remember it is grace we are talking about, not force. Absolute and unconditional grace has by very definition to be irresistible, one would think. Did you ever meet someone with irresistible grace? All that means is that you are utterly and completely captivated and so cannot finally "resist." Certainly God's whole purpose in coming was to make grace irresistible, was it not? Do we not hope that in the end all enemies will be overcome, all opposition stilled, grace completely triumphant and God all in all? How can that be if grace is not finally irresistible?

The questions are the death rattle of the old self who knows itself to be under the most radical attack from without. But the old self can only be drowned in the gracious water, not coddled. The answer is ever repeated and asserted yes. It is God's yes, and so he will go on saying it until finally we die of it and begin to whisper "Amen, so be it Lord." And then we shall be saved. Just so does baptism regenerate, put the old to death to raise up the new. And just so it is to be proclaimed. And just so we must hear it unto salvation. It must be heard and renewed daily. It will likely take a lifetime, but it will save.

In some such fashion baptism must enter into the proclamation. It participates in the attack on the old self all turned in upon itself. It calls us out of the self, out of bondage to the devil, the world, and the flesh into the newness of life. Proclamation must never take the tack of much so-called evangelical preaching that attempts to promote itself by calling baptism or its efficacy into question. If baptism has not been efficacious in people's lives, then the place to start is with the baptism, not by denigrating it. If people have "fallen away" from baptism, the place to start is with the fact that God has not turned away from them. To lead people away from baptism by substituting some propaganda about decisionism and so forth is only to lead them back into the Slough of Despond once again. To be saved is to be drawn out into the glorious light of the day of grace begun and continued in God's act of making new beings. Baptism embedded in the proclamation will do this. It is simply the gospel.

The Last Supper

The Last Supper presents the task of proclamation today with a problem somewhat different from that of baptism. The tendency in the case of baptism is to slight it or even to polemicize against it in favor of the preached Word. In the case of the Last Supper the tendency, especially among the more sacramentally inclined or perhaps one could say hierarchical churches, is to elevate the sacrament above the preached Word as the primary means of grace, or even as the central constituting event of the church. There is a tendency, in such instances, to speak in rather precious terms of "the most Holy Eucharist" as the sole or major grace-bestowing and church-forming event.

This tendency is perhaps understandable where proclamation has lost its graceful power as a Word that kills and makes alive, but it does not auger well even for the sacrament itself, and certainly not for the understanding of church and ministry. Where the supper is sundered from the life-creating proclamation it tends to become something we do rather than a sheer gift from God. It becomes, say, a "sacrifice" that we perform or in which we participate rather than God's gift to us. Ordained ministers, in turn, become a cadre of specially endowed priests ecclesiastically authorized to do the sacrifice, constitute and preside over the church. Where such views intrude, the supper rapidly loses its character as proclaimed and distributed gift, and the proclaimed Word likewise degenerates into explanation, something like instructions on the eucharistic box.

This kind of development set in rather early in the life of the church. In the desperate defense against gnostic and manichean dualisms the defenders of orthodoxy tended also to become suspicious of the eschatological dualism of the apostolic message. Unwittingly they became the enemies of the new age. The result was that the Word lost its force as a bearer of the eschatologically new here and now and became more or less information and explanation about an end which would come in due time. In such a strait, the sacraments became virtually the sole bearers of grace, events in which grace is "really" given.

Sundered from the eschatological framework the sacraments had difficulty holding their ground against alien commitments. Instead of eschatological signs and events creating faith they became bearers of supernatural grace that was to effect the appropriate transformation of life in the pursuit of virtue. Taken out of the eschatological time table they ran afoul of this-worldly time lines. Baptism, as we have already noted, was supposed to remove original sin. But then the question arose about sins committed after baptism in this world's time line. Early on there was some temptation to postpone baptism until one's deathbed when one was supposedly through with sinning. But that would only produce a church of unbaptized procrastinators, a rather unsatisfactory state of affairs, to say the least.

In general it seems that the sacrament of penance came to the rescue. Penance was popularly touted as the "second plank" to save after the "shipwreck" of baptism. But that only had the effect of further gutting the eschatological power of baptism and reducing it to a rite of initiation into the church and its penitential discipline. Whereupon the church and its priests becomes a hospital for sick souls, a rather joyless surrogate for the eschatological kingdom.

The belief that baptism is shipwrecked on the rocks of untimely sin could not but affect the supper as well. Since penance was viewed as the remedy for chronic and persistent sin there was strong pressure, especially in the West, to interpret the death of Christ as the supreme and infinitely worthy penitential sacrifice for sin. But once again such a construction runs afoul of this world's time line. Since there is no proclamation of the death and resurrection of Christ which kills and makes alive in the living present, the sacrifice slips away into the past. It is not once-for-all, it is just "once upon a time." But then there is no way we can participate in it. It becomes "history."

So other means must be devised to allow present participation. Enter the theology of the mass with its idea of the repeated or re-presented sacrifice. Since we were not there when they crucified our Lord, steps must be taken to bring him here. Popular Roman Catholic theology and piety inclined to the idea that the sacrifice was "repeated" in unbloodly fashion in the eucharistic ritual. More sophisticated scholastic and recent ecumenical theology prefers the idea that though not repeated, the sacrifice is made present again (represented) in the properly ordered ritual action of the mass. This, in turn, involves the idea of a priesthood specially endowed ontologically with the power to perform the ritual action of representation. Since Christ is not essentially present with his body and blood someone must have the authority and power to make him so. The failure to set the sacrament within the framework of eschatological time has a chain of consequences disastrous for the understanding of the church and its ministry.

The doctrine of the re-presentation of the sacrifice of Christ in the eucharistic ritual has made much headway in current ecumenical circles. Many think it to have removed the obstacles posed by the old ideas of repeated sacrifice and so to have provided a basis for ecumenical rapprochement. This is a disastrous miscalculation. The move from repetition to re-presentation is really only a cosmetic alteration.

The whole remains quite unaffected by eschatology. The basic idea of penitential sacrifice remains, together with all the assumptions about the meaning and direction of it, i.e., that it is offered by us to appease God, etc. The time line remains essentially unaltered requiring the same understanding of a priesthood specially endowed to make present what is essentially absent. It is quite consequent therefore that pressure is stepped up in ecumenical circles to adopt an understanding of ecclesiastical orders consonant with such views. Ministry and ecclesiastical orders becomes the crucial ecumenical question. Acceptance of the idea of ritual representation is at the root of the ecumenical problem today.

Usual Protestant objection has been a frontal attack on this position. Since the sacrifice of Christ was made once-for-all it cannot be repeated and need not be re-presented. Furthermore, as a consequence, there is then neither the necessity for nor the possibility of an ordained clergy endowed with the power to do it. The sacrifice remains a once-for-all event. But the traditional understanding of sacrifice was nevertheless retained. Given that, it just recedes into the past once again. One simply accepts the old framework and denies the ecclesiastical machinery set up to bridge the time gap. So the supper loses whatever present tense it had and recedes into the past once again. The old time line remains essentially intact. The only way one can participate in the past sacrifice is by memory. But that only means that the individual is to perform the feat of making the self contemporary by leaping over the time line to the past. The supper is not sheer gift but a rather prodigious task. To be sure, in any view of the supper, memory is invoked. We do this in remembrance of the Lord as we are mandated. But what we remember is his promise to be present here and now for us with his body and blood. We trust his promise to bridge the gap between then and now. When there is no presence remembrancing collapses back on itself. The supper becomes something we do. It loses its character as proclamation.

If the supper is to retain its place in the proclamation as sheer gift it would seem that considerable reformulation is necessary. This is what the Lutheran Reformers tried to initiate. In the first place, the very idea of the mass as a sacrifice came under insistent and repeated attack, especially in Luther. The mass was not to be understood as a sacrifice (*sacrificium*) but as a gift (*beneficium*).[9] The entire direction

174 Theology Is for Proclamation

of the ritual proceeding is to be reversed. At its very heart, the sacrament is not a sacrifice from the human side to God in any way, but rather a gift from God to us. This is, of course, quite consonant with what we have said in the section on atonement. Christ was sacrificed for us, not for God. Thus the supper is the body and blood of Christ given for you, not for God. The only possible sacrifice one could talk about as a result would be our sacrifice of praise and thanksgiving for such a gift. One might even, if one wished, say that in receiving this absolutely free gift we are sacrificed in such receiving. The old is put to death with Christ so the new can be raised. But it can be such only because in the supper the completely free gift is given to us.

The objection to the idea that sacraments work just by being done (*ex opera operato*) was therefore leveled not against the idea that the sacrament worked "magically" on us, but rather against the idea that it worked magically on God. The objection was to the idea that the ritual gives the priest, in pagan fashion, some means for manipulating God. That is, there was certainly no objection to the objectivity and from-withoutness of the sacrament, and certainly not against the idea that it works powerfully on us. Indeed, the charge of "magic" is reprehensible only when it is understood as a means placed in human hands for manipulating the gods. It is quite another matter when it is understood, so to speak, as God's "magic," God's way of getting to us to end the old and begin the new.

It is quite consequent, therefore, that the conceptuality which Luther liked to use to interpret the Last Supper was not sacrifice or even covenant but, leaning on Heb. 9:15-22, that of *testament.* What was established on the night when Jesus was betrayed was his last will and testament, promised to his heirs. When the testator dies, the will goes into effect and so is to be distributed as promised. Thus what is to go on in the church repeatedly and throughout all time is the distribution of the testament to the heirs according to the will of the one who has died. Therefore, what is to be remembered and repeated in this sacrament is not primarily what occurred on Calvary, but what occurred on the night in which he was betrayed, the Last Supper.[10] Thus the preferred terminology for this sacrament is just that: "the Last Supper" or "the Holy Communion" rather than "Eucharist," "Sacrifice," and the like. The idea that the event of Christ's death is to be repeated or even re-presented in the ritual action results from a too hasty and unquestioned conflation of what happened on the night in which he was betrayed with what happened on Calvary. The whole is then subsequently interpreted in terms of the rather obscure conceptuality of sacrifice with its attendant problems. The net result is that the reality of the sacrament as gift (*beneficium*), tends to disappear behind the facade of analogies, ritualism, and ecclesiastical pretension.

The conceptuality of testament, however, provides a more simple and straightforward understanding that supports and drives directly to the proclamation and distribution of the sheer gift. The sacrament is not a ritualistic analogy of what happened long ago on Calvary. The sacrament is what it claims to be, the distribution of the last will and testament of our Lord and Savior, the body and blood of Christ given to his heirs. We meet to remember and receive the promised inheritance, not to "play Calvary." We are making a reality claim in this event: "This is. . . ." The conceptuality of testament enhances that reality claim. The theology of eucharistic sacrifice does not.

But this claim puts all the more pressure on the question of the presence of the body and blood of Christ in the supper. How is it so that the body and blood are here given and received? It is important to stress that the specific benefit of this sacrament is the body and blood as the words promise and declare. That is, the question is not that of the more general or what one might call "spiritual" presence of Christ in our gatherings. No one disputes that. Every Christian communion believes that where two or three are gathered in Christ's name, he is there. But that is not at question here and that is not what the argument was about at the time of the Reformation or subsequently. The question is that of the presence of the body and blood "in, with, and under" the bread and wine so that there is not only "spiritual" participation but oral and physical eating according to the promise. How is this to be conceived?

The Western tradition prior to the Reformation, as we have seen, tried to solve this problem ecclesiastically, that is, by claiming that the church through its holy orders, its ordained priesthood, had the power to make the body and blood present again in the Eucharist. This opened the way to much nonsense about the church being the "extension of the incarnation," or "the true sacrament" through the Holy Orders and so forth. Reformed Protestantism simply denied this ecclesiastical claim flat out but then reverted to more "spiritual" understandings of presence. Christ's body and blood are mediated spiritually to faith, with the danger that the whole will collapse inward upon itself once again. The presence does not create faith, but depends on it.

The Lutheran Reformers, however, proposed that the question should be dealt with christologically (that is, by developing the consequence for presence flowing out of the incarnation, death, and resurrection of Christ himself). The starting point for all this was simply the Word of promise, the testament, given by Christ himself: "This is my body, this is my blood," and subsequent biblical witness to the reality of our partaking of and participating in this gift. It must always be remembered that it is the testament of Christ and the biblical Word that stands first in their deliberations. Whatever comes subsequently is simply an attempt to rearrange one's thinking so as to accord with the biblical witness. Reflecting in the light of faith in the promise led them to challenge the basic assumptions about the time line and presence that had militated against that promise.[11] The advent, death, and resurrection of Christ, if it is not just a once-upon-a-time but a once-for-all event, must bring with it some fundamental and permanent alterations. Christological reflection must take account of this so as to lead back to appropriate proclamation in both Word and sacrament.

Thus the Lutheran Reformers came to deal with the questions of presence christologically rather than ecclesiologically or spiritually. This they did by the teachings about the ubiquity of Christ in his human nature and the communication of the divine attributes to the human nature in the person of Christ (*communicatio idiomatum, genus maiestaticum*). Because of the unity of the person in the incarnate Son, the human nature—the body and the blood—can be as present everywhere as the divine nature is and wills to be. Whether this presence was, so to speak, automatically guaranteed or only according to the will of the divine was, apparently, arguable. But the point here is that the Lutherans made the move to solve the problem by asking what difference the incarnation, death, resurrection, and glorification of Christ makes permanently, rather than through a doctrine of Holy Orders or by spiritualizing. The body and blood of Christ are present for us in the supper because his incarnation, death, and resurrection have made permanent alteration in the structure of reality.

This development of Christology has met, however, with rather vigorous opposition, especially from the side of Reformed Protestantism. If divine attributes such as ubiquity or omnipresence are communicated to a human nature, then that nature is no longer human. It is simply obliterated. The old Alexandrian temptation to swallow up the human in the divine stands near at hand. Either that or it creates a metaphysical monstrosity. The communication of attributes, whatever it is trying to say, becomes the warrant of all sorts of ecclesiastical abuse if it is understood as an abstract universal, a permanent condition.

Clearly these objections need to be heard. But what is needed is a reconstruction in the understanding of presence which supports and drives to the proclamation in both Word and sacrament. This is what the christological developments in the direction of ubiquity and communication of attributes were designed to do. Where there is no such presence and communication, the time gap is not bridged. Then not only is the presence in the sacrament lost, but also there is no warrant for the claim that the quite human word of the church and its ministers is in fact the very Word of God. In other words, the entire basis for the claim that the Word of direct and concrete proclamation, the "I declare unto you . . . ," is the Word of God here and now is swept away. Not only is one left with only a memory in the supper, but the words of the preacher are also just "memory work," information about the past with exhortations to do something about it.

How shall we deal with this impasse between obliterating the human by dissolving it in divine ubiquity and letting it remain human so that it just lapses into "history"? Perhaps it is necessary and possible to make something of the same move here as we have suggested in our treatment of Christology itself, the move from the language of being to the language of act. The permanent change that the incarnation, death, and resurrection of Christ brings is to place this age under its eschatological end (*telos*). Christ, as the one universally rejected and yet vindicated in the resurrection, sacrifices himself into sheer and unconditional presence for us. The fact that the divine is communicated to the human means that in and through his quite human story, he does God, does the end and new beginning to us. Because we killed him and God nevertheless raises him, he is now always present for us. His story is the story of God for us. To borrow from Bonhoeffer, Jesus does not need to have ubiquitous presence added to his being in some abstract or extrarevelational fashion, but just is, by virtue of death and resurrection, the one who is now always for us.[12] Or, as Robert Jensen has put it, the more abstract notion of omnipresence translates into the proclamation that "neither death nor life, . . . nor things present, nor things to come, . . . nor height, nor depth, . . . will be able to separate us from the love of God in Christ Jesus."[13] The time line, the spatial limitation of this age is broken by the eschatological proclamation of the new and its reality breaking in upon us.

But just as in the Christology proper, this move will avoid collapse into low Christology and sacramentology only where it is understood and proclaimed as death and life. The Last Supper must be understood and proclaimed also as such. Just as in baptism we meet our death and the promise of new life, so also here we encounter the death of the old and the hope of the new. "When you eat this bread and drink this cup you proclaim the Lord's death until he comes" (1 Cor. 11:26). It is death-dealing to pretentious god-seekers to be reduced to eating a bit of bread and drinking a sip of wine for salvation. But just so it is also life-giving in the promise. It is the breakthrough of the new in the midst of our time.

Perhaps one could say that in the sacrament God invades even the matter of our time to reclaim it for the promise of the new. In the fallen world water does not wash us clean from sin. Remember Lady Macbeth! In baptism, however, water is reclaimed to cleanse utterly. And so it shall be one day. In the fallen world bread and wine do not satisfy. They are that for which we struggle and fight and kill, that which we must earn in the sweat of our brows. Now they are reclaimed. This is my body, my blood, and it is free, it is for all. It is the end to sin and the beginning of the new life in him who died and rose and so made all things new. It is a foretaste of the heavenly banquet in which all things, body and spirit, will be put back together. Where this eschatological "flavor" is recaptured, the sacraments can take their appointed and proper place in the proclamation. Systematic theology ought to be so constructed as to make this possible.

Ministry

Now we can briefly draw things together in a view of the ministry and mission of the church which flows from all this. Ministry is first and foremost the ministry of proclamation, the concrete speaking of the Word of God, doing of the sacramental deed, in the living present. The primary paradigm for ministry is absolution—concrete, present-tense, I-to-you declaration in Word and sacrament authorized by the triune God: "I declare unto you the gracious forgiveness of all your sins in the name of the Father, the Son, and the Holy Spirit." That is the culmination of all we have been saying. Ministry is the actual doing of the deed.

Almost since the beginning churches in the Reformation tradition have had difficulty establishing a solid and perhaps we could say appropriately high doctrine of ministry in the shadow of more Roman Catholic understandings of holy orders. Lutheranism in particular has vacillated between a low understanding of ministry in terms of purely functional operations where ministry is necessary merely for the sake of "good order" and ostensibly "higher" views supported by episcopal and Roman claims to ontological status. In the former case, ministry is a function assigned to one called merely for the sake of order. The called and ordained minister tends to be looked on as a more or less dispensable "hired hand" of the congregation. In the latter the called and ordained ministry acquires something of an ontological status necessary and "constitutive" for the church. The clergy are the "real" church, or at least church makers. The question from which discussion must start is whether it is possible to arrive at a view of ministry that avoids the pitfalls of these two alternatives.

In the terms of this study a major contributing factor to this constant vacillation is a failure to comprehend just what ministry is and what it is supposed to accomplish. The view of ministry, that is, has not been sufficiently rooted in an understanding of what proclamation is all about. The ministry of proclamation, as we have repeatedly insisted, is the concrete doing of the divine election in the living present. In the words of the text at the beginning of this chapter, to minister is "to preach . . . the unsearchable riches of Christ, and to make all people see what is the plan of the mystery hidden for ages in God who created all things; that through the church the manifold wisdom of God might now be made known to the principalities and powers in the heavenly places." Through the church and its ministry, that is, in the here and now, the mystery is to be made known, to be made public. What was hidden is to be revealed even to the principalities and powers in high places. All this is according to God's eternal purpose in Jesus Christ. Ministry is doing the deed of election here and now, publicizing the mystery in and through the church. It has to do with the concrete, present-tense, public doing of the deed. Everything has been accomplished in Christ so that this is now to be done.

Ministry is obedient service to the divine deed accomplished in Jesus Christ in the living present. Ministers ought to operate in the consciousness that this is what they are supposed to be doing. Where this consciousness is absent, one of two things seems to happen. Either ministry degenerates into the mere dissemination of information about the past deed of reconciliation, explaining rather than proclaiming, in case it is not clear what called and ordained ministry is for, since most any sufficiently intelligent and pious person can do that. Or, ministry is elevated to the status of a special ontological class endowed with the ability to complete what is supposedly lacking in the divine deed of reconciliation. The minister, that is, has to be elevated to an "order" of beings who can "re-present" the sacrifice of Christ because Christ did not quite manage to overcome the problem of time. The ministers, somehow, are elevated to a class of being able to do what Christ could not do. The mark that distinguishes them from the laity, therefore, is that they can "preside" at the eucharist.

But if ministry is the public doing of the divine deed of election in the living present, why is ordained ministry necessary? Is not every Christian obligated to do the deed? In the first place, it should be clear that ministry is the task of the church and thus of all the baptized. All are called by virtue of baptism to the ministry of making public the mystery hidden from the ages but now revealed in Jesus Christ. All are authorized and obligated to do it. This is entailed in the priesthood of all believers. Baptism, not ordination, as the Reformers insisted, is what makes priests.

Some care must be taken at this point, however. The fact that all are called to ministry does not mean that everything the baptized do is ministry as such. If ministry is service to the divine deed of election, one ought to avoid the current inflation of the terms that inclines to call anything and everything ministry. Where everything is ministry, specific and concrete service to the deed of God in Christ easily gets lost, on the one hand, and the quite worldly nature of God-given tasks in this world gets obscured, on the other. Our priesthood as believers gets turned topsy-turvy with our call to minister. As believers, as the baptized, we are priests to and for one another. It is the business of priests to sacrifice—in this case to sacrifice ourselves in deeds of service and love for one another. We should, in this regard, speak of the priesthood of the baptized rather than the ministry of the baptized when referring to our daily tasks. A minister, however, is different from a priest. It is the task of a minister strictly to follow the orders of the sovereign. One should not confuse priesthood and ministry. Such confusion would be avoided if the understanding of priesthood were more clearly worked out in terms of the doctrine of vocation, and distinguished from the call to minister. We are called to be priests in our worldly tasks for one another. We are, in addition, called to do ministry, to follow the orders of the Lord. But not everything the Christian does should be called ministry lest such calling simply be lost.

Ordained ministry takes the cause of making the mystery public one last step. Here the drive to publicize the mystery culminates in a public office. In ordained ministry, the Christian vocation to minister "crosses the line," converges upon, or coins itself in an office in this world and all that is involved in that. In the public office the age to come, the kingdom of God, makes its claim known in this age. Ordained ministry is consequently a precarious and at the same time audacious move. It is precarious because on the one hand the possibilities for abuse, pretense, perversion, high-handed clericalism, and the like, are legion. The temptation to politicize the office, to usurp for it too much of this world's power, always lies near at hand. Formerly that was done by claiming power over the state and appropriating royal forms of authority—swine rights, succession, and so forth. More recently, it seems, the urge is to involve the office in political advocacy. Such abuse of the office generally leads to its discrediting, to slighting, demeaning, disdaining, to anticlericalism. The audacity of the move to public office must be recognized, however, because here a claim is made, an authority is asserted in the trappings of this age, so to speak, which is not of this age. The public office announces the end, the limit, the goal (*telos*) of all offices. The precariousness and audacity of the move to public office means that the church must take utmost care in how it orders this office.

Ordained ministry is ordered ministry. It is that in a double sense. It is a ministry one is ordered (called) to do, and it is to be done in ordered (carefully regulated) fashion. Ordained ministry is ministry incarnated, so to speak, in the orders of this age, this public. It is crucial, therefore, to look upon it not as a being elevated above this world as such but rather as an instance in which the new age invades, and stakes out its claim over and against the public order of this world. This is the view of ministry presented in the Augsburg Confession. Articles 5 and 14 set it forth quite tersely and plainly. Article 5 says that in order to obtain the justifying faith claimed in Article 4, "God has instituted the office of ministry, that is provided the Gospel and the sacraments." Through these concrete and external means God the Holy Spirit works faith when and where he pleases. But Article 5 does not yet explicitly speak of ordained ministry though it seems strongly to imply it. Article 14, however, provides the conclusive move to the public office: "Nobody should publicly teach or preach or administer the sacraments in the church without a regular call."

It is important to look carefully at these articles to get the point of what they are trying to say. In the first place, the office is a divine institution, not a human invention. It is not an option that churches may or may not exercise. The office is God's idea, not ours, because God provided the gospel and the sacraments. God insisted on making the mystery public through the proclamation. The German version says it quite clearly: "*Gott hat das predigtamt eingesetzt ...*" ("God established the office of preaching"). The office, that is, is instituted by virtue of the fact that God has gone public in and through Jesus Christ, the gospel and the sacraments. God has invaded the age in just this way and staked out his claim. The confession, therefore, avoids the usual impasse created by arguments about whether Jesus "ordains" a special class of followers whose "rights" are guaranteed by a line of succession, or whether Jesus envisaged or intended such. By virtue of what happened to Jesus, the gospel and the sacraments are given, and with them ministry is entailed and demanded. The gospel and the sacraments demand the office. God thereby instituted the office.

The sole difference between clergy and laity is comprehended in the fact that the clergy are called and ordered to a public exercise

of the office. The move from Article 5 to Article 14 is quite consequent
and natural. "Nobody," says Article 14, "should teach or preach or
administer the sacraments publicly without a regular call." The confessors see no inconsistency between divine institution and churchly
calling to the public office. All public offices, for them, are divinely
instituted, even though the particular mode of filling such office is left
to the needs and demands of times and places. On this score the public
office of ministry is no different from other public offices. God institutes, the church orders, just as in the state God institutes the office
of the head of state, magistrate, and so forth, and these are ordered
according to existing political structures. Nor can there be any real
cause for competition between lay and clerical exercise of the office.
The whole church, all its members, are to be involved and concerned
about the public exercise of the office, the drive to make the claim
of God public. Since it is the concern of all the baptized, no one can
arrogate the public exercise of the office to himself or herself. It is
not a private matter. It is God's gift to the church. Therefore, the
church through its quite public ordering calls and approves those
appropriately qualified to exercise the public office.

This means, however, that the congregations of the church do
not own the office nor do they "transfer" their authority to it. The gift
of the office has been given by God to the church and demands filling
in responsible fashion. The church through its structures is to do this,
but the church does not give the office its authority. It is helpful to
make a distinction here between the authority to fill the office and
the authority of the office itself. The church has the authority to fill
the office, but the authority of the office is rooted in the Word its
holders are called to proclaim. The church in its ordering is to see
that the Word may have free and public course in its midst and in the
world.

But at this point it is necessary to be clear about what a public
exercise of the office entails so as to complete the understanding of
ordained ministry. Public exercise of the office does not simply mean
that it is done "in public." It gets its meaning rather from the fact that
for the confessors Christianity was a public cult (*cultus publicus*). It
belonged, that is, to the "republic" (*res publica*). The ordained minister
was in that sense akin to a public official who was authorized to do
the public acts of the cult in and for the people. The ordained minister

was to make public proclamation of and public argument for the Word of God, to care for the public witness and theology of the church, to administer the sacraments as public acts, and to call the public and its magistrates to public account before divine law.

Such public exercise of the office was set in contrast to a more private exercise in family, between individuals, among Christians. In such instances one had to do with Christianity as a private cult. This may be somewhat confusing since we have spoken throughout about publicizing the mystery. The point is that the mystery is to be made known, publicized, both in more "private" ways and through the explicitly public exercise of the office. Everyone is called to a "private" exercise of the office. The public exercise of the office, however, has to be publicly ordered. Only those regularly called are so ordered.

The difficulty encountered in the modern world with this distinction is that Christianity, or any religion for that matter, is no longer accorded the status of a public cult. The modern state has more or less taken over the public sphere altogether. It is concerned for the most part only with what affects the physical well-being of its citizens, the economy, defense of the realm, just distribution of goods and services, and so forth. Only such matters are considered "public affairs." The modern state cares little about religion as long as it does not interfere with public affairs. The result is that religion is banished to the sphere of private or individual matters. Christianity, too, quickly becomes a private cult.

The general result of banishment to the sphere of the strictly private is that the rationale for ordained ministry tends to disappear altogether. When the church becomes simply a private cult it is difficult to say just why any Christian cannot perform most if not all the "functions" ordinarily assigned to the ordained. A democratic society will find it perhaps presumptuous to assume that some are raised to a different level by ecclesiastical fiat. Since religion is a private matter, what difference can ordination make? Furthermore, when clergy no longer understand the office as public doing of the deed authorized in Jesus Christ, when they no longer do what could be called public proclamation, teaching, or absolution, but rather just make public display of private emotion and experience or invest most of their time in private counseling, what does one need ordination for? Ordination per se does not automatically confer any noticeable skills or make a person "nice." Cannot properly "sensitized" lay people do just as well? Ironically, the state itself turns out to be one of the last holdouts here. The state still clings to the vestigial remains of the public office when it refuses to allow just anyone to marry, acquire tax exemptions, perform chaplain's duties in institutions, and the like. For more public duties, the state wants to know about ordination.

Since the idea of a public office has largely been lost, ordained ministry has to go begging for a rationale. Quite naturally it tends to take refuge in the one manifestly public act left, the Sacrament of Holy Communion. Even here there are pressures to privatize of late, to do the eucharist in cozy and private groups. The church becomes a "support group." Even in more public celebrations the ordained are more and more marginalized by lay substitutes. Since ministry is no longer the eminently public act of doing the electing deed, it becomes more a matter of our private "sharing" with one another. So it is more meaningful, no doubt, to receive the bread and wine from someone "just like me" than from one ordained to public office. The sole function left for the ordained minister is to "preside." Why one has to be ordained to do that remains something of a mystery. Cannot intelligent lay people read the words in the book? Since the most eminently pastoral act, that of the actual distribution, has largely been taken over, it is not strange that clerics have to fall back on the old idea that ordination somehow mysteriously imparts the power to re-present the sacrifice. Having lost its status as a public office, ministry seeks validation in the hidden agenda, the behind-the-scenes theology. The public office becomes mystified. Ministry gets its rationale from a theory of the eucharist, and as such becomes constitutive for the church, and the church in turn, is understood primarily as the "eucharistic community."

Where the public office of ministry is understood as the doing of the divine deed in the living present, however, it is possible to recover a "high" doctrine of ministry without succumbing to mere occasional functionalism on the one hand or an ontologizing view of holy orders on the other. We do indeed need to be careful about what we say of this office today. What is needed is a doctrine that comprehends its crucial importance at the same time as it avoids the ecclesiastical mythology which only provokes anticlericalism. Ordination does not mean elevation to some higher order, but rather invasion of the order of this world with the Word of the gospel to announce God's claim upon the world. In spite of pressures to privatize, the church must not surrender this claim to public office. Here the church carries through on God's eschatological claim.

To be called and ordained to the public office is to be called through the church to give public voice to the Word of God. It is not the office holder as such who transcends the congregation by elevation to a higher order, but the Word of God. The only ultimate defense against anticlericalism is the proper preaching of this Word so that the gospel is heard. To be called and ordained is to take up this public office. The ordained pastor is not a guru or a shrink or a perpetual optimist or nice person, but a public proclaimer. The ordinand, therefore, is to be properly examined and ordered to do the task. One is not called to this public office to peddle private opinions, but to serve, proclaim, and care for the public witness and theology of the church in a particular time and place, to have the guts (or the Spirit, in theological terms), to say it and do it. To that end the church through the holders of this office lays on hands, prays, and invokes the Spirit on those called so to do.

The Church

Finally, we need to say a word about the understanding of the church that flows from all this. We confine ourselves to the basics. We can do no better at the outset than follow the definition of the church given in the Augsburg Confession: The church "is the assembly of all believers among whom the Gospel is preached in its purity and the holy sacraments are administered according to the Gospel."[14] The church, that is, is the assembly in which the proclamation of the gospel in Word and sacrament occurs. It is this proclamation that calls the church, the assembly of hearers and receivers, into being. Upon hearing and receiving, the believers undertake to speak again what they have heard, give what has been received, and make appropriate arrangements to do so.

In other words, the church is not just any assembly that happens to call itself by the name of Jesus for whatever reason or purpose, or where there may be orders calling themselves holy and so on. To counter a current heresy, the church is not just "people." That assertion may rightly controvert the idea that the church is a building or even an institution, but it too easily forgets that the church is a gathering called and shaped by the gospel of its Lord, Jesus Christ. The Christian church occurs where the quite specific activity known as speaking the gospel occurs and the sacraments are administered according to that gospel. Where that does not occur there is no such thing as the church of Jesus Christ.

It is vital, however, at the conclusion of this study in which the necessity of proclamation has been so relentlessly promoted, to resist the claim being touted more and more in ecumenical circles that the office of ordained ministry is somehow "constitutive" of the church. The office constitutes nothing. Christ is the head of the church and the sheer giver of all good. The office is called forth and "instituted" by the sheer act of giving. It is the giving of the gift that constitutes the church and the office, not vice versa. The office is simply ministry: service called forth by the divine giving. To say more than that is to confuse the giving and the gift. The delivery of the gift, and, indeed, a "delivery boy" is quite necessary, but it does not constitute anything.[15]

The claim gaining currency in ecumenical dialogues that ordained ministry is constitutive of the church results only in a messy confusion between this age and the next. The office and its holders take on a status that suggests a transcendence of the eschatological limit. A "hierarchy" emerges that reaches beyond this age and/or mirrors that "of heaven," and so threatens the nature of the gospel. Soon one begins to invest theological capital in the status and authority of the delivery boy rather than in the gift. One spins theories and argues about the delivery systems. The "office of delivery" intrudes itself as a more or less independent reality between the giver of the gift and the receiver. Soon the delivery boys begin determining the nature of the gift and the conditions under which it can be given. The church becomes dominated by and defined as a delivery system ruled by the delivery boys, not the assembly constituted by the actual giving of the gift. It is as though the postal service were to intercept, regulate, censor, or perhaps set its own conditions for the delivery of the correspondence between the lover and the beloved. If the correspondence were merely human there might, of course, be some instances where censorship or interception is allowable. But surely where the lover is God, all must simply stand aside and serve. "The mail must go through!" "Woe is me if I preach not the gospel!" Recall the words of Luther,

That the gospel is preached and your king comes is not due to your power or merit, God must send it out of sheer grace. Thus there is no greater wrath of God than where He withholds the gospel and nothing but sin, error, and darkness remain. . . . "Behold," that is: "Your King comes"; you do not seek him, he seeks you. You do not find him, he finds you. Because the preachers come from him, not from you. Their sermon comes from him, not from you. Faith comes from him, not from you. And everything that faith works in you comes from him, not from you, so that you see clearly that where he does not come, there you remain on the outside, and that where the gospel is absent, there is no God, but only sin and corruption, though free will does, suffers, works, lives, as it pleases and wants.[16]

The church thus knows itself to be the hearer of the gospel. If it knows itself properly it will have no illusions about itself. It will know that it is constantly in the position of the hearer and that it will desire and have to hear ever and again. It will know that such speaking and hearing cannot be taken for granted. It will know itself to be the company of those who are always sinners who live from the concrete, present-tense proclamation (*simul iustus et peccator*). It will know that it cannot live today on yesterday's gospel. It must hear again and again and assembles so as to hear, and takes what steps it can to guarantee that it will indeed hear the gospel. It orders, cares for, and gathers around the public office.

As such, the church is hidden and revealed. It is hidden because the hearing of faith is not directly discernible or certifiable by the canons of this age. As such the church of "true believers" is an object of faith. It is the "body of Christ," the company of those who have been put to death and raised in Christ. The way of that company can never be readily comprehensible to this age. Its existence is a matter of faith. We believe in the holy catholic church.

This church is revealed in the preaching of the Word and the administering of the sacraments. Those are its predominant "marks." Should anyone want to know where it is, one can say it is where those things occur. The church, that is, is revealed in those acts that set us free from the power of sin, death, and the devil. It is revealed only in such acts of genuine liberation. One might add subsequent marks of such liberation such as the keys, prayer, suffering, bearing the cross, and so on, but these are mentioned only because they are marks of the liberation, not possibilities for tyranny. Where there are no such "marks" it is not the church with which we have to do but some other organization and its agenda, however pious or useful it might be.

The church, therefore, as hearer of the Word and receiver of the sacraments concerns itself, as pointed out in the previous section, with ministry, with the business of making the mystery known, both in its own "private" life and in its more "public" witness. It concerns itself with caring for and building up its members in the faith, and with filling the God-given office of ministry, with calling and ordaining appropriately qualified ministers to public proclamation. It takes steps to guarantee as best it can that what it has heard will be heard again, that the gospel be proclaimed. It arranges its organizational life to serve and foster the ministry of the gospel in Word and deed. It knows that this is its mission and believes that this is finally the only way it has to help the world: to "put an end" to it, a limit, and a goal (*telos*).

It is important to stress this hidden/revealed nature of the church today when proclamation seems to be on the decline in favor of other ways to make the church "visible." The hidden/revealed understanding of the church should replace the tendency to think in terms of the "invisible" and "visible." The invisible/visible conceptuality tends to convey too much an idealist understanding where the invisible is the ideal supposedly to become at least partially visible in our projects. The result is a strong drive for the church to become visible in this world's agendas. This appears especially to be true today in the constant pressure exerted for the church to align itself with movements for social reform, liberation, or even conservative and reactionary causes. But that only means that the church identifies itself with acts of tyranny, not of genuine liberation. Where the hidden/revealed nature is denied the eschatological vision is generally lost and the church's mission obscured.

> The lesson of the "German Christians" during the Third Reich should not be forgotten. A very strong case could be made for the "liberation" of Germany from the tyrannies imposed by its imperialistic neighbors. Where it is thought essential for the church to involve itself in such "liberation" movements it was only consequent, no doubt, for the German Christians to do so. The result was disaster both for the church and for Germany. That other or more current cases for "liberation" can be made and shown to be more worthy alters the matter for the church only in degree but not in kind. The church cannot identify itself with such causes, no matter how just. It must always and forever stand for

and proclaim a gospel that is the end, limit, and ultimate goal of this age. It will indeed insist that its members engage in activity to care for the world, but it will always insist also on constant vigilance to guard against the temptation for such activity to substitute itself for the kingdom of God and thus to become tyranny. So it will preach the gospel as the end of and limit to this world's hopes and know that to be the best thing it can do for the world.

Where the temptation is present to make the church visible in current causes the only result is that the church begins to look more and more like the world. The world certainly does not come to look like the church. However worthy the causes, the church cannot identify itself with them. To be sure, those who belong to the church will want to support and work for worthy causes in the world, but they will do so with the clear-eyed recognition that such causes are not the revelation of what is hidden. The hidden remains hidden to this world and is apprehended only by faith. Revelation comes through the gospel, not the world's causes. The church preaches the gospel and waits. Its members work to take care of creation and world in the meantime, but they know that the kingdom comes only by the power of the God of the gospel, not by human endeavor.

The church is therefore an absolutely unique body in the world. It is the place where the absolutely strange and unheard-of kind of speaking—gospel speaking—takes place. Thus the church is where the gospel is preached and the sacraments administered according to that gospel. This is its primary business and this is what it must see to. To those whose perception of the gospel is jaded or dimmed this will not seem like much. But it is really all there is to do. For those who are always impetuously anxious to be about the business of helping the world it must be said that this is also the primary way in which the church can help the world. The world needs above all to know that in the gospel of the crucified and risen Lord it too comes up against its limit, end, and goal. Only where and when the gospel is heard will people be set free to turn back to the world and genuinely care for it. As the "outpost" of the new age, the kingdom of God, the church must proclaim this gospel so that all, including the world, may be saved.

Abbreviations

BC
: *Book of Concord: The Confessions of the Evangelical Lutheran Church,* ed. and trans. Theodore G. Tappert (Phildadelphia: Fortress Press, 1959).

CD
: *Christian Dogmatics,* 2 vols., ed. Carl E. Braaten and Robert W. Jenson (Philadelphia: Fortress Press, 1984).

Christ
: Dietrich Bonhoeffer, *Christ the Center,* trans. Edwin H. Robertson (San Francisco: Harper & Row, 1987).

Lutheranism
: Eric W. Gritsch and Robert W. Jenson, *Lutheranism: The Theological Movement and its Confessional Writings* (Philadelphia: Fortress Press, 1976).

LW 31
: *Luther's Works,* vol. 31, *Career of the Reformer, I* (Philadelphia: Fortress Press, 1957).

LW 33
: *Luther's Works,* vol. 33, *Career of the Reformer, III* (Philadelphia: Fortress Press, 1972).

LW 42
: *Luther's Works,* vol. 42, *Devotional Writings, I* (Philadelphia: Fortress Press, 1969).

Notes

Introduction

1. Gotthold Ephriam Lessing, "On the Proof of the Spirit and of Power," in *Lessing's Theological Writings*, trans. and introduction by Henry Chadwick (London: Adam and Charles Black, 1956).

2. Immanuel Kant, *Religion Within the Limits of Reason Alone*, trans. T. M. Greene and H. H. Hudson (San Francisco: Harper and Bros., 1960).

Chapter 1: The Preached God

1. Ronald Goetz, "The Suffering God: The Rise of a New Orthodoxy," *The Christian Century*, 103/13 (April 16, 1986), 385.

2. Ibid.

3. Ibid.

4. Ibid.

5. Ibid., 386.

6. Ibid., 388.

7. Ibid., 389.

8. Ibid., 388.

9. James Turner, *Without God, Without Creed: The Origins of Unbelief in America* (Baltimore: The Johns Hopkins University Press, 1985).

10. Ibid., xiii.

11. Ibid., 265.

12. Ibid., 267.

13. St. Augustine, *City of God,* trans. Marcus Dods (New York: Random House, 1950), 153.

14. Martin Luther, *The Bondage of the Will. LW* 33:53.

15. The reader will notice that we are perilously close to preaching here. But that is perhaps just an illustration of my point. Systematic theology drives to proclamation, leaving one in the position in which that has to be the next move because every other road is cut off!

16. *LW* 33:136. Erasmus quoted Ezek. 18:23, 24, 27. Luther summed it up with Ezek. 33:11, as then translated: "I desire not the death of the sinner . . ."

17. *LW* 33:137.

18. *LW* 33:139.

19. *LW* 33:170.

20. See the study by Klaus Schwarzwaeller, *"Sibboleth,"* in *Theologische Existenz Heute*, 153, ed. K. G. Steck and G. Eichholz. (Muenchen: Kaiser Verlag, 1969).

21. *LW* 33:140.

22. Ibid.

23. Regin Prenter, *Spiritus Creator,* Trans. John M. Jensen (Philadelphia: Muhlenburg Press, 1953), 19 ff.

24. Immanuel Kant, *Religion Within the Limits of Reason Alone* (New York: Harper and Brothers, 1960), 111. This is, of course, not all that could be said about Kant's volume; I believe that this passage is a watershed in the history of modern hermeneutics and systematics: from that point in time, all scriptural assertions which smacked of election had to be trimmed to fit the dimensions of "practical reason" and the religion of the autonomous self. Not even biblical fundamentalists or so-called evangelicals seem to have escaped. Theology so construed turns the whole into a matter of our decision rather than God's.

25. *LW* 33:161

Chapter 2: The Hard of Hearing

1. See Hannah Arendt's cogent discussion in *Willing,* vol. 2 of *The Life of the Mind* (New York: Harcourt Brace Jovanovitch, 1978), 13ff.

2. *LW* 33:70.

3. *LW* 33:68.

4. See Philip Watson's introduction, "The Lutheran Ripost," in *Luther and Erasmus: Free Will and Salvation,* Library of Christian Classics 17, trans. and ed. E. Gordon Rupp and Philip Watson (Philadelphia: Westminster Press, 1969), 18.

5. See Luther's "Disputation on Scholastic Theology," *LW* 31:10, Thesis 17: "Man is by nature unable to want God to be God. Indeed, he himself wants to be God, and does not want God to be God."

6. In what has come to be called New Age religion this identification of self and God is apparently commonplace.

7. See the works by Ernest Becker, *The Denial of Death* (New York: Free Press, 1973) and Arthur McGill, *Death and Life: An American Theology,* ed. Charles A. Wilson and Per M. Anderson (Philadelphia: Fortress Press, 1987).

8. See the discussion in Robert Jenson, *Alpha and Omega: A Study in the Theology of Karl Barth* (New York: Thomas Nelson & Sons, 1963), 38–39.

9. See the discussion by Paul Ricoeur, "Guilt, Ethics, and Religion," in *Royal Institute of Philosophy Lectures: Talk of God,* vol. 2 (New York: St. Martin's Press, 1969), 100–77.

10. *LW* 33:103. Even Luther, who adamantly insisted on the bondage of the will, nevertheless also insisted that the will is vertible. It is most accurate, he held, to define the will as bound but vertible, but not as a free will.

Chapter 3: The Preacher

1. *Christ,* 35.

2. Willi Marxsen, *The Beginnings of Christology: A Study in Its Problems,* vol. 22 in Facet Books, Biblical Series, ed. John Reumann, trans. Paul J. Achtemeier (Philadelphia: Fortress Press, 1969), 33–35 passim.

3. See the remarks on historical heteronomy above in the introduction, 7.

4. The most prominent contemporary example of this is *The Myth of God Incarnate,* ed. John Hick (Philadelphia: Westminster Press, 1977). On the one hand the authors go to great lengths critically to dismantle the "myth" that God actually became enfleshed in a man, but on the other hand they go on to make quite extravagant claims about the religious superiority of Jesus. Dennis Nineham notes this in the epilogue.

5. Jürgen Moltmann, *The Crucified God,* trans. R. A. Wilson and John Bowden (New York: Harper & Row, 1974), 123.

6. Martin Hengel, *Crucifixion in the Ancient World and the Folly of the Message of the Cross* (Philadelphia: Fortress Press, 1977), 89–90.

Chapter 4: The Preached God

1. *CD* 1:128–29.

2. Athanasius, *c. Ar.* I. 14–16, 21, 28; *de Syn.* 41, 51. See the discussion in *The Letters of St. Athanasius Concerning the Holy Spirit,* trans. C. R. B. Shopland (New York: Philosophical Library, 1957), 99–103.

3. See *CD* 1:511–14, for critical estimates of the Chalcedonian decree.

4. See R. A. Norris, *Manhood and Christ* (Oxford: At the Clarendon Press, 1963), 39–41.

5. Ernest Becker, *Denial of Death* (New York: Free Press, 1973).

6. The discussion here parallels Pannenberg's view that Jesus' relation to the Son of God is "indirect" and that his unity with the Father consists in the fact that he, in our terms, "does Sonship" by his obedience to the eschatological calling involved in God's imminent kingdom. See Wolfhart Pannenberg, *Jesus— God and Man,* trans. Lewis L. Wilkins and Duane A. Priebe (London: SCM Press LTD, 1968), 334ff. I would, however, insist that Jesus' "doing Sonship," or "doing God" to us must involve the fact of death—that he "does us to death" to bring new life—if it is to carry the burden of the shift from substantial to active language. Pannenberg, I think, does not adequately encompass the cross and death in his Christology.

7. The classic statement is in Luther's "The Bondage of the Will," in *LW* 33:62.

8. *LW* 33:62–63.

9. Moltmann, *The Crucified God,* 204–05.

10. In Pannenburg, *Jesus—God and Man,* 348.

11. Ibid., 333–34.

12. Ibid., 141.

13. This treatment of atonement, which is absolutely central to the argument, is perhaps not so extensive as it might be. The relative brevity is attributable to two factors. First, the construing of Jesus as the man who does God to us already moves into the arena of atonement implicitly when not explicitly. It is not possible to make a neat distinction between person and work when one tries to move from the language of substance to the language of action. Second, I have already expressed myself at considerable length on atonement elsewhere: *CD* 2: 5–99, and "Caught in the Act: Reflections on the Work of Christ," *Word and World* 3, no. 1 (1983): 22–31.

14. *Christ,* 35.

15. *LW* 42:9.

16. See Søren Kierkegaard, *Philosophical Fragments: Johannes Climacus,* ed. and trans. Howard V. Hong and Edna Hong (Princeton: Princeton University Press, 1985). The title page asks: "Can a historical point of departure be given for an eternal consciousness; how can such a point of departure be of more than historical interest; can an eternal happiness be built on historical knowledge?"

17. See *CD,* 2:88f.

Chapter 5: Hearing

1. Karl Barth, *Epistle to Romans,* tr. Edwin C. Hoskins (Oxford: Oxford University Press, 1933), 332.

2. Eberhard Jüngel, *God as Mystery of the World,* tr. Darrell L. Guder (Grand Rapids: William B. Eerdmans, 1983), 14–35.

3. Ibid., 29.

4. Ibid., 192.

5. *LW* 33:268.

6. Arthur C. McGill, *Death and Life: An American Theology.* (Philadelphia: Fortress Press, 1987), 48.

7. *WA* 24, 18, 26–33. Preface to Sermons on Genesis, 1527. My translation.

8. McGill, *Death and Life,* 49–59.

9. Ibid., 49.

10. Ibid., 50.

11. Ibid., 51.

12. Again, for a more complete picture of my views on justification and the Christian life, the reader is directed to other works: *CD* 2:390–469; Forde, *Justification by Faith: A Matter of Death and Life* (Philadelphia: Fortress Press, 1982); Forde, "Forensic Justification and Law in Lutheran Theology," in *Justification by Faith: Lutherans and Catholics in Dialogue 7,* ed. H. George Anderson, T. Austin Murphy, and Joseph A. Burgess (Minneapolis: Augsburg Publishing, 1985), 278–303.

Chapter 6: Proclaiming

1. For further detail and documentation see my article, "Law and Gospel in Luther's Hermeneutic," *Interpretation* 37, no. 3 (1983): 240–52.

2. For an extended exposition of my attempts in the matter of preaching, see my essays on "Preaching the Sacraments," *Lutheran Theological Seminary Bulletin* 64, no. 4. (1984): 3–27.

3. *BC* 440, 31.

4. *BC* 439, 24.

5. *BC* 436, 1.

6. John Bunyan, *Pilgrim's Progress* (New York: Grosset & Dunlap, n.d.) 24–25.

7. *BC* 440, 28.

8. *BC* 444, 30.

9. Vilmos Vatja, *Luther on Worship* (Philadelphia: Muhlenberg Press, 1958), 27–63.

10. See James S. Preus, "Neglected Problems in the Eucharistic Dialogue," *Currents in Theology and Mission* 3, no. 5 (1976): 279–87.

11. *Lutheranism,* 101–109.

12. *Christ,* 57 passim.

13. *Lutheranism,* 108.

14. *BC,* 32.

15. See the article by Klaus Schwarzwaeller, "Rechtfertigung und Ecclesiologie in den Schmalkaldischen Artickeln," *Kerygma und Dogma* 35, no. 2 (1989): 95–105.

16. *WA* 10 I/2:30, 13–28. Sermon on Matt. 21:1-9 (Advent I) from the Church Postils, 1521. The translation is my own.

Index

Nature. *See* Creation

Old being, 51, 54, 77–78, 126, 136–
37, 168–70
Ordination, 184–85, 186

Paul, 75–81
Predestination. *See* Election
Physical presence, 175–76

Repetition/re-presentation, in the
Last Supper, 172–73

Sin, as bondage, 53
condition of, 50
confession of, 50–51
death and the law, 79
defined, 142–43
essence of, 77
original, 50–55
See also Creation; Creation, fall,
redemption
Spirit, Holy, convicter of sin, 123
that gives life, 154
proceeding from Father and Son,
93
the work of, 33, 138

Tense, past/present, 6, 29. *See also*
Discourse; Language; Word of
God
Text, doing the, 155–58
Titles, christological, 64–65. *See
also* Christology; Tri-polar
relation
Tri-polar relation, 63–64, 67, 69, 76,
87, 88. *See also* Christology;
Titles
Two kingdoms, doctrine of, 145

Universalism, 33–34

Will, the, 43, 47, 55. *See also*
Bondage of the will; Free will
Word of God, concrete, incarnate,
29
the doing of, 149, 157
eschatological, 157–58
external, 158–64
sacramental character of the,
147–49
See also Discourse; Language,
Tense
Wrath of God, 15, 29, 118, 119,
130–31